The GREENHOUSE EXPERT

Dr. D. G. Hessayon

All Editions & Reprints: 830,000 copies

Published by Expert Books
a division of Transworld Publishers

TRANSWORLD PUBLISHERS
61-63 Uxbridge Road, London W5 5SA
a division of the Random House Group Ltd

EXPERT BOOKS
www.expertgardening.co.uk

Contents

Reproduction by Spot On Digital Imaging Ltd, Gomm Road, High Wycombe, Bucks HP13 7DJ
Printed and bound by Butler Tanner & Dennis, Frome & London

CHAPTER 1

INTRODUCTION

Perhaps the greatest joy in owning a greenhouse is the one which receives least attention in the textbooks. The point is that when you go through that metal or wooden doorway and then close the door, you are entering a private world which isolates you from your workaday worries as well as the weather.

Outdoors you must share your plants with neighbours, passers-by, family and so on, and all around you there is an environment you cannot control — frost, wind and rain dictate your activity. Not so in the greenhouse — all you have here are you, a protected environment and a group of plants which rely upon you for their very existence. Watering, feeding, pricking out, potting on ... without you they must surely die.

There is something very comforting about working in a well-run greenhouse. You are warm and dry when the wind is blowing or the rain is falling outside, and your results depend entirely on your skill rather than on the vagaries of soil type and weather. But don't be oversold by some of the glowing pieces in books, articles or catalogues.

First of all, greenhouse growing is not simply a matter of common sense — there is nothing obvious about the right way to train a Cucumber or the reason why you have to ventilate on a cool day. Do read books like this one and its companion volumes to find out what to do. Next, don't be fooled into believing that not much work is involved. Constant attention is needed at most times of the year, and this means every day in summer unless you install an automatic ventilator and an automatic watering system. Finally, take the money-saving claims with a pinch of salt. An average-sized heated house will certainly not "pay for itself quite easily in a year". The greenhouse fitted with staging etc will cost you about £300 and the fuel a further £100 a year to keep the temperature at a minimum of 42°–45°F during an average winter.

So it is not a money-making proposition nor is it a simple pastime calling for occasional action. It is instead an absorbing hobby which enables you to produce a range of plants at a time when their garden counterparts are far behind or their growth outdoors is impossible. There is a steady stream of jobs to do, but none of these is strenuous, which makes greenhouse growing especially suitable for the not-so-young and the disabled.

All sorts of shapes and a wide range of sizes are available, but the fundamental difference between one type and another is the minimum temperature at which it is kept. The cold house is the simplest — no artificial source of heat is provided and so in the depths of winter the temperature will almost certainly fall below freezing point. Despite this, the cold house extends the growing season by trapping the sun's heat during the day. Here you can work protected from the elements with plants which are sheltered from wind and rain and can enjoy day temperatures which are appreciably higher than outdoors. Tomatoes are the favourite crop — during the rest of the year there are cuttings to take, seeds to sow and vegetables to grow. You can have Strawberries, Turnips and Potatoes weeks before the outdoor crops are ready and a wide range of annuals can be grown to provide colour.

Still, the cold house is rather limited. You cannot grow frost-sensitive plants between early winter and mid spring unless you provide heat. The usual practice is to turn the structure into a cool house in which winter temperatures do not fall below 42°–45°F. A whole new world opens up because you can now grow 'greenhouse plants' — Azalea, Cineraria, Cyclamen, Freesia, Primula, Streptocarpus and many, many more. Half hardy bedding plants can be raised for the garden and a succession of blooms can be created for either greenhouse or living room. The installation of a heater transforms growing under glass from a place for Tomatoes, Cucumbers and hardier plants into a place of great variety in which to exercise a year-round hobby.

So buy that greenhouse if you have the money to spare, enough free time to care for it properly and a liking for growing things. If possible, buy the next size larger than you have planned as most people who buy a greenhouse soon run out of space for all the exciting things they want to grow. Keep it as a cool house — the attraction of having a warm house with a minimum temperature of 55°F is obvious if you want to grow exotics, but such warm conditions are undesirable for some plants and you will also have a fuel bill of about £300 a year. The stove house with a minimum temperature of 65°F is for the tropical specialist and not for you.

What you grow is up to you. Perhaps you just want to produce fruit and vegetables with little thought for floral display. On the other hand you might want nothing more than blooms and foliage attractively arranged all year round — in this case your greenhouse has become a conservatory. Although there are no strict rules about what to grow, you should avoid trying to grow too varied a mixture — you cannot place shade lovers like ferns next to sun lovers such as Geraniums. Finally, don't let your greenhouse become a place which houses a row of Tomato plants, an assortment of house plants which have finished flowering, a few trays of shop-bought annuals awaiting bedding out and a collection of pots and gardening equipment. A greenhouse offers you a way to extend the joy of gardening — use it properly.

Conservatory or Greenhouse?

There is no single feature which separates a conservatory from a greenhouse. A conservatory is usually a more ornate structure and is generally attached to the house wall, but there are exceptions — the great conservatories of the past were situated well away from the stately home. A green-house is generally a place where plants are raised and cultivated rather than set out for display — but greenhouses used solely for alpines or orchids illustrate that this feature has its exceptions.

The difference between these two types of plant house is a combination of several factors, and these are set out below.

THE CONSERVATORY

- The well-being and comfort of people are the prime consideration

- The basic purpose is the display of orna-mental plants with showy leaves, stems and/ or flowers

- In most but not all cases the structure is attached to the house

- In most but not all cases the structure is decorative and with external ornamentation

- Some form of decorative flooring is present, ranging from simple matting to marble tiles

- Wood and uPVC are the favourite framing materials — glazing bars are usually sturdy

- A small but well-designed version is expensive

THE GREENHOUSE

- The well-being and comfort of plants are the prime consideration

- The basic purpose is the propagation and cultivation of plants which may or may not be ornamental

- In most but not all cases the structure is detached from the house

- In most but not all cases the structure is practical and without external ornamentation

- Some form of practical flooring is present, such as compacted soil or concrete

- Aluminium is the favourite framing material — glazing bars are usually slender

- A small but well-designed version is relatively cheap

CHAPTER 2
STRUCTURE & EQUIPMENT

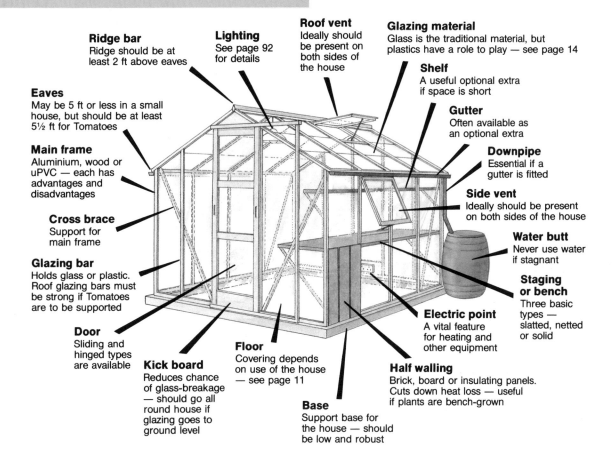

Ridge bar
Ridge should be at least 2 ft above eaves

Lighting
See page 92 for details

Roof vent
Ideally should be present on both sides of the house

Glazing material
Glass is the traditional material, but plastics have a role to play — see page 14

Shelf
A useful optional extra if space is short

Eaves
May be 5 ft or less in a small house, but should be at least 5½ ft for Tomatoes

Main frame
Aluminium, wood or uPVC — each has advantages and disadvantages

Cross brace
Support for main frame

Glazing bar
Holds glass or plastic. Roof glazing bars must be strong if Tomatoes are to be supported

Door
Sliding and hinged types are available

Kick board
Reduces chance of glass-breakage — should go all round house if glazing goes to ground level

Floor
Covering depends on use of the house — see page 11

Base
Support base for the house — should be low and robust

Half walling
Brick, board or insulating panels. Cuts down heat loss — useful if plants are bench-grown

Electric point
A vital feature for heating and other equipment

Staging or bench
Three basic types — slatted, netted or solid

Water butt
Never use water if stagnant

Side vent
Ideally should be present on both sides of the house

Downpipe
Essential if a gutter is fitted

Gutter
Often available as an optional extra

MEASUREMENTS

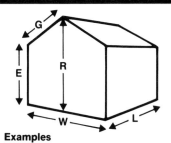

Examples

MEASUREMENT	CALCULATION
Volume	W x L x ½ (E + R)
Surface area	2 x G x L + 2 x E x L + (E + R) x W
Approximate glass area (all-glass house)	95% of surface area

Length (L)	Width (W)	E	R	G	Volume	Surface area	Approximate glass area
6½ ft	4½ ft	5 ft	7 ft	3 ft	175 cu. ft	158 sq. ft	150 sq. ft
8 ft	6 ft	5 ft	7 ft	3½ ft	288 cu. ft	208 sq. ft	195 sq. ft
8 ft	8 ft	5 ft	7 ft	4½ ft	384 cu. ft	248 sq. ft	235 sq. ft
10 ft	8 ft	5 ft	7 ft	4½ ft	480 cu. ft	286 sq. ft	270 sq. ft
12 ft	8 ft	5 ft	7 ft	4½ ft	576 cu. ft	324 sq. ft	305 sq. ft

GREENHOUSE TYPES

SPAN ROOF

The traditional style has vertical sides. Use of space and heat is efficient, and enclosed lower part cuts down winter heat loss. Choose an all-glass version for growing-bag and border crops.

THREE-QUARTER SPAN

Lighter and more airy than a lean-to — useful for growing wall plants such as Grapes and Figs. Expensive, however, so the choice should be between a span roof house or a lean-to.

LEAN-TO

Useful for a south or west wall, which stores heat so the fuel bill is reduced. An interconnecting door makes it part of the home. Heaters can be linked to domestic central heating.

DUTCH LIGHT

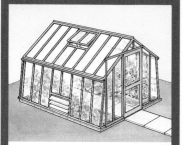

Sloping sides and an even span roof — angled glass makes it warmer and brighter than a traditional span roof house. Also more stable, but supporting upright plants from floor to roof is more difficult.

CURVED HOUSE

There is floor to roof glass with glazed panels. These form a smooth curve up to the ridge without the distinct angle at the eaves as occurs in the span roof and Dutch light. Supporting upright plants is difficult.

POLYGONAL

Many sides — six, seven or nine. Basically ornamental — attractive when filled with pot plants and sited close to the house. Expensive, however, and not a good buy if you want maximum space for your money.

DOME

Three advantages — attractive appearance when filled with flowers, maximum stability and maximum light absorption. The major drawback is its unsuitability for growing tall crops effectively. Ornamental rather than practical.

MINI-HOUSE

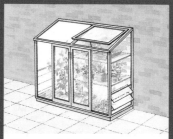

Very useful where space is limited — a lean-to which will accommodate the plants but not you. Treat as a cold house, but small size can mean a very rapid rise in temperature in summer. Keep an eye on the thermometer and open vents as necessary.

POLYTUNNEL

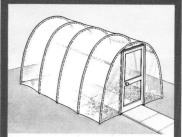

Plastic sheeting is stretched across a series of metal hoops — this is the cheapest form of greenhouse. Good for low-growing crops such as Lettuce and Strawberries, but not really suitable for Tomatoes and Cucumbers.

Greenhouses Illustrated

*The ornamental greenhouse.
No Tomatoes or other vegetables and
fruits in this small greenhouse — it has
been used entirely for pot plants such
as Impatiens, Plumbago, Iresine,
Hypoestes, Streptocarpus, Begonia etc* ▷

◁ *The productive greenhouse. The standard scene
in most greenhouses in July — lines of Tomato
plants in full growth. These specimens are
planted in pots, although growing bags are now
much more popular*

△ *The mixed greenhouse. Here there are both ornamentals and
fruit growing together. Grape vines reach up to the ridge and
the benches hold Pelargonium, Fuchsia and so on in full flower*

CONSERVATORY TYPES

GEORGIAN

The two distinct features are a flat roof and plain windows with small panes of glass. The roof is usually solid and not glazed, and the shape is generally semi-circular. A good garden room and suitable for most house plants, but not ideal for sun lovers.

VICTORIAN

The classic conservatory, once made of wood and cast iron but now more likely to be constructed of aluminium or uPVC. Ornate, with decorative ridge cresting. The usual shape is rectangular with a rounded 'octagon' bay at the end.

EDWARDIAN

A simpler and less ornate style than the Victorian, but the decorative ridge cresting is sometimes retained. The shape is rectangular, with additional square or rectangular bays where space permits. The windows are generally plain.

CONTEMPORARY

A modern-style conservatory which comes in all sorts of shapes and sizes. The two key features are an absence of cresting, ornamentation or fancy windows plus framing which is generally thinner than on the traditional structure.

GOTHIC

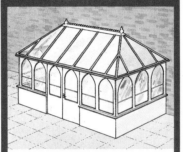

Easy to recognise — the windows are topped by a distinct gothic (pointed) arch which gives an old-fashioned and rather solid look to an Edwardian or Victorian conservatory. Still popular, but there are no advantages for the plants within.

STATELY HOME

The grand orangeries with solid roofs of the 18th century were followed by the cast-iron and all-glass grand conservatories of the 19th century. They were often vast buildings — the Great Stove House at Chatsworth was 65 ft high.

Windows

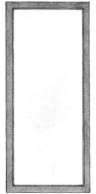 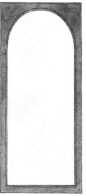   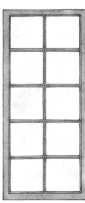

Plain **Arched** **Gothic** **Ogee** **Georgian**

Conservatories Illustrated

The jungle conservatory.
A conservatory is for the comfort of
people as well as plants, but here the
plants clearly predominate. Vines, ferns,
bulbs and other ornamentals crowd in
around the chairs ▷

◁ The well-balanced conservatory. Here
there are both space and comfort for
people and a range of ornamentals.
An attractive tree-seat surrounds the
central planting with flowers in pots
above and below the staging

△ The garden room. This conservatory is an extra living area.
Light and airy, with hanging baskets and house plants on the sills,
it is a dining room rather than a home for plants

Recommended minimum dimensions

Eaves
5–5½ ft high

Ridge
7–7½ ft high

Door
6 ft high.
2 ft wide —
3 ft if barrow
is used

SIZE

You can buy a greenhouse which is no more than 6 ft long and 4½ ft wide or you can choose one which measures 20 ft x 10 ft. Picking the most suitable size is not easy, and you should consider various factors. A tiny house saves money, of course, but there are two serious disadvantages. First of all, it is much more difficult to control the environment in a small house than in a larger one — draughts and sudden fluctuations in temperature are serious problems. The second difficulty is that most gardeners find that they need more space after a season or two, and regret that they didn't buy a larger model. If space is available, it is advisable to buy a modular greenhouse which can be extended if the greenhouse growing bug bites you.

The most popular size is 8 ft long x 6 ft wide and this is a good selection where space is restricted — choose a 10 ft x 8 ft house if you plan to have staging on both sides of the house. You will often read that you should buy the largest size you can afford, but do think before taking this advice. The size should be in keeping with the area of the garden — a large greenhouse can be very costly to heat and a structure which is more than 8 ft x 6 ft will usually need a concrete base.

The rules are different for a conservatory. Choose a size which fits in with the home and make sure that eaves and ridge height will be comfortable for tall visitors. The recommended minimum size is about 10 ft x 8 ft, but 12 ft x 10 ft is preferable if you plan for a table and chairs as well as plants.

FRAME

ALUMINIUM ALLOY

Aluminium alloy has taken over as the most popular material for greenhouse frames for several reasons. It is cheaper than wood, requires no painting or other treatment and the thin glazing bars mean more light within the house. Warping of the ridge bar does not occur and the clip-on system has made reglazing a relatively simple matter. There are a number of minor drawbacks. Aluminium greenhouses lose slightly more heat at night than wooden ones and condensation drips are more likely to occur. The frame is received in bits and the instructions may be difficult to follow for the non-DIY fan. If an aluminium unit is badly designed and constructed it may twist in windy or hot weather and panes may be broken. Finally it is difficult to fix shelves, hooks etc to the solid metal frame, but many models nowadays have a series of pre-drilled holes in the main frame. A bloom occasionally appears on aluminium frames — this is normal and nothing to worry about. The more expensive models have an anodised or impact-proof painted surface.

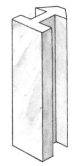

WOOD

Wood is considered by many to be the most attractive material. The main problem is that rot-proof timber is expensive — teak and oak are very costly and the cheaper western red cedar is still appreciably more expensive than aluminium. These rot-proof frames should be rubbed with linseed oil every few years to enhance their appearance. Always use brass or galvanised iron fittings. Most wooden greenhouses are made from the softwoods ('Yellow Deal', 'Baltic Pine' etc) which are less expensive than western red cedar but which also readily rot after a few years. Make sure that the wood has been pressure-treated with a preservative before you buy a softwood greenhouse. Paint or treat with a plant-safe preservative every few years. Untreated softwood is a poor buy.

uPVC

Unplasticised (rigid) PVC is the latest material. It is generally quite expensive, but it does not decay so little maintenance is needed. This maintenance consists of an occasional washing down to remove dust, bird droppings etc. uPVC is becoming increasingly popular for the construction of conservatories. Its main drawback is that it is not a strong material, which means that glazing bars have to be as thick as wooden ones and with large buildings the uPVC frame requires a metal core.

GALVANISED STEEL

Galvanised steel is still used in the manufacture of commercial greenhouses, but is no longer popular for home models. The great advantage of this material is its rigidity and strength which means it can support a large roof. This is of little advantage for an ordinary 8 ft x 6 ft house, and the fact that the galvanised or painted surface can become scratched and then pitted with rust is a distinct disadvantage.

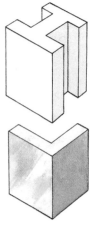

FLOOR

Shingle to keep down weed growth, prevent mud underfoot and to hold water after damping down

Central path of concrete or concrete slabs laid on sand

The traditional pattern for the floor of the greenhouse was to have one or both sides as border soil for growing plants and a central pathway covered with pea shingle, concrete, concrete slabs or wooden slats (duck-boarding). The pathway remains as important as ever (rammed soil is not satisfactory) but most experts no longer recommend using border soil for growing annual plants such as Tomatoes. The problem is a build-up of diseases, pests and other troubles in the soil. Growing bags and pots are preferred these days. If you plan to use the border soil, dig in 4 oz per sq. yard of Growmore plus a liberal amount of garden compost well before planting time. Do not plant the same crop in the border year after year. If you don't intend to have borders then concrete the whole area or cover the ground on either side of the pathway with shingle.

The floor of the greenhouse is entirely functional, but the floor of a conservatory needs to be decorative. Carpeting is not practical as occasional damping down will lead to rotting, and so stone or reconstituted stone slabs are quite popular. At the luxury end of the market is a wide range of tiles above underfloor heating — terrazzo, glass mosaics, marble etc. Do choose carefully — you will need a non-slip surface if damping down is to take place. Terracotta tiles are a good choice.

GUTTERING

Guttering is a useful extra as rainwater dripping from the roof can undermine the foundations. Some models have built-in guttering as a standard fitting — check before you buy. The water from the gutters should be channelled to a soakaway or into a plastic water butt. The butt should have a tight-fitting lid to keep out leaves and other debris. Experts do not agree whether such water is safe to use for watering greenhouse plants — never use it if the water is obviously polluted.

DOOR

Hinged or sliding — both types have their disciples. Sliding doors don't slam shut and they can be used as extra ventilators in an emergency. But they do get stuck occasionally and the nylon bearings may need replacing. Hinged doors generally fit better and so are less likely to be a source of draughts. Sadly in some areas a lock has become an essential piece of equipment.

LIGHTING

Lighting is not essential, but horticultural lamps (see page 92 for details) can increase the range of activities under glass. An electric point will be required within the house.

VENTILATORS

Hinged ventilator   **Louvred ventilator**

There are times when a series of rapid air changes is necessary within the greenhouse. If the temperature rises above 80°F or the humidity approaches 100 per cent it is essential to have about 40–60 air changes per hour. Unfortunately the ventilators fitted on most standard models are inadequate. There should be at least one roof ventilator ('ridge vent') and one side ventilator ('side vent') — a single ventilator along the ridge is not enough. The roof ventilators are all-important — hot air rises and this is the means of escape. The total ventilator area along the ridge should be 16–20 per cent of the total floor area — these hinged ventilators should open to at least 55°. Side ventilators need not open so widely and louvred ones are generally better than the traditional hinged type. Make sure that they close properly. Extra ventilators can be bought as optional extras, but with many greenhouses they are in fact essential items. Side ones should be set low down to ensure proper air circulation. As noted on page 5 it is a good idea to have ventilators on both sides of the house.

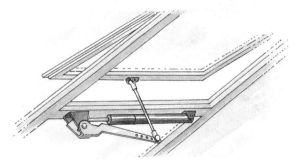

Automatic ventilator

An automatic ventilator, like extra hinged ones, may be described as an 'optional extra' in the catalogue, but it is a vital piece of equipment if you take your greenhouse seriously and cannot spare the time to go out daily to open and close the ventilators by hand. It is a non-electrical item which has a tube containing a heat-expanding compound as the control unit. A plunger within the tube moves as the temperature changes, and this opens or closes the ventilator.

An extractor fan is sometimes fitted. Set it close to the ridge at the end opposite to the door. This item is a horticultural version of the domestic extractor fan. It is a low-speed model which does not create strong draughts but still produces enough air movement to remove hot and cold air pockets in the greenhouse. A thermostat switches on the fan when the air reaches a set temperature. Noisy and quite expensive to run — not usually necessary unless the house is a large one.

WATERING EQUIPMENT

A greenhouse is a rainless place which relies on you for water. Watering by hand is more time-consuming than any other aspect of greenhouse and conservatory gardening, and is probably the most difficult to master. Unless your greenhouse is very small and attached to the home you will find it a tiresome chore to carry cans of water each day in summer from the kitchen to the Tomatoes, Cucumbers or other plants. The first requirement to make things easier is a tap within the greenhouse or conservatory. If you are a handyman you can run the plastic tubing from the tap to the mains pipe, but the connection will have to be made by a plumber. Note that the plastic tubing will have to be buried about 2 ft below the surface to prevent freezing in winter. To make things even easier you can use one of the automatic systems described below.

WATERING CAN

Insert spout *under* the leaves — pour water steadily and gently. Fill the space to the top of the pot — leave to drain

A watering can enables you to satisfy individual needs better than any other method, but it is only practical for a small collection of plants. Buy a 1 gallon good-quality can — the spout should be long and an extension spout is a useful extra. Use the spout for watering established plants and a fine rose for seedlings.

HOSE PIPE

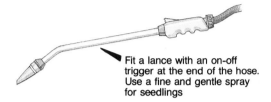

Fit a lance with an on-off trigger at the end of the hose. Use a fine and gentle spray for seedlings

A hose pipe connected to an external water supply or a tap inside the house will save you a lot of time. The use of a lance will enable you to reach the pots or trays at the back of the staging and a variable spray head will enable you to apply a fine spray when required. Use a gentle trickle — do not turn the water full on.

Automatic Watering

There are several ways of making watering easier — the **automatic** ones work from the mains either directly through a tap or indirectly through a reservoir tank. All the plants are kept watered until the system is switched off. This switching on and off is usually done by hand, but you can buy a simple timer or a complex water computer which can be set to give watering periods of various lengths on different days. In the most sophisticated arrangements a number of sensors are inserted into the compost and these turn on the water computer when watering is necessary.

Nearly all amateur set-ups are much simpler and are **semi-automatic** — the reservoirs have to be filled with water manually and may need switching on every time water is required. Like the more sophisticated systems they are great time savers, but as with all these methods every pot generally receives the same amount of water — a problem in a mixed collection in summer and often a menace in winter.

Water computer

SAND BENCH

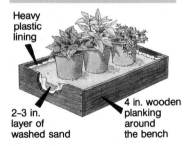

Heavy plastic lining

2–3 in. layer of washed sand

4 in. wooden planking around the bench

The sand (or capillary) bench has been around for many years, but it has never become popular. The staging holding the tray must be level and stout. The sand is kept moist by means of a watering can or a pipe connected to a manually-filled reservoir or header tank. Plastic (not clay) pots without crocks are screwed into the moist sand.

CAPILLARY MATTING

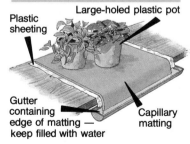

Large-holed plastic pot

Plastic sheeting

Gutter containing edge of matting — keep filled with water

Capillary matting

A modern alternative to the sand bench — lighter, easier to install and more popular, but it has to be replaced after a time as it becomes clogged with algae. Polythene sheeting is laid on the bench and the matting is placed on top of it — this is kept permanently moist by means of a watering can, pipe fed from a tank, or a water-filled gutter.

TRICKLE IRRIGATION

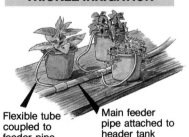

Flexible tube coupled to feeder pipe

Main feeder pipe attached to header tank

Greatly favoured by commercial growers, but an unsightly technique for a display greenhouse. The main pipe is fed from a header tank and small pipes wind from this in spaghetti-like fashion to exit points inserted in each pot. Water trickles into each pot either continuously or on a time-controlled basis. Check frequently for blockages.

BLINDS

Plants must be protected from the sun's rays in summer — overheating can be a serious problem and so can the scorching of delicate foliage. The simplest and cheapest answer is to apply a shading paint to the outside of the glass, but this can't be simply whisked away when a period of cloudy and cool weather arrives. Blinds are generally regarded as the best answer — you can choose from a wide selection of roller types made of wooden slats, plastic slats or plastic-coated sheeting. When fitted on the outside the temperature inside the house is reduced and the harmful glare of the sun is eliminated. An advantage of using inside rather than outside blinds is that the opening of the ventilators is not hampered, but inside blinds do not keep down the internal temperature. Blinds are pulled up or down depending on the weather — there are automatic blinds available which are operated by the temperature within the greenhouse.

STAGING & SHELVING

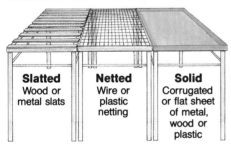

Slatted	Netted	Solid
Wood or metal slats	Wire or plastic netting	Corrugated or flat sheet of metal, wood or plastic

Benches or staging are essential if you grow pot plants — constant stooping to ground level would add backache to greenhouse gardening. The two terms are interchangeable in popular use, but strictly speaking staging is a permanent structure whereas a bench can be folded up and removed. The traditional form is slatted wooden staging about 2½ ft above the ground. Air can circulate in winter, cutting down the risk of disease. Netted staging has the same virtues, but both the slatted and netted forms have the disadvantage of making a poor work surface when potting and are not suitable for automatic watering. Solid staging with a shallow lip overcomes these drawbacks — it conserves heat in winter, holds compost when transplanting or filling pots and can be filled with water-holding material for automatic watering. Shelving is a miniature form of bench which is secured at head height to hold small pots or trays when space or sunlight is restricted. Nowadays you can buy metal benches and shelves as optional extras. A collapsible bench enables you to grow bedding plants and bulbs at a convenient height in spring and then you can dismantle it in summer to grow Tomatoes in growing bags.

INSULATION

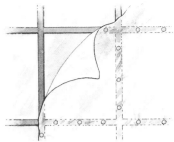

The general principle is to put an inner lining of transparent plastic close to the glass — even a simple arrangement will cut fuel bills by 20–25 per cent. Tailor-made panels are offered by some greenhouse manufacturers, but the usual practice is to attach polythene sheeting to the sides of the house with drawing pins, staples or adhesive strip so that a ½–1 in. layer of air is trapped between glass and plastic. Not all experts are enthusiastic about this technique — about one-sixth of the sun's illumination is cut out and condensation may be a problem. If maximum light is desired then plastic insulation should be confined to the north side of the house. Another method which gives maximum heat retention and minimum condensation is bubble polythene which has air trapped within it. The best solution for the conservatory is double glazing.

PROPAGATOR

Cuttings need a moist and reasonably warm atmosphere in order to root satisfactorily. Seeds of some important plants, including Cucumber and Tomato, require a temperature of 60°–75°F in order to germinate properly. Obviously it would be ridiculous to create these conditions throughout the greenhouse — a heated propagator is the answer. A propagator is a plastic or aluminium container with a glass or transparent plastic cover. Choose one heated by electricity rather than by paraffin, and look for thermostatic control and one or more ventilators at the top of the cover. There are mini-greenhouses in which you can keep tropical plants in stove house conditions, but you will probably need something much simpler. There should be enough floor area for at least 2 seed trays and enough headroom to hold pots containing 6 in. high plants.

THERMOMETER

A maximum/minimum thermometer is vital. Suspend it close to the plants but make sure that air can circulate freely around the thermometer. It should be close to eye-level at the north side of the house. There are 2 types — the traditional mercury thermometer with internal tiny iron bars which you set with a magnet and the digital type which you reset by pressing a button.

GLAZING MATERIAL

Until fairly recently glass was the only glazing material, and it still remains the most popular choice for greenhouses and conservatories. This may seem surprising as plastics would seem to have two important advantages. They are shatterproof, which is so necessary if a greenhouse is sited near to a children's play area or close to a road. They are also lightweight, which means that stout window lights are not required. The problem is that the early glazing plastics had a number of drawbacks and led to disappointing results. They had poor insulating properties and so the house cooled down rapidly at night, clarity was often quite poor and tended to get worse as dust was attracted by the electrostatic charge, and they cracked in a year or two as a result of breakdown by ultra-violet rays. Things have improved with modern plastics. UV inhibitors are added which means that a 10–15 year life can be expected. Twin-walled materials have good insulation properties and some of the newer types have a clarity almost as good as glass. Plastic glazing materials have now become popular for several purposes such as the roofing of conservatories, and their use is likely to increase in the future.

Glazing has also improved in recent years. In the modern aluminium greenhouse the introduction of glazing clips and glazing bars means that replacing glass has become a simple job. Wooden frames call for the use of the traditional method of glazing sprigs plus a sealant. Putty is now largely a thing of the past — it has been replaced by non-hardening mastic.

GLASS

Glass is the usual choice. It has excellent clarity — good quality glass allows 90 per cent of the sun's radiation to enter. The next important feature is heat retention — even in frosty weather the temperature in an unheated glass-covered greenhouse will be about 8°F higher than outside. It is not affected by ultra-violet rays and it can be shaded with paint-on materials. But as stated above, it is heavy and breakable. For greenhouses buy horticultural grade glass which is described as 3 mm (its thickness) or 24 oz (the weight of 1 sq. ft). This is good quality glass which should be free from air bubbles.

For conservatories both insulation and safety are even more important. The usual way to secure improved insulation is to buy a double-glazed building. More expensive, of course, but certainly worth the difference. A cheaper way to reduce heat loss is to buy Low Emissivity (LE) Glass which is only slightly dearer than ordinary glass. To prevent accidents do insist on safety glass — this will be described as either Toughened or Laminated.

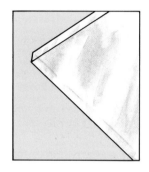

POLYCARBONATE

The rising star in the glass substitute world — because of its lightness and toughness it has become the most widely used glazing material for conservatory roofing. The popular form is twin-wall or double-skinned polycarbonate — because of its cellular structure the light is diffused, but actual light transmission is about 80 per cent. Its outstanding property is heat retention — the 'double glazing' effect means that it is superior to 3 mm glass in keeping heat from escaping. Choose the 3 or 4 mm grade for greenhouse sides and the 10 mm grade for roofing.

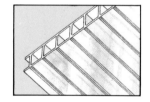

ACRYLIC

The 2 and 2.5 mm sheet has light transmission properties which are almost equal to glass. It is not quite as strong as polycarbonate and it is less expensive, although it should last just as long (12–15 years minimum). It can be moulded, and is therefore widely used to produce curved panes for conservatories. When cutting to size mark lines and drilling holes on the protective paper — use a tenon saw for cutting and a hand drill (not a power one) for making holes. Sawn edges should be smoothed with glasspaper after which the protective cover should be removed.

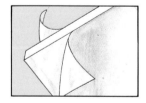

FLEXIBLE PLASTIC

The two most important uses are the covering of polytunnels (see page 6) and the insulation of greenhouses (see page 13). Polythene sheeting is the most popular and inexpensive form — the material produced for horticultural use these days contains a UV inhibitor and it should last for 3 or 4 seasons before becoming discoloured and brittle. Its main faults as a glazing material are that it can be torn by strong winds and has poor heat-retention properties. Fluoroplastic film is the best of the flexible sheeting materials — its light transmission equals glass and its heat retention is reasonable.

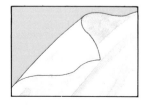

Glazing an Aluminium Greenhouse

Usually a straightforward job as putty is not required. There are a number of different systems available involving clips, bars etc — shown here is one of the popular clip methods.

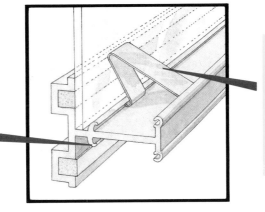

STEP 1:
REMOVE BROKEN PANE
Put on a pair of strong gloves. Unhook the glazing clip and remove the broken pane. In some greenhouses the panes overlap — in this case the upper pane will also have to be removed

STEP 2:
SECURE THE NEW PANE
Place the new pane in position and replace the clip. A straightforward job requiring no skill, but take great care when reglazing an awkward spot on the roof. Stretching and then slipping can cause a nasty accident

Glazing a Wooden Greenhouse

STEP 1:
REMOVE BROKEN PANE
Wear gloves to remove broken glass. Use a screwdriver or chisel to get rid of all old putty or mastic. Remove any glazing sprigs, metal clips or beading and then brush away dirt and dust

STEP 2:
PLACE PUTTY OR MASTIC IN REBATE
Buy the right grade of mastic — putty is not popular these days. Mould in your hands until it is soft — squeeze a ¼ in. thick strip into the rebate

STEP 5:
INSERT GLAZING SPRIGS
Place new glazing sprigs in position. Knock the sprigs into the rebate with the side of an old chisel — slide the blade along the surface of the glass. Do not use a hammer

STEP 6:
ADD MORE PUTTY OR MASTIC
Run another strip in the angle between the new pane and the wooden frame. This step and Step 7 are optional — the neat bevelled edge is decorative but not essential

STEP 3:
PUT NEW PANE INTO OPENING
The new pane should be ⅛ in. smaller than the width and height of the opening. Make sure you buy the right grade and thickness — see page 14

STEP 4:
PRESS GLASS INTO PUTTY OR MASTIC
Press the glass into the mastic until it is firmly bedded in place. Put the bottom of the pane into position first and then press forward — always press the edges and never the middle of the glass

STEP 7:
SMOOTH PUTTY OR MASTIC
Use a putty knife to smooth the mastic as a neat bevel. Mitre the corners and then remove all excess mastic from glass surface and glazing bars

STEP 8:
CLEAN GLASS
Wipe off remaining traces and fingerprints with a cloth soaked in methylated spirits. If putty is used run a moist brush along the surface and leave for 2 weeks to harden

HEATING EQUIPMENT

The unheated or cold greenhouse is generally a place for Tomatoes and Cucumbers in summer, Chrysanthemums in autumn and alpines, bulbs and hardy house plants such as cacti in winter.

If you wish to extend this range of plants to include early fruit and vegetables, winter Chrysanthemums and half hardy pot plants then you will need some form of heater to maintain a minimum temperature of 45°F (7°C) during the depths of winter. This is the cool greenhouse and is the one which the experts recommend for the ordinary gardener. The position is a little different with the conservatory — the cool house is popular, but for the cultivation of many ornamentals it is necessary to maintain warm or even stove house conditions. In addition it will be necessary to maintain human-comfort temperatures during winter evenings if the conservatory is used as a living as well as a plant area.

A wide choice of fuels is available for heating purposes — coke, coal, wood, natural gas, paraffin, oil and electricity. Gone are the days when everyone had to rely on hot water pipes heated by a coal- or coke-fed boiler — nowadays the popular choices are paraffin, natural gas, bottled gas and electricity.

Electricity is the best source of heat — fume-free, easy to control and not a source of water vapour which can promote disease in winter. A word of caution — installing electricity outdoors is a job for a professional electrician. The burning fuels (paraffin, natural gas and bottled gas) require adequate ventilation when used within the house. The appeal of paraffin is obvious — the heaters are inexpensive and there is no need for electrical wiring, gas pipes or heavy cylinders. Still, the problems outweigh the advantages — thermostatic control is not practical and regular attention is essential. Bottled gas heaters are more satisfactory, but the cylinders are heavy and the heaters are large and cumbersome. A natural gas boiler can be used to heat a hot water system in the lean-to or conservatory — see 'Linked Central Heating' on page 17.

Minimum Temperature

COLD GREENHOUSE
Unheated except by the sun

minimum temperature 28°F (–2°C)
when outside temperature falls to 20°F (–7°C)
Overall benefits: Plants are protected from wind, rain and snow
Growth is approximately 3–4 weeks ahead of outdoor plants
Drawbacks: No growth occurs in the depths of winter
Unsuitable for overwintering frost-sensitive plants

●

COOL GREENHOUSE
Heater required during the cooler months

minimum temperature 45°F (7°C)
Overall benefits: Plants are protected from wind, rain, snow and frost
Growth is approximately 3–4 weeks ahead of cold greenhouse plants
Minimum temperature is just high enough to support plant growth
Frost-sensitive plants can be overwintered
Drawback: Some form of heating is required between autumn and spring

●

WARM GREENHOUSE
Heater required during most months

minimum temperature 55°F (13°C)
Overall benefits: A wide range of plants can be grown during the winter months
Exotic flowers and fruits can be planted
Drawback: Fuel costs are about three times higher than cool greenhouse costs

●

STOVE HOUSE
Heater required all year round

minimum temperature 65°F (18°C)
Overall benefit: Tropical plants can be grown — definitely one up on the Jones's
Drawbacks: Fuel costs are prohibitive for the average gardener
Too warm for some plants

Heater Types for a Cool Greenhouse

Make sure the heater you choose is sufficiently large to heat the greenhouse to 45°F when the temperature outside is only 20°F. There are several formulae to calculate the size of the heater required to ensure this heating capacity. Use the simple one below, after having worked out the surface area as shown on page 5.

Type of heater	Size of heater
Paraffin Oil Gas	Surface area x 33 = BTUs per hour required
Electricity	Surface area x 10 = Watts required

As an example, an 8 ft x 6 ft greenhouse (surface area 208 sq.ft) requires 6864 BTUs per hour (paraffin, oil or gas) or 2080 Watts (electricity) when the outside temperature falls to 20°F. Remember that all equipment should be designed for greenhouse use.

Electric tubular heater

Electric fan heater
(horticultural type)

Heat source	Details
ELECTRIC FAN HEATER	The popular choice for a small greenhouse. There are many advantages — no fumes, no transporting of fuel and good thermostatic control. These advantages are shared with other electric heaters, but fans have the added benefit of circulating the air quickly. Warm air is provided in winter, cool air in summer. Choose a model with a fan which continues to run when the thermostat switches off the heating element
ELECTRIC TUBULAR HEATER	The preferred type for heating a large house or where high temperatures are required. The warmth is distributed from the lines of pipes around the walls — these pipes should be set at least 4 in. from the wall. Heat is much more evenly spread than from a fan heater. A single 'black heat' tube can be installed to warm up a cold spot
ELECTRIC CONVECTOR HEATER	Convector heaters are popular for home heating but have found little favour with greenhouse or conservatory owners. This form of heater has neither the air-circulating properties of a fan nor the evenness of warmth of a tubular heater. Night-storage heaters are economical to run, but they provide day-heat and not the night-heat which is required in a greenhouse
PARAFFIN HEATER	Cheap to buy and generally cheap to run, but the advantages stop there. Water vapour is produced and this increases the risk of grey mould in winter. Buy a blue-flame model and trim the wick regularly. Never allow it to run dry and ensure adequate ventilation. Make sure the heater is large enough to maintain 42°–45°F in icy weather. Not recommended, but a useful standby in case of power failure
GAS HEATER	Flueless heaters are available which use either natural or bottled gas. They have their merits — carbon dioxide is produced which stimulates plant growth and thermostatic controls are fitted. But there are drawbacks. As with paraffin the production of water vapour can be a problem and regular maintenance is essential. For a bottled gas heater use propane and make sure the cylinders are placed on a firm and level surface
PIPED HOT WATER	The traditional type of greenhouse heater — once the standard and now very much the exception. Water is heated in a boiler by solid fuel, oil or gas and the hot water is circulated along horizontal pipes around the sides of the house. Pipes are 1½–4 in. in diameter and heat distribution is excellent if an equal gap is left at the back of the staging. The major drawback is the cost of the installation
LINKED CENTRAL HEATING	Installing one or more radiators in a conservatory or lean-to greenhouse and linking them to the domestic central heating system seems like an excellent idea. However home central heating systems operate during the day and switch off at night, which is the wrong way round for the greenhouse. This problem is solved by installing a separate feed with its own timer and thermostat — consult a central heating engineer
ELECTRIC HEATING CABLE	Two types are available. The popular one is the soil-heating cable which is placed on the staging or in the soil. Economical, as the heat is directed exactly where you want it — frosting of plants in a cold house is prevented. Also available is the air-warming cable, clipped on to the walls of a cold frame or a small greenhouse

Paraffin heater

Gas heater

Electric heating cable

CHOOSING

Your first major decision is to choose between a greenhouse and a conservatory — page 4 outlines the basic differences between the two. They come in all sorts of shapes, sizes ... and prices. Picking the right one is difficult, and if you make a mistake you will have to live with it for a long time. Before deciding read the advertisements and study the catalogues by all means, but the best plan is to look at a range of buildings which have been erected. Go to a garden centre, DIY store or to a large horticultural show such as Chelsea, Hampton Court or Southport.

● IS IT THE RIGHT TYPE?

Both the lean-to and free-standing types have advantages and drawbacks. The free-standing structure allows maximum light transmission and maximum ventilation, and may be the only type you can have if wall space is not available. The problem is that it is away from the domestic water and heating supplies. The lean-to overcomes this drawback, and the house wall traps heat — a distinct advantage in winter. But it is a drawback in summer, and so good ventilation and shading are essential. For a greenhouse weigh up the advantages and drawbacks and make your choice — for a conservatory the best choice is a lean-to with direct access to the house.

● IS IT RIGHT FOR THE USES I HAVE IN MIND?

If you plan to concentrate on tall plants like Tomatoes and Cucumbers, choose a greenhouse with vertical sides and floor-to-roof glass. On the other hand if you wish to concentrate on plants which are active in winter it is a good idea to have a structure with sloping sides, as it will be warmer than a vertical-sided house when the sun is low. Half-timbered sides are suitable if you want to reduce fuel costs and you propose to grow only pot plants.

● WHERE SHALL I BUY IT?

Many small aluminium greenhouses are ordered directly from catalogues and newspaper advertisements, but it is advisable to inspect the model before purchase, as noted in the introduction. If you are buying a DIY kit, do make sure you have the experience, fitness and helpers for such an undertaking. If not, choose a supplier who offers an erection service. You have to be even more careful when selecting a supplier if you plan to purchase a conservatory. You can buy an inexpensive model from a DIY store or garden centre — the designs are usually simple and you are expected to erect it yourself or to use the services of a local builder. At the other end of the scale are the conservatory specialists who will design you a building from scratch to meet your specific requirements. The company will do everything, but at a price. This route may be necessary if you have an awkward space to fill, but the best source is usually the conservatory company which has a range of off-the-peg models which can be adapted to your needs.

● IS IT THE RIGHT SIZE?

Too big or too small — both pose a problem. The greenhouse should not dominate the garden nor should it provide much more space than you can fill. But it must be large enough for your needs — a popular rule is to buy the next larger size than the one you originally planned to buy. If you have the space, consider a double-pathed square model rather than a long rectangular one. It is not just a matter of length

and width. If you are above average height, is it tall enough to allow you to work without stooping? Is the door wide enough for your width, and for your wheelbarrow if you plan to work in the border soil? If you are thinking about a conservatory, do remember that it is meant to be a place where you can sit in comfort with your family or friends surrounded by your plants. Where space is severely limited it is worth considering a popular-sized greenhouse rather than a tiny conservatory.

● DO I LIKE THE LOOK OF IT?

Wood has a more traditional appeal than aluminium and a domed house is much trendier than a standard span roof one. Above all, the question you must ask is — does the greenhouse appeal to you and the family? Remember you will have to live with it as part of the permanent garden display. The question is even more important with a conservatory, because that will become part of the home.

● CAN I AFFORD IT?

Making your own house from scratch is not an economical option these days — the wood and glass will cost you more than a home-assembly greenhouse. In general you will get what you pay for — so do not regard 'bargain offers' as great value. When money is no object you can think of a double-glazed hardwood greenhouse, but that can cost up to 10 times more than the same size house in the cheapest materials. If funds are limited the best choice is an aluminium house covered with glass from a reputable supplier. Thin plastic sheeting instead of glass will reduce the price, but this is false economy as heating will cost you so much more. Don't forget these fuel costs — there is not much difference between the various types of fuel, but keeping it at a minimum of 55°F instead of 45°F in winter can be costly. Another point to bear in mind is that to remove the chore of opening ventilators and daily watering by automation is an extra but often an essential expense.

● IS IT SOUNDLY MADE?

You cannot expect top-quality craftsmanship if you have bought a low-priced model, but it should still be soundly constructed. Do the ventilators and door fit properly? Is the ridge bar rigid and firmly held? Press the glazing bars — are they unyielding?

● ARE ESSENTIALS INCLUDED IN THE PRICE?

Make sure that essentials are not classed as 'optional extras' unless you can afford the additional cost. Check exactly what is included in the price. Glazing material, staging and an adequate number of ventilators are essentials, but are not always included in the basic price. A foundation may be offered as an optional extra, but treat it as an essential feature. Make sure that you are told about any delivery or erection charges.

SITING & ERECTING

The new greenhouse should be set well away from trees — 30 ft is the recommended minimum distance. An overhanging branch casts shade, drops dirt on the glass below and may break off in high wind. If the structure is a free-standing one place it well away from buildings, fences etc which could shade out winter sun

Do not site a glass greenhouse close to the road or a play area — replacing broken panes is always annoying. Other sites to avoid are waterlogged soils and frost pockets — never try to erect a greenhouse on recently-dug soil

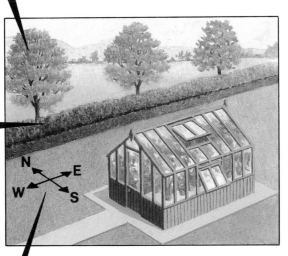

A windbreak such as a hedge is useful on the north and east sides, as strong winds can damage the structure and even ordinary winds will increase the heating bill. The greenhouse should be sited at least 15 ft away from the hedge

A free-standing green-house should be located as close as practical to the home — electric wiring is costly and carrying other forms of fuel to the far end of the garden is a chore in winter

Most experts recommend that a free-standing greenhouse should be set so that the ridge runs from East to West. A few believe that the house should run North to South, but all agree that orientation is not a key factor for an average-sized house. The situation is quite different with a lean-to structure. Built against a south wall it will be a sun trap — fine in winter but too hot for comfort in summer. The best site for a lean-to is a west-facing wall

Doing the Work

A firm and level site is essential — if the structure is larger than 8 ft x 6 ft you will need a concrete foundation. Buy the recommended base if one is offered by the manufac-turer. Mark out the outline of the building with pegs and string.

Read the instructions carefully before you start. Lay out the parts and number them if necessary. Erect the framework first — do not attempt to glaze at this stage. Make sure that the structure is firmly anchored.

Choose a still, dry day for glazing — begin in the morning and try to finish the job in a single day as a strong wind can cause havoc to a partly glazed greenhouse. Make sure the frames are square — never use the glass to straighten aluminium glazing bars.

Getting Permission

PLANNING PERMISSION

Permission from the Planning Department of your local authority is not usually necessary for an average-sized structure in a standard location. Still, it is best to check as there are situations where you will need to obtain formal permission. Any one of the following conditions calls for an application to be made before you start erecting the building:

● The volume of the greenhouse or conservatory will increase the volume of a detached or semi-detached house by more than 70 cubic metres or 15 per cent — these figures are reduced to 50 cubic metres or 10 per cent for a terraced house.

● Part of the structure will project beyond the front of the house facing the road, or will be higher than the top of the roof.

● The structure will cover more than half the garden if the house is a listed building or is located in a conservation area.

BUILDING REGULATIONS

Building regulation approval is not usually required if the greenhouse or conservatory is at ground level and the floor area will be less than 30 sq. metres. It is still wise to check.

NEIGHBOURS' PERMISSION

Not compulsory, but a good idea if the new structure interferes with the view from their house. A different model or a change in the site plan may be necessary to avoid a great deal of friction, but in many cases a discussion before you begin is all that is necessary in order to prevent a dispute.

CHAPTER 3

PLANTS

It is difficult to define just what we mean by a 'greenhouse' plant. There are some plants which live their whole lives within the confines of a greenhouse or conservatory. Then there are others which produce their ornamental display or their crop under glass, but have to start their life outside the greenhouse or must spend part of their adult life in the open. The final group of plants have a life pattern which is just the opposite — they produce their ornamental display or their crop in the garden. For them the greenhouse is a place which provides a protected environment. This is either at the start of their life as seedlings or cuttings, or when they are established plants in pots and in need of frost-free conditions.

The first group described above are true greenhouse plants in every sense of the word. They spend their whole life under glass, although there are a few which benefit from being stood outdoors in the fresh air during the summer months — examples include Citrus, Jasmine and Passion Flower. In this 'true' greenhouse plant group are the vegetables which need protection in order to crop satisfactorily in this country or to ensure an earlier crop than would be produced outdoors. Here you will find the greenhouse varieties of Tomatoes and Cucumbers, the short-rooted types of Carrots, the winter and spring varieties of Lettuce and tender vegetables such as Aubergines and Capsicums. In addition to these vegetables there are the greenhouse fruits — Grapes of course, but also Figs, Peaches, Melons etc.

These food crops dominate the average small greenhouse in summer, but in the conservatory it is the ornamental plant which is king. Depending on the size of the structure and personal preference, these ornamentals can be as small as a tiny rock plant or as large as a stately palm. However, even when money and space are no problem you cannot choose just any ornamental plant for your greenhouse or conservatory — its minimum temperature requirement will have to be met in winter. As noted in the lists beginning on page 23 there are hundreds from which to make your choice for a cool house (minimum temperature 45°F), and most people aim for a mixed collection of widely different sorts. But then there are the hobbyists who devote all or a sectioned-off part of the greenhouse to a specialist collection. There is much to be said for this approach if you are a keen collector of alpines, cacti, ferns or orchids — you can enjoy your hobby to the full and you can adapt and run your greenhouse to satisfy the specific needs of your specialist collection.

The second major group of plants for growing in a greenhouse is a small but important one — these are the types which bloom or fruit in the greenhouse but must spend part of their lives outdoors. Included here are the hardy spring-flowering bulbs which are grown in bowls that begin life in a plunge bed outdoors. There are the pots of Strawberries which are brought into the cool greenhouse from the garden in January and there produce fruit which is ready for picking in April. A final example is the late-flowering Chrysanthemum which spends its summer in a pot outdoors and is then brought into the greenhouse in late September.

The final group of plants is large and complex — these are garden plants which are either raised or overwintered under glass. They are not 'greenhouse' plants in any sense of the word — your lean-to is merely a place where they can stay to keep out of the wet and cold of winter weather outdoors. Here you will find seedlings of half hardy vegetables and bedding plants, cuttings of Chrysanthemums and pots of bedding Geraniums and Fuchsias waiting for the return of frost-free nights in the spring.

The ideal is to have *two* structures, a purely practical greenhouse for producing seedlings, resting sick plants and growing vegetables etc, and a decorative conservatory to show off your ornamentals at their best. But that is a counsel of perfection — in your single quite small greenhouse you can have a variety of plants to delight you all year round.

Ornamentals : General

Plants which are grown for the sole or primary purpose of providing a decorative display within the greenhouse or conservatory. Bulbous types and specialist groups (alpines, ferns, cacti and orchids) are dealt with elsewhere.

Pages 22–47

Ornamentals : Bulbs

Plants which are raised from swollen underground parts (corms, tubers, rhizomes or true bulbs). **Greenhouse Bulbs** are half hardy types grown under glass. **Hardy Spring Bulbs** are started outdoors and then brought inside for display.

Pages 48–55

Ornamentals : Alpines

A group of low-growing plants which are grown under glass to protect them from winter snow, frost, wind and rain. Cool temperatures and extra ventilation are necessary — an adapted cold greenhouse is satisfactory.

Pages 56–57

Ornamentals : Cacti

A distinct group of succulents which are almost all leafless and bear woolly or bristly cushions on their stems. **Desert Cacti** require little or no winter watering. **Forest Cacti** have their own special requirements.

Pages 58–59

Ornamentals : Ferns

A large group of non-flowering plants which range from ground-hugging varieties to tree-like specimens. Most require high air humidity, shade and compost which is kept moist at all times. Temperature requirements vary.

Pages 60–61

Ornamentals : Orchids

A group of plants noted for their colourful and exotic blooms. A prominent lower petal ('lip') is often present and most have a thickened stem base. Each has its own requirements and they range from 'fairly easy' to 'extremely difficult'.

Pages 62–63

Bedding Plants

Plants which are raised from seeds or cuttings in the greenhouse and are then planted out in the garden as temporary occupants to provide a colourful display. Bedding plants may be annuals, biennials or perennials.

Pages 64–65

Garden Perennials and Shrubs

Plants which spend all their active adult lives in the open garden but occupy the greenhouse either at the start of their lives or during the winter months when frost threatens their existence.

Pages 66–67

Tomatoes

For many years the most popular greenhouse plant and likely to remain so. Once grown in border soil and pots — now primarily cultivated in growing bags. Seed is sown in early March for planting in early May.

Pages 68–72

Cucumbers

Second only to Tomatoes in popularity. Once a difficult crop, requiring higher temperatures and moister air than Tomatoes, but new F_1 hybrids have made Cucumber cultivation much simpler.

Pages 73–74

Vegetables

Greenhouse Vegetables spend all their lives under glass, from seed sowing to harvest. **Garden Vegetables** are hardy or half hardy varieties which are raised as seedlings under glass, prior to planting out in the garden.

Pages 75–78

Fruit

Plants which are grown solely or primarily for fruit production. Some, such as Melons and fan-trained Peaches, spend all their lives in the greenhouse — others spend part of their lives in the garden.

Pages 79–81

Ornamentals : General

Greenhouse ornamentals are a vast collection of plants of every shape and size, but they all share a single feature. Their sole or primary purpose is to provide a decorative display within and not outside the greenhouse or conservatory. Described here is the major group of them — the general ornamentals. They are the non-bulbous sorts and exclude the specialist types (alpines, ferns, cacti and orchids) which have fairly specific requirements and are often grown on their own.

The range of general ornamentals is enormous, but year after year the same mainstays appear — varieties of Chrysanthemum, Pelargonium, Carnation, Impatiens, Fuchsia, Begonia, Cineraria and Primula. Other popular ones include Streptocarpus, Kalanchoe and a host of foliage house plants. There are two basic reasons for this restricted range in common use — limited space and limited availability. Shortage of bed or staging area is a real problem for the owner of a small and overcrowded greenhouse, and here the bolder specimens and showy climbers are generally out of the question. But it is no excuse if you have a large and underused conservatory. The difficulty in finding the more unusual indoor plants is another real problem, as garden centres seem to offer the same rather limited range of greenhouse and conservatory plants. The answer is twofold. Many types can be raised from seed, which also is an economical way of stocking your greenhouse, and you can send off for the catalogues of the conservatory plant nurseries which advertise in the gardening magazines. Look in the Plant Finder if you want to find a supplier of a specific plant. Of course there is a third source of unusual plants if you are lucky — cuttings obtained from a friend with a well-stocked conservatory.

There is no need to create a steamy jungle — many of the plants in this section will be happy in a cool greenhouse or conservatory. The usual plan is to have a kaleidoscope of colourful blooms all year round, but in the conservatory you should aim for a permanent background of 'architectural' plants to show off these flowering types — foliage specimens with interesting shapes and/or leaves. And do be bold if space permits — grow shrubs such as Camellia or Hydrangea in tubs and have tall climbers such as Lapageria and Passiflora.

The general ornamentals fall roughly into two groups with no clear-cut dividing line between them. Conservatory plants are generally eye-catching and often tall or spreading. House plants on the other hand are usually smaller and are capable of growing quite happily in the rather shadier conditions found in the average living room. Two groups, then, but the split is of more value to textbook writers than to conservatory owners.

ABUTILON   Flowering Maple
Minimum temperature: 45°F

Abutilons are not difficult to grow. The Maple-like leaves are often blotched with yellow or white and the bell-like pendent blooms appear all summer long. **A. megapotamicum** is a 4 ft climber which needs support. The lantern-like flowers are red and yellow — the variety **'Variegatum'** has yellow-splashed leaves. The tree-like **A. hybridum** needs space. It quickly reaches 5 ft and the flowers are available in various colours — **'Ashford Red'** (rose-red), **'Canary Bird'** (yellow), **'Boule de Neige'** (white) etc. These plants are best treated as annuals — sow seed in February.

Abutilon megapotamicum

ACACIA   Mimosa, Wattle
Minimum temperature: 45°F

The Mimosa used by flower arrangers is **A. dealbata**. It is an easy-to-grow shrub which can reach 20 ft if space is available — prune back after flowering to avoid legginess. The flowers appear from December to March — small yellow powder-puffs above the 9 in. long feathery fronds which are silvery-grey. **A. armata** (Kangaroo Thorn) also bears fluffy yellow blooms in late winter, but the growth is more compact and there are spiny 1 in. long phylloclades (false leaves) instead of true leaves.

ACALYPHA   Acalypha
Minimum temperature: 65°F

The two conservatory Acalyphas are quite different in appearance but they do share several features. Both are woody shrubs which need moist air and stove house conditions. **A. hispida** (Chenille Plant) bears 1 ft long tassels of tiny red flowers in late summer. Prune back hard in early spring. **A. wilkesiana** (Copperleaf) has large coppery leaves blotched with green or brown.

Acalypha hispida

AESCHYNANTHUS   Basket Vine
Minimum temperature: 55°F

An eye-catching hanging plant with 1½–2 ft long trailing stems, waxy leaves and red flowers. The easiest to find is the Lipstick Vine **A. lobbianus** — the tubular 2 in. red flowers arise from the brown 'lipstick' cases in summer. They are fussy plants — you must keep water and direct sunlight off the leaves. Other dislikes include cold draughts, dry air and wet soil in winter.

AGAPANTHUS   African Lily
Minimum temperature: 35°F

Agapanthus needs cool conditions in winter — apart from this requirement it is an easy plant to grow. Ball-like flower-heads on 2 ft stalks appear above the strap-like leaves. It is often sold as **A. africanus**, but this name seems to cover **A. campanulatus** and many hybrids. The 1½ in. long tubular flowers are usually blue, but white varieties are available. Plant in a tub and repot every 5 years.

Agapanthus africanus

AGAPETES   Agapetes
Minimum temperature: 55°F

This member of the Heather family with arching stems is suitable for the larger conservatory. The lance-shaped glossy leaves are about 1 in. long, and in spring the stems bear pendent urn-shaped blooms on short flower-stalks. The usual species is **A. serpens** — the flowers are rose-red and bear dark red V-shaped markings. The drooping branches will need some form of support.

AGLAONEMA   Aglaonema
Minimum temperature: 65°F

House plants which need moist air, shade from sunlight and warmth in winter. They will grow under shrubs in a heated conservatory. See The House Plant Expert, page 65.

ALLAMANDA   Golden Trumpet
Minimum temperature: 55°F

An excellent climber for the conservatory — **A. cathartica** bears 3 in. wide flaring yellow trumpets in summer. It needs moist air and some direct sunlight — water sparingly in winter.

Allamanda cathartica

ORNAMENTALS: GENERAL

Anigozanthos manglesii

Anthurium andreanum

Aphelandra squarrosa 'Louisae'

Aristolochia elegans

ALOCASIA　Kris Plant
Minimum temperature: 65°F

This showy foliage plant needs really warm conditions if it is to survive from year to year. It is quite spectacular — **A. amazonica** bears 1–2 ft long arrow-shaped leaves which are dark green with bold white veins. **A. sanderiana** differs by having scalloped-edged leaves which are purple below. With both these species you will need to keep the air moist and the compost constantly damp during the growing season.

ALYOGYNE　Alyogyne
Minimum temperature: 45°F

You will find this one in the catalogues of some conservatory plant nurseries. It is free-flowering and bears 3 in. wide Mallow-like blooms. The favourite one is **A. huegelii 'Santa Cruz'** — an erect shrub which needs to be cut back in winter to keep it in bounds. The spring-summer flowers are pale blue. **A. hakeifolia** has red-centred mauve flowers.

ANIGOZANTHOS　Kangaroo Paw
Minimum temperature: 35°F

A clump-forming evergreen which has Iris-like leaves and unusual flowers. Each bloom is a long tube which is split at the end into 6 segments, giving a kangaroo paw-like effect. **A. flavidus** grows about 2 ft high and bears yellowish-green flowers in late spring. **A. manglesii** is more colourful — the 3 in. long green flowers are bright red at the base.

ANTHURIUM　Anthurium
Minimum temperature: 55°F

A popular plant for the warm conservatory. The flowering ones have a distinctly exotic look with their palette-like flowers in summer. **A. scherzerianum** (Flamingo Flower) is the easiest to grow. The leaves are lance-shaped and the waxy 2 in. long flower has a curly orange tail. The larger **A. andreanum** (Oilcloth Flower) has heart-shaped leaves with 4 in. puckered flowers which bear a straight or arched yellow tail. **A. wendlandii** can grow to 6–8 ft across. The foliage species is **A. crystallinum** which bears 1–2 ft long velvety leaves with prominent silvery veins.

APHELANDRA　Zebra Plant
Minimum temperature: 55°F

A popular house plant, but this tropical American genus really needs conservatory conditions if it is to survive from one year to another. The best known variety is **A. squarrosa 'Louisae'** with its white-veined leaves and cone-shaped flower-heads made up of red-edged yellow bracts. These flowers appear in autumn and last for about 6 weeks. The plant grows about 2 ft high — choose the variety **'Dania'** for a more compact bush. Cut the stems back to about 4 in. in spring.

ARAUCARIA　Norfolk Island Pine
Minimum temperature: 35°F

An easy-to-grow conifer for the conservatory. **A. heterophylla** (**A. excelsa**) grows to about 5–6 ft, bearing its stiff branches in tiers. The needle-like leaves are ½ in. long. Do not repot too frequently — every 3–4 years is frequent enough. Dry compost or constantly dry air will cause leaf drop.

ARDISIA　Coral Berry
Minimum temperature: 45°F

Another specimen tree, but this one bears glossy leaves and fragrant white or pale pink flowers which are followed by red berries. **A. crenata** (**A. crispa**) is the popular species — keep it cool in winter and prune back in early spring.

ARISTOLOCHIA　Dutchman's Pipe
Minimum temperature: 55°F

An unusual climber which bears pipe-shaped flowers — hence the common name. The one to look for is **A. elegans** which produces 3 in. wide white-blotched maroon flowers in summer and autumn. Prune back hard after flowering.

ARUNDINARIA   Bamboo
Minimum temperature: 35°F

The conservatory Bamboos are grown in tubs to provide handsome specimen plants — they have Reed-like stems and short branches bearing grassy leaves. Examples include **A. auricoma** (3 ft, yellow-striped leaves), **A. variegata** (2 ft, cream-striped leaves) and **A. nitida** (8 ft, purple stems).

ARUNDO   Giant Reed
Minimum temperature: 35°F

Like Bamboo this grassy plant bears cane-like stems. **A. donax 'Variegata'** is the one to buy — 6 ft arching stems with leaves which bear broad white stripes. Plumes of tiny white flowers appear in autumn.

Arundo donax 'Variegata'

ASCLEPIAS   Blood Flower
Minimum temperature: 45°F

It is strange that this American plant is so rarely seen in the conservatory. **A. curassavica** is a 3 ft shrub which has lance-shaped leaves and in summer and autumn there are round heads of starry flowers. Each flower has bright orange petals and an inner yellow crown. Asclepias is easy to raise from seed.

ASPARAGUS   Asparagus Fern
Minimum temperature: 45°F

Asparagus Fern is not really a fern — the 'leaves' are needle-like branches and it belongs to the Lily family. There are many types which can be used to provide a green foil for more colourful plants — see The House Plant Expert, page 69.

Asclepias curassavica

ASPIDISTRA   Cast Iron Plant
Minimum temperature: 35°F

The Aspidistra is usually thought of as a house plant rather than a conservatory one, but it is an extremely useful subject when you are trying to create a Victorian look with palms, cane chairs etc. See The House Plant Expert, page 70.

BANKSIA   Banksia
Minimum temperature: 45°F

This one is a challenge, but well worth the trouble. The flowers are spectacular — globe- or cone-shaped flower-heads containing hundreds of tiny but colourful blooms. Now for the special needs — good ventilation, rather dry air, bright light and a compost of ⅔ moss peat/⅓ grit. Water sparingly in winter. Even if conditions are perfect some species take 3 years before reaching the flowering stage. **B. grandis** grows 6 ft high and produces 6 in.–1 ft high orange flower-heads in spring.

Banksia grandis

BEAUCARNEA   Pony Tail
Minimum temperature: 45°F

An interesting plant which needs space — in time it will grow 6 ft high and the plume of strap-like leaves has a 5 ft spread. The key feature of **B. recurvata** is the swollen bulb-like base which stores water. An easy plant which will stand some neglect.

BEGONIA   Begonia
Minimum temperature: 55°F

The types of flowering Begonias are many and varied, and identification is often difficult. The showiest blooms are borne by the tuberous types — see page 49. Described here are the fibrous-rooted flowering ones and also the foliage varieties. The most popular flowering Begonias with fibrous roots are the bushy types. These are the ones which are usually thrown away after flowering — here you will find the Lorraine Begonias which bloom at Christmas and the brightly coloured Hiemalis hybrids such as **B. 'Fireglow'** which can be bought in flower at any time of the year. The favourite bushy type is the Wax Begonia (**B. semperflorens**) which can be kept from year to year. Apart from the bushy types there are the cane-stemmed varieties (e.g **B. coccinea**) and the trailing types such as **B. glaucophylla**. Finally there are the foliage Begonias, dominated by **B. rex**. For details see The House Plant Expert, pages 74–79.

Begonia glaucophylla

Bougainvillea glabra

Bouvardia domestica

Guzmania lingulata

Browallia speciosa 'Major'

BELOPERONE   Shrimp Plant
Minimum temperature: 55°F

There is just one species — **B. guttata**. It is a popular house plant but prefers the brighter light of the greenhouse or conservatory. Both stems and leaves are downy, and the 4 in. long curved flower-heads are made up of orange bracts and small white flowers growing between them. These prawn-like flower-heads will appear almost all year round if you water regularly between spring and autumn, and sparingly in winter.

BOUGAINVILLEA   Paper Flower
Minimum temperature: 45°F

A distinctly exotic climber which produces brightly coloured bracts all summer long — it can be seen flowering outdoors in sub-tropical and tropical areas throughout the world. The woody and spiny stems will need some form of support and good light is essential. Plant in the border soil or a 12 in. pot. Keep the compost moist at all times during the growing season — in autumn cut back the stems and keep the compost almost dry in winter. The basic species is the rose-purple **B. glabra**, but it is much more usual to grow one of the many hybrids such as **'Mrs. Butt'** (rose-crimson), **'Orange King'** (orange), **'Scarlett O'Hara'** (orange-red) and **'Jamaica White'** (white).

BOUVARDIA   Bouvardia
Minimum temperature: 55°F

This plant is not easy to find at the garden centre as it is a disappointing house plant, but in the warm, sunny and moist atmosphere under glass it blooms freely. The tubular flowers are ¾ in. across and are borne in large clusters above the leaves in summer and autumn. The hybrid **B. domestica** grows about 2 ft high and was very popular in the Victorian conservatory. The variety **'President Cleveland'** is bright red — there are also pink and white types. Some are very fragrant.

BREYNIA   Leaf Flower, Snow Bush
Minimum temperature: 55°F

This shrub was introduced as a house plant in the 1980s but it never became popular. The problem is that it is not happy in the dry air of the living room — it needs a conservatory or greenhouse. **B. nivosa 'Roseopicta'** bears 1 in. oval leaves which are pure white splashed with pink and green — hence the common names. Protect from direct sunlight and repot every 2 years.

BROMELIADS
Minimum temperature: 55°F

The bromeliads are a group of interesting and sometimes spectacular plants which will flourish in the conservatory if you look after their unusual watering requirements. The general growth pattern is a rosette of leathery and strap-like leaves with a central water-holding 'vase' — this foliage may be green and plain or patterned and highly decorative. A showy flower-head is produced on top of a stalk by many varieties. The floral display may last for months but once it has faded the leaf rosette dies and is replaced by another. This flower-head is composed of colourful bracts — the true flowers are not significant. The basic point to remember is that bromeliads have tiny root systems — this means that they should not be repotted and watering consists of filling the central 'vase' every 1–2 months. The compost should be kept slightly moist — never wet. There are many genera and species — see The House Plant Expert (pages 86–89) for details of **Aechmea**, **Ananas**, **Billbergia**, **Guzmania**, **Tillandsia**, **Cryptanthus**, **Neoregelia**, **Nidularium** and **Vriesea**. In recent years the air plants ('Grey Tillandsias') have become popular as they literally live on air. Water is absorbed from the moist atmosphere and nutrients are obtained from dust.

BROWALLIA   Bush Violet
Minimum temperature: 55°F

A perennial bushy plant which is generally grown as an annual — sow seed in early spring for summer flowers or delay sowing until summer for winter flowering. Pinch out the growing tips occasionally to maintain bushiness — staking is often necessary to support the 1½–2 ft stems. **B. speciosa** has 2 in. wide star-shaped violet flowers with white throats. **'Silver Bells'** is a dwarf white-flowered variety. **'Major'** is a blue-violet type which can grow 3 ft high.

BRUNFELSIA   Brunfelsia
Minimum temperature: 55°F

You should grow this one — with care it will stay in flower almost all year round and the blooms change colour as they mature. The popular one is **B. calycina** (Yesterday, Today and Tomorrow) — a 2 ft high shrub with purple blooms which fade to pale violet and then finally white. Protect from direct sun in summer and provide moist air. Stand the pot outdoors occasionally in warm weather. The taller **B. americana** (Lady of the Night) has flowers which change from yellow to cream and finally to white.

CAESALPINIA   Caesalpinia
Minimum temperature: 35°F

There are a number of showy exotic plants you can grow in a cool house which is kept at just a few degrees above freezing in winter — **C. gilliesii** (Bird of Paradise Flower) is a good example. It is a tall-growing shrub with ferny leaves, but it can be kept in check by pruning. In summer the 1 ft high flower-heads appear — a cluster of yellow flowers with a mass of long red stamens.

CALADIUM   Angel's Wings
Minimum temperature: 65°F

You can grow this plant for summer display in a cool house, but to keep it as a permanent resident you will need stove house conditions. From late spring to early autumn the varieties of **C. hortulanum** provide a colourful display of arrow-shaped leaves — paper thin and variously coloured in green, white, red, pink, orange and purple. Stop watering when the foliage dies down — replant the tubers in spring.

CALCEOLARIA   Slipper Flower
Minimum temperature: 45°F

This temporary pot plant is grown for its pouch-like flowers which last for about a month in spring or summer. **C. herbeohybrida** has large downy leaves and grows about 1½ ft high — there are a number of varieties with yellow, red or orange puffed-up flowers which are often spotted or blotched. They can be raised from seed. Sow in summer for flowering next year, but it is more usual to buy potted plants in flower.

CALLISTEMON   Bottlebrush Plant
Minimum temperature: 45°F

A good plant for the cool house or conservatory. The key feature is the display of fluffy floral spikes in summer — the common name describes their appearance. **C. citrinus** is the most popular one — it grows about 3 ft high and bears 4 in. cylindrical red flower spikes. **'Burning Bush'** is a more compact red variety — **'Mauve Mist'** is pink.

CAMELLIA   Camellia
Minimum temperature: 35°F

A fine winter-flowering shrub when grown in a large pot or tub. The 3–5 in. wide single or double blooms of **C. japonica** appear amongst the glossy leaves. It is not an easy plant for the conservatory — the house must be a cold one and you will have to use lime-free water and compost. Stand the pot outdoors once flowering has finished and bring it indoors in autumn.

CAMPANULA   Bell Flower
Minimum temperature: 45°F

The popular one is the Italian Bellflower **C. isophylla**. It is a trailer with grey-green hairy stems which grow about 1½ ft long — the usual colour is blue but there is a white variety (**'Alba'**) and a mauve one (**'Mayi'**). **C. pyramidalis** (Chimney Campanula) is a tall upright plant with white or blue flowers.

CAMPSIS   Campsis
Minimum temperature: 45°F

Campsis is a feathery-leaved climber for the conservatory. It may grow 10–15 ft high but can be kept in check by pruning. **C. tagliabuana 'Madame Galen'** produces clusters of pink trumpet-shaped flowers from late summer to autumn. The leaves fall in winter.

Brunfelsia calycina

Caladium hortulanum 'White Queen'

Callistemon citrinus

Campsis tagliabuana 'Madame Galen'

Cassia corymbosa

Cestrum elegans

Chorizema ilicifolium

Chrysanthemum morifolium

CAPSICUM   Christmas Pepper
Minimum temperature: 35°F

A popular house plant bought in December for the display of green, orange and red cone-like fruits. The display lasts until early spring — see The House Plant Expert page 112 for details.

CASSIA   Cassia
Minimum temperature: 45°F

This free-flowering shrub grows about 6 ft high, but can be pruned annually if it gets out of bounds. It blooms in late summer to winter — clusters of cup-shaped yellow flowers which may be followed by flattened pods ('Senna pods'). It is listed in the catalogues as **C. alata, C. corymbosa** or **C. didymobotrya**.

CELOSIA   Plume Flower
Minimum temperature: 35°F

Sow seed in February at 60°–65°F for a summer display. **C. plumosa** bears its yellow or red plumes of tiny flowers for many weeks provided you do not allow the compost to dry out. The usual height is 1½ ft, but 8 in. dwarfs are available. **C. cristata** has a velvety cockscomb head rather than a plumed one.

CESTRUM   Jessamine
Minimum temperature: 45°F

The Jessamines grow 6–10 ft high — the weak stems need some form of support. All the species have oval shiny leaves and in summer large clusters of tube-like flowers. The most fragrant one is the white-flowering **C. nocturnum** with blooms which open at night and can fill the conservatory with their fragrance. **C. auranticum** bears fragrant 1 in. long orange flowers — **C. elegans** has red flowers.

CHLOROPHYTUM   Spider Plant
Minimum temperature: 45°F

A very popular house plant, but its role in the greenhouse or conservatory is to provide a background for showier specimens. See The House Plant Expert, page 114.

CHOISYA   Mexican Orange Blossom
Minimum temperature: 35°F

This neat evergreen shrub is well known as a garden plant but is hardly ever mentioned in greenhouse textbooks or catalogues. It does make an excellent tub plant, producing its white starry flowers in spring and occasionally in summer and autumn. **C. ternata** is available in the Shrub section of your garden centre.

CHORIZEMA   Chorizema
Minimum temperature: 45°F

A rarity, but you will find it in some of the specialist catalogues. It is a weak-stemmed 2 ft high shrub which will need some support. The leaves are spiny and the flowers of **C. ilicifolium** are borne in long clusters in spring and summer. Each bloom is about ½ in. wide and is a mixture of orange, yellow, pink and pale purple.

CHRYSANTHEMUM   Chrysanthemum
Minimum temperature: 45°F

The Greenhouse Chrysanthemums (**C. morifolium**) are the late-flowering sorts, producing blooms from October to late December. For large flowers choose an Exhibition variety and begin the year in February by taking cuttings — alternatively buy rooted cuttings in early spring. In April transfer the rooted cuttings from 3 in. to 5 in. pots. In mid May move into 8 in. pots and insert one or more stout canes to support the stems. Pinch out ('stop') the tips of the stems when they are about 8 in. high. In early June move the pots outdoors. Water regularly and in late September bring the pots back in. Disbud as necessary and feed until the buds show colour. Other types are the Pot varieties which are bought in flower at any time of the year for temporary display, the seed-raised Charm varieties covered with masses of flowers and the Cascade types with pendent stems, and the Marguerites (**Argyranthemum** or **C. frutescens**) with their yellow-disced flowers in summer.

CINERARIA   Cineraria
Minimum temperature: 45°F

Cineraria (proper name **Senecio cruentus**) is bought between late winter and mid spring. Buy a specimen with some open flowers and masses of unopened buds — the display will last for 4–6 weeks after which the plant should be discarded. The large heart-shaped leaves of the 9 in.–2½ ft high plant are covered by the Daisy-like flowers. Many colours are available — the showiest strain is the Grandiflora group with 2–3 in. wide blooms. For a compact plant grow the Multiflora Nana strain. Cineraria can be raised from seed sown in May.

Senecio cruentus

CLERODENDRUM   Glory Bower
Minimum temperature: 55°F

The Glory Bower has long, weak stems which can reach 8 ft or more — allow to trail or twine around an upright support. Keep in check by pruning in winter if space is limited. Provide a moist atmosphere and water very sparingly in winter. **C. thomsoniae** produces clusters of inflated red-tipped white blooms all summer long. **C. ugandense** (Blue Glory Bower) bears blue flowers in spring.

CLIANTHUS   Clianthus
Minimum temperature: 45°F

These shrubs have feathery leaves and in late spring or summer an unusual floral display. The 4 in. long blooms are distinctly beak-like, the lower petal being curved and pointed. The low-growing **C. formosum** (Glory Pea) grows 2 ft high and bears bright red flowers in summer — treat as an annual. **C. puniceus** (Parrot Bill or Lobster Claw) is an 8 ft straggling shrub with red flowers which open in late spring.

Clerodendrum thomsoniae

CLIVIA   Kaffir Lily
Minimum temperature: 35°F

An old favourite. **C. miniata** displays its cluster of bell-shaped orange flowers in spring on top of a tall stalk above the strap-like leaves. Yellow, red and cream varieties are available. A rather temperamental plant — keep cool in winter and water sparingly between late autumn and early spring.

COBAEA   Cup and Saucer Vine
Minimum temperature: 35°F

The Cup and Saucer Vine **C. scandens** is grown outdoors as an annual, but under glass it is a rampant perennial climber. The flowering season extends from midsummer to autumn — each mature flower consisting of a 3 in. high purple 'cup' in a pale green 'saucer'. Cut back hard once flowering is finished.

Clianthus puniceus

CODIAEUM   Croton
Minimum temperature: 65°F

This foliage house plant needs tropical-like conditions in order to flourish — if the temperature goes below 60°–65°F or if it fluctuates widely then the plant will stop growing and may lose its lower leaves. The air must be moist. **C. variegatum pictum** (Joseph's Coat) is the basic Croton, but there are scores of different types. The standard leaf form is multicoloured with distinctly coloured veins. Some of the popular Crotons are illustrated on page 119 of The House Plant Expert.

COLEONEMA   Coleonema
Minimum temperature: 45°F

You will have to go to a specialist supplier for this one, but it is not difficult to grow. **C. pulchrum** is a 3 ft spreading shrub which is Heather-like in appearance and bears masses of starry pink flowers in spring and summer.

Cobaea scandens

COLEUS   Coleus
Minimum temperature: 55°F

The Poor Man's Croton — it is easily raised from cuttings or seed and is much simpler to care for than its rival. However, it is not as impressive and the plants soon become leggy — it is best to treat Coleus as an annual. Many named hybrids of **C. blumei** are available — nearly all have foliage with two or more colours.

Columnea banksii

Coronilla glauca

Crossandra undulifolia

Cupressus cashmeriana

COLUMNEA   Goldfish Plant
Minimum temperature: 55°F

A showy conservatory plant — grow it well and its 3 ft trailing stems will bear rows of red flowers in winter or early spring. Each 3 in. long bloom is a hooded tube with a yellow throat or mouth. Columnea is not an easy plant — the smooth-leaved types such as **C. banksii** and **C. 'Stavanger'** are less difficult than the hairy-leaved ones (e.g **C. gloriosa**, **C. microphylla** and its variegated variety **'Tricolor'**). Keep the compost moist at all times between spring and autumn.

CORONILLA   Coronilla
Minimum temperature: 35°F

An attractive evergreen shrub which is almost hardy and so is useful for a conservatory which is kept just above freezing on cold winter nights. **C. glauca** grows about 4 ft tall and in spring and summer bears clusters of yellow Pea-like flowers. These blooms have a Peach-like fragrance.

CORREA   Correa
Minimum temperature: 35°F

These unusual Australian shrubs are easy to grow and bear their flowers early in the year. **C. backhousiana** produces small clusters of 1 in. long pendent bell-like flowers which are white or cream. **C. reflexa** grows to about the same size (3 ft x 3 ft) but has more colourful flowers — red with a narrow white mouth.

COSTUS   Spiral Ginger
Minimum temperature: 55°F

Costus is an interesting but rarely seen conservatory plant. It gets its common name from the way the large leaves spiral around the stem. The ragged-petalled flowers are about 2–3 in. across — they appear in summer. **C. igneus** grows about 1½ ft high — the leaves are glossy and the flowers orange and yellow. **C. speciosus** will reach 4–6 ft with yellow-centred white blooms.

CROSSANDRA   Firecracker Flower
Minimum temperature: 55°F

The Firecracker Flower is a colourful plant and blooms from spring to autumn, but it needs humid air around the 3 in. long lance-shaped leaves. **C. undulifolia** (**C. infundibuliformis**) is the usual one — the orange open-faced tubular blooms are borne in clusters on top of 2 ft high flower-stalks.

CUPHEA   Cigar Plant
Minimum temperature: 55°F

You will often see this one in the House Plant section of the garden centre — a pretty but not a particularly eye-catching plant. **C. ignea** grows about 1 ft tall and the bush bears pendent 1 in. tubular flowers from spring to autumn — red with white and purple mouths. Cut back hard in early spring to prevent the plant from becoming leggy, but Cuphea is easily raised from spring-sown seed and is best grown as an annual.

CUPRESSUS   Cypress
Minimum temperature: 45°F

There is an excellent conifer for growing under glass — **C. cashmeriana** or the Kashmir Cypress. This small tree bears weeping branches of silvery-blue foliage. Another suitable species is **C. macrocarpa**. Prune in early spring if space is limited.

CYPERUS   Umbrella Plant
Minimum temperature: 55°F

An interesting foliage plant to grow amongst showy specimens. Cultivation is easy if you remember the golden rule — stand the pot in a saucer of water and keep the compost soaked at all times. **C. alternifolius** is the popular one with 3 ft stalks and grassy leaves radiating from the top like the spokes of an umbrella. **C. diffusus** is more compact (1 ft) with wider leaves. **C. papyrus** (Papyrus) grows to 5–8 ft and bears thread-like leaves — it requires stove house conditions.

CYTISUS   Genista
Minimum temperature: 45°F

This is the well-known Broom of the shrub border — it is less well known in the conservatory where it is usually called 'Genista'. Long sprays of yellow flowers appear in spring at the end of arching branches — these blooms are Pea-like and fragrant. The pot should be stood outdoors during the summer months. Choose from **C. racemosus**, **C. canariensis** or **C. 'Porlock'**.

Cytisus racemosus

DATURA   Angel's Trumpet
Minimum temperature: 55°F

The name has been changed in some of the catalogues but the beauty remains. You may now find it listed as **Brugmansia** and it is an excellent choice for the larger conservatory, provided you remember that all parts are poisonous. It is a tub-grown shrub which bears very large pendent trumpets with flaring mouths in summer and autumn. Prune back hard once flowering has finished. **D. candida** is a popular species which will grow to 15 ft or more if space is available — the white flowers are highly fragrant and 8–10 in. long. **D. suaveolens** is another white-flowering species — for red-mouthed blooms grow **D. sanguinea**.

Datura suaveolens

DESFONTAINEA   Desfontainea
Minimum temperature: 35°F

This shrub is grown outdoors in mild areas of the country, but it is much more reliable in a frost-free greenhouse. **D. spinosa** is the species which is available — a plant with Holly-like leaves and tubular yellow-mouthed scarlet flowers in summer. The variety **'Harold Comber'** has orange-red blooms.

DIANTHUS   Dianthus
Minimum temperature: 55°F

Annual Pinks (hybrids of **D. chinensis**) and Sweet William (**D. barbatus**) are sometimes grown as temporary pot plants, but the true conservatory types are the Perpetual Flowering varieties — these are the ones you see at the florist shop. Choose a **'Sim'** variety — buy rooted cuttings in spring. Remove the tips to induce the formation of side shoots and move to a 5 in. and finally a 7 in. pot as growth proceeds. Provide adequate support for the long stems and remove the side buds to ensure large blooms. Cut flowers can be obtained at any time of the year if the temperature does not fall below 55°F. The plants will remain productive for about 3 years — replace with rooted cuttings taken from young plants.

Desfontainea spinosa

DIEFFENBACHIA   Dumb Cane
Minimum temperature: 65°F

The Dumb Cane will grow to 5 ft or more and is used as a specimen plant in the conservatory. The large fleshy leaves on stout stalks are a blend of green and cream or white, varying from the nearly all-green **D. amoena** to the nearly all-white **D. picta 'Rudolph Roehrs'**. Take note of the common name — the sap is extremely unpleasant if swallowed. Dieffenbachia will lose its lower leaves if the night temperature falls below 60°–65°F or if the air is too dry. For further details see The House Plant Expert, page 127.

DIOSCOREA   Ornamental Yam
Minimum temperature: 65°F

The conservatory needs plants with spectacular foliage as well as those with showy flowers, and **D. discolor** is an excellent choice for stove house conditions if you want eye-catching leaves. The twining stems bear 6 in. long heart-shaped leaves which are velvety green with silvery veins above and purple below. Growth dies down in autumn — keep the compost dry until early spring.

DIZYGOTHECA   False Aralia
Minimum temperature: 55°F

A graceful and tall-growing bush which has a distinctly lacy effect. Each long-stalked leaf of **D. elegantissima** is divided up into 7–10 finger-like serrated leaflets which are coppery when young and near-black when mature. A temperamental plant which cannot stand dry air, cold draughts or overwatering. Repot in spring every 2 years — it can grow 6 ft high in a warm conservatory.

Dieffenbachia picta 'Rudolph Roehrs'

Eccremocarpus scaber

Episcia cupreata

Erica hyemalis

Erythrina crista-galli

DRACAENA   Dracaena
Minimum temperature: 55°F

There are many species and varieties of Dracaena and the closely-related Cordyline. Most of them are false palms, the leafless woody trunk and crown of strap-like leaves giving a distinctly palm-like appearance. For a tall architectural plant choose one of the coloured-leaf varieties of **D. marginata** — where space is limited there are **D. sanderiana** and the well-known Ti Plant **Cordyline terminalis**.

DREGEA   Dregea
Minimum temperature: 35°F

There is just one species — you will find it labelled as **D. corrugata** or **Wattakaka sinensis**. It is a Hoya-like climber with twining stems and clusters of fragrant flowers in summer. Each flower is white and star-shaped with an inner corona which is white with red streaks.

ECCREMOCARPUS   Chilean Glory Flower
Minimum temperature: 45°F

An easy-to-grow climber which does not need warm conditions. **E. scaber** is quick-growing, reaching 10 ft or more in a single season. It flowers from spring to autumn, producing deep orange tubular blooms in clusters above the evergreen leaves. Cut back by about a half when flowering is over.

ECHIUM   Viper's Bugloss
Minimum temperature: 45°F

The annual **E. plantagineum** is hardy and can be grown in the garden, but the shrubby species need the winter warmth of the greenhouse or conservatory. **E. fastuosum** (Pride of Madeira) is an evergreen which grows about 4 ft high. It has downy leaves and the flowers in spring and summer are deep blue.

EPISCIA   Episcia
Minimum temperature: 55°F

This attractive trailer demands high air humidity — it can be grown in a hanging basket but it is better to use it as ground cover between taller plants. There are only 2 species you are likely to find, both bearing 1½ ft long stems and tubular flowers in summer. With **E. dianthiflora** (Lace Flower) the velvety green leaves are small and are borne in groups, and the white flowers have feathered edges. The foliage of **E. cupreata** (Flame Violet) is much showier — it has a quilted surface and distinct veins. The flowers are orange-red.

ERICA   Cape Heath
Minimum temperature: 45°F

The usual pattern with Cape Heaths is to buy them in bloom in autumn and winter as house plants and then throw them away when blooming is over. However, these indoor Heathers can be kept from year to year in a conservatory. Grow in lime-free compost and keep it moist at all times. Stand the pot outdoors in summer. The tiny flowers are globular or tubular and the foliage is needle-like. **E. gracilis** and **E. hyemalis** are the popular species.

ERYTHRINA   Coral Tree
Minimum temperature: 35°F

This tub plant is not often seen, but it is easy to grow in a frost-free house if you have the space. The thorny stems of **E. crista-galli** grow about 6 ft high. Red claw-like flowers are produced in autumn. The stems die down in winter — cut back and keep the compost dry until new buds appear in spring.

EUCALYPTUS   Gum Tree
Minimum temperature: 45°F

Young specimens are grown for their bluish foliage which has a distinct aroma when crushed. Pinch out the growing tips to keep in check and stand out of doors in summer. Grow **E. gunnii** (Cider Gum), **E. citriodora** (Lemon-scented Gum) or **E. globulus** (Tasmanian Blue Gum).

EUPHORBIA   Euphorbia
Minimum temperature: 55°F

The indoor Euphorbias come in a variety of quite dissimilar types. There are Poinsettia (see page 41) and the Succulent forms mentioned on page 46. The two here are the non-succulent flowering Euphorbias. **E. milii** (Crown of Thorns) has 3 ft high thorny stems and tiny flowers which are surrounded by showy bracts in red, orange or yellow. With care this plant will bloom nearly all year round, but **E. fulgens** (Scarlet Plume) is winter flowering. Its stems are arched and thornless.

Euphorbia fulgens

EXACUM   Persian Violet
Minimum temperature: 55°F

Raise the Persian Violet (**E. affine**) from seed or buy it as a pot plant with plenty of buds and only a few open blooms. The flowering season extends from midsummer to late autumn. It grows about 8 in. high — the fragrant flowers are pale purple with a gold centre. Discard after flowering.

FATSIA   Castor Oil Plant
Minimum temperature: 35°F

A good choice for a cool conservatory where you want to provide a Victorian feel, but too space-consuming for the ordinary greenhouse. **F. japonica** bears deeply lobed 1 ft wide leaves. The variety **'Variegata'** has white-edged leaves. Creamy flower-heads are produced in winter.

Exacum affine

FEIJOA   Pineapple Guava
Minimum temperature: 35°F

A plant which is definitely worth growing in the cool house. **F. sellowiana** is a 3 ft x 3 ft shrub with dark green leaves which are felted below. The 1½ in. wide late spring flowers have 4 petals, red on the inside and white outside. At the centre is a prominent display of yellow-tipped red anthers.

FELICIA   Blue Daisy
Minimum temperature: 45°F

If you keep the compost moist at all times it is possible to have this 1 ft high sub-shrub in bloom from spring to autumn. **F. amelloides** bears 1 in. wide yellow-centred blue Daisies — a pretty plant but the flowers will only open when the sun is shining. Pinch back regularly to keep it bushy.

Feijoa sellowiana

FICUS   Ornamental Fig
Minimum temperature: 55°F

The species of Ficus have long been one of the basic providers of ornamental foliage and stately shapes in the conservatory. There are the ground cover types with small leaves such as **F. pumila** and the tall and upright **F. lyrata** with 1½ ft long leaves. Between these two are the popular Rubber Plant (**F. elastica decora**) and the Weeping Fig (**F. benjamina**). For details see The House Plant Expert, pages 142–143. The secret of success with upright varieties of Ficus is to avoid overwatering — the compost must dry out to some extent between waterings.

FITTONIA   Net Plant
Minimum temperature: 65°F

A ground cover plant for the heated house — it does not flower but its oval leaves bear colourful veins which may be white (**F. argyroneura**), pink (**F. verschaffeltii**) or red (**F. verschaffeltii 'Pearcei'**). For success the plants need constant warmth, partial shade and moist air around the leaves. The easiest one to grow is the dwarf **F. argyroneura 'Nana'** (Snakeskin Plant) which has white-veined 1 in. long leaves.

FREMONTODENDRON   Fremontodendron
Minimum temperature: 35°F

You will find this one in the Shrub section of the catalogue or garden centre — it grows outdoors in mild areas. **F. californicum** is also a useful conservatory plant with lobed leathery leaves and cup-shaped yellow blooms from spring to autumn. Train the shrub against the wall.

Fremontodendron californicum

Fuchsia hybrida 'Ballet Girl'

Gardenia jasminoides

Grevillea banksii

Hardenbergia violacea

FUCHSIA   Fuchsia
Minimum temperature: 55°F

Most Fuchsias grown in the garden or as house plants are thrown away once the attractive pendent flowers have faded, but with a greenhouse these plants can be kept for several years. The rules are to cut back the stems and to water sparingly in winter — then repot in early spring. Take cuttings in spring and summer — pinch the tips of young stems to induce bushiness. It takes about 8 weeks for plants to bloom after stopping. Stake or leave to trail — remove dead blooms to ensure regular bud formation. There are numerous species and hundreds of named varieties of **F. hybrida** — see The House Plant Expert, pages 148–149.

GARDEN ANNUALS
Minimum temperature: 35°F

A number of annuals sold for the garden rather than the greenhouse can be grown in pots or hanging baskets to provide a display under glass. Sow seed or buy as bedding plants in spring for a summer display — hardy annuals can be sown in autumn to flower in the spring. Feed regularly with a high potash feed. Successful types include **Ageratum, Antirrhinum, Calendula, Clarkia, Convolvulus, Godetia, Lathyrus, Lobelia, Matthiola, Nemesia, Nicotiana, Phlox, Tagetes, Tropaeolum, Viola** and **Zinnia**.

GARDENIA   Gardenia
Minimum temperature: 65°F

A beautiful but fussy glossy-leaved shrub which really needs stove house conditions for free flowering. **G. jasminoides** bears 3 in. wide semi-double or double white flowers with a very strong fragrance. Use lime-free compost and water, provide an even temperature and keep the air moist.

GERBERA   Barberton Daisy
Minimum temperature: 45°F

The species grown is **G. jamesonii** — a clump-forming perennial with deeply lobed leaves and 4 in. wide Daisies on 2 ft leafless stalks. The petals are yellow, orange, red, pink or white around a central yellow disc. For more compact growth choose the variety **'Happipot'**. Keep almost dry in winter.

GREVILLEA   Grevillea
Minimum temperature: 55°F

The Silk Oak (**G. robusta**) is a popular feathery-leaved house plant, but there are shrubby flowering types for the conservatory. These are harder to grow than the Silk Oak but are worth the effort. **G. banksii** bears red flower-heads — each one is a crowded cluster of blooms with long curved styles.

GRISELINIA   Griselinia
Minimum temperature: 35°F

You will find this plant in the Shrub section of the catalogue or garden centre. **G. littoralis** (Broadleaf) is the species which is usually offered and can be grown outdoors in mild areas. Under glass it will grow about 4 ft high. The flowers are inconspicuous — the leathery leaves are the display feature. Choose a variegated variety such as **'Variegata'**, **'Dixon's Cream'** or **'Bantry Bay'**.

GYNURA   Velvet Plant
Minimum temperature: 45°F

A popular trailer which contrasts well with plants bearing pale green foliage — the leaves of **G. sarmentosa** are dark green and covered with glistening purple hairs. Pinch out the tips occasionally to prevent the growth from becoming too straggly. Remove the small flowers at the bud stage as their aroma is unpleasant.

HARDENBERGIA   Sarsparilla
Minimum temperature: 45°F

A scrambling shrub which grows about 6 ft high — it should be more widely grown. **H. violacea** is a free-flowering species which produces masses of mauve Pea-like blooms in late winter and spring. Pruning should take place after flowering.

HEDERA   Ivy
Minimum temperature: 35°F

Ivy is a very popular house plant rather than a conservatory one, but it can be used for ground or wall cover under glass. There is a wide range of varieties of **H. helix** — plain and variegated, heart-shaped and needle-pointed. See The House Plant Expert for details of Hedera — also for details of **Glechoma** (Ground Ivy), **Senecio** (Cape and German Ivy), **Plectranthus** (Swedish Ivy) and **Hemigraphis** (Red Ivy).

HEDYCHIUM   Ginger Lily
Minimum temperature: 45°F

A spectacular clump-forming plant growing 5 ft or more. **H. gardnerianum** produces its floral spikes in summer and autumn — more than 1 ft long and composed of scores of 2 in. long red-stamened yellow flowers. Other species include **H. greenei** (deep orange flowers) and **H. coronarium** (white flowers).

HELICONIA   Heliconia
Minimum temperature: 65°F

This plant needs tropical conditions if it is to produce its colourful 1–2 ft long flower-heads made up of red bracts ('lobster claws') and small flowers. You will need a lot of space — **H. bihai** has 3 ft long leaves. Do not water in winter.

HEPTAPLEURUM   Parasol Plant
Minimum temperature: 55°F

Once the genus name for the smaller Umbrella plants — now grouped with Schefflera (page 44).

HIBBERTIA   Guinea Flower
Minimum temperature: 55°F

A fast-growing glossy-leaved climber which produces 1½ in. wide yellow flowers mainly in summer but occasionally throughout the year. **H. scandens** is the only species you are likely to find.

HIBISCUS   Rose of China
Minimum temperature: 55°F

A common sight in warm countries and much used in conservatories to give a tropical look. **H. rosa-sinensis** grows about 3 ft high and from spring to autumn produces a succession of short-lived blooms. These flowers are easily recognised by the central prominent column. Named varieties are available in white, yellow, orange, pink and red. The variety **'Cooperi'** has variegated foliage. For frilly-edged blooms grow **H. schizopetalus**.

HOYA   Wax Flower
Minimum temperature: 55°F

An evergreen climber with clusters of starry flowers which are fragrant and waxy. The flowering season is May–September. **H. carnosa** has glossy 3 in. long leaves and red-centred pink flowers in a neat round cluster. Water very sparingly in winter and do not repot unless it is essential. The Miniature Wax Flower (**H. bella**) produces white flowers and needs more heat and humidity.

HYDRANGEA   Hydrangea
Minimum temperature: 45°F

This familiar garden shrub can be grown in the greenhouse in a large pot or tub. Keep cool in winter and water copiously during the growing season. The familiar mop-heads of **H. macrophylla** appear in spring and autumn.

HYPOESTES   Freckle Face
Minimum temperature: 55°F

A plant grown for its pink-spotted leaves. **H. sanguinolenta** is a popular house plant but it can be used in the conservatory — see The House Plant Expert, page 159.

Hedychium gardnerianum

Heliconia bihai

Hibiscus rosa-sinensis

Hoya carnosa

ORNAMENTALS: GENERAL

Nepenthes coccinea

Ipomoea acuminata

Jacobinia carnea

Jasminum polyanthum

IMPATIENS   Busy Lizzie
Minimum temperature: 55°F

The traditional type of Impatiens for growing under glass is **I. wallerana** and related species. The succulent stems grow about 2 ft high and the flat-faced blooms are produced almost all year round. Nowadays it is more usual to grow one of the F_1 hybrids which are much more compact, much more free-flowering and much used as bedding plants. Even more exciting are the New Guinea types which are taller than the compact hybrids and the flowers are larger, but the key feature is the bicoloured or multicoloured foliage.

INSECT-EATING PLANTS

Some people find the insectivores fascinating, but they are generally not particularly ornamental. There are 3 types — the Fly Traps with spiny-edged leaves which are hinged in the middle, the Sticky-leaved Plants with hairs which produce sticky fluid, and the Pitcher Plants with leaves which form water-filled funnels. It is impossible to generalise about temperature requirements, but all are difficult to grow. Keep the compost constantly moist and use rainwater. Genera include **Dionaea**, **Drosera**, **Darlingtonia**, **Sarracenia** and **Nepenthes**.

IPOMOEA   Morning Glory
Minimum temperature: 45°F

You can grow the annual **I. tricolor** for a short-term display but there are perennial types for the conservatory. The popular one is **I. acuminata (I. learii)** which is a vigorous twiner — between June and October a succession of 4 in. wide mauve-purple funnel-shaped flowers appears.

IRESINE   Iresine
Minimum temperature: 55°F

Iresine is a foliage plant to add colour to a dull foliage display. Two species are available — with both you should pinch out the growing tips to induce bushiness. **I. herbstii** (Bloodleaf) grows about 2 ft high and bears wine red notched leaves. **I. herbstii 'Aureoreticulata'** (Chicken Gizzard) has red stems, green leaves and yellow veins.

IXORA   Flame of the Woods
Minimum temperature: 65°F

Grow this one if you like a challenge — it needs moist air, absence of cold draughts and careful watering to keep the soil moist during the growing season. **I. coccinea** grows 3–4 ft high and in summer round flower-heads appear above the glossy leaves. The ½ in. wide tubular blooms are white, yellow, pink or red.

JACOBINIA   Jacobinia
Minimum temperature: 55°F

There is a confusion of plant names here. The well-known King's Crown has a plume-like 5 in. flower-head in late summer and is labelled as **Jacobinia** or **Justicia carnea**. A quite different species is **J. pauciflora (Justicia rizzinii)** which bears lots of individual yellow-tipped scarlet flowers along the stems during the winter.

JASMINUM   Jasmine
Minimum temperature: 45°F or 65°F

Most Jasmines will flourish quite happily in a cool house. The favourite one is **J. polyanthum** — a vigorous climber with twining stems and in spring the pink buds open into star-faced tubular flowers which are fragrant. **J. primulinus** bears non-fragrant yellow flowers in spring and summer. The popular Jasmines are often trained round a wire hoop inserted in the pot. **J. sambac** (Arabian Jasmine) needs stove house conditions — the flower clusters are white and fragrant.

JOVELLANA   Jovellana
Minimum temperature: 45°F

Numerous shrub and conservatory catalogues offer **J. violacea**. It is an erect and neat shrub which in summer produces terminal flower-heads of mauve blooms with purple-spotted yellow throats.

KALANCHOE Kalanchoe
Minimum temperature: 45°F

Kalanchoe is one of the most popular European flowering house plants, and it is also popular as a compact ornamental for the greenhouse or conservatory. The favourite ones are the hybrids of **K. blossfeldiana** with large heads of tiny tubular flowers in a wide variety of colours. Hybrids of **K. manginii** are now also available — the flower-heads carry ¾ in. long bell-shaped blooms. For details see The House Plant Expert, page 166.

LAGENARIA Bottle Gourd
Minimum temperature: 65°F

A thing of interest rather than beauty. **L. vulgaris** is an annual climber — plant the seeds in spring. White flowers appear in summer and these are followed in autumn by the large bottle-shaped or round fruits which are used as calabashes or bottle gourds in tropical countries.

LANTANA Yellow Sage
Minimum temperature: 55°F

The key feature of this rather straggly plant is the display of 1–2 in. flower-heads which change colour as the tiny blooms mature. **L. camara** blooms from spring to autumn — red, yellow and white varieties are available. Cut back the stems after flowering.

LAPAGERIA Chilean Bell Flower
Minimum temperature: 45°F

The experts will tell you that the best way to grow this twining climber is along wires under the roof of the building so that the 3 in. long waxy bell-like flowers can hang down. **L. rosea** is the species (rose-pink) and there are a number of varieties — white, dark pink and streaked. Flowers appear almost all year round. Remember to grow this one in lime-free compost.

Lapageria rosea

LEPTOSPERMUM New Zealand Tea Tree
Minimum temperature: 35°F

This plant can sometimes be found in the Shrub section of the garden centre. The bush bears small leaves and in spring the foliage is covered by a mass of small 5-petalled flowers. **L. scoparium** has white flowers, but the coloured varieties are more popular — **'Keatleyi'** (pink) and **'Red Damask'** (double, red) are examples.

LISIANTHUS Prairie Gentian
Minimum temperature: 45°F

Lisianthus is making a come-back — you will find it labelled as **L. russelianus** or **Eustoma grandiflorum**. The compact varieties now offered bear single or double Poppy-like blooms in white, purple or blue. It is grown as a summer-flowering annual or biennial as it is difficult to grow as a perennial.

Lisianthus russelianus

LOTUS Lotus
Minimum temperature: 45°F

A trailer for the conservatory — excellent in hanging baskets. **L. berthelotii** (Coral Gem) bears silvery needle-like leaves along its 2 ft stems and in early summer the orange-red 'lobster claw' flowers appear. Be careful not to overwater. **L. maculatus** has a similar growth habit but the flowers are yellow and black. Both are unusual and attractive, but they are not easy to grow.

Lotus berthelotii

LUCULIA Luculia
Minimum temperature: 45°F

A shrub with large oval leaves and crowded heads of wide-mouthed tubular flowers. The most popular species is **L. gratissima** from the Himalayas — the pink blooms appear during winter. The stems should be cut back by half when flowering is over and the plant should be kept rather dry until active growth starts in spring. For summer flowers grow **L. grandiflora**.

Luculia gratissima

Mandevilla sanderi 'Rosea'

Medinilla magnifica

Mimulus aurantiacus

Musa coccinea

MANDEVILLA   Mandevilla
Minimum temperature: 55°F

Mandevilla (other name **Dipladenia**) is a woody climber which bears open trumpet-shaped flowers. Grow in a large pot — it can reach 10 ft or more but it is better to cut the stems back once flowering is finished to keep it bushy. **M. laxa** (**M. suaveolens**) bears fragrant white flowers all summer long — **M. 'Alice du Pont'** has pink blooms and **M. sanderi 'Rosea'** produces yellow-throated pink flowers.

MANETTIA   Firecracker Plant
Minimum temperature: 55°F

The twining stems will need support or can be left to trail. **M. inflata** (**M. bicolor**) has yellow-tipped red tubular flowers — each bloom is not particularly eye-catching, but they may be numerous enough to cover the leaves and appear nearly all year round. Pinch out the tips to maintain bushiness.

MARANTA   Maranta
Minimum temperature: 55°F

The Maranta group are foliage house plants which bear oval or lance-shaped leaves with coloured veins or prominent blotches. The background colour varies from near white to almost black. All need partial shade, moist air, freedom from draughts and some winter warmth. **Maranta** is the most popular genus, but **Calathea** species are often more ornate — **C. makoyana** bears the apt common name Cathedral Windows and **C. crocata** has orange-red flowers. Less usual genera are **Ctenanthe** and **Stromanthe**. See The House Plant Expert pages 171–172 for details.

MEDINILLA   Rose Grape
Minimum temperature: 65°F

Few conservatory flowers are more spectacular than **M. magnifica**. This evergreen grows about 3–4 ft high, and if you can keep the air moist and maintain near-tropical conditions then the magnificent pendent blooms appear in late spring — each one a 1½ ft long pink flower-head with tiered bracts and masses of small flowers.

MIMOSA   Sensitive Plant
Minimum temperature: 55°F

This plant is grown for its habit of folding its feathery leaves and drooping its branches when touched — a great favourite with children! It takes about an hour to recover and as a bonus fluffy pink flower-heads are borne in summer. **M. pudica** is the only species you will find.

MIMULUS   Mimulus
Minimum temperature: 35°F

Mimulus is best known as a bedding plant or rockery perennial, but there is an evergreen shrub (**M. aurantiacus**) which is sold for the conservatory. It grows about 3 ft high — the lance-shaped leaves are sticky and the deep yellow, funnel-shaped flowers open from spring to autumn.

MONSTERA   Swiss Cheese Plant
Minimum temperature: 55°F

Often seen as a foliage house plant, but in a warm and humid conservatory **M. deliciosa** can grow to jungle-like proportions with huge split and perforated leaves, hanging aerial roots, Lily-like flowers and cone-shaped fruit ('breadfruit'). The form **'Variegata'** has cream-splashed leaves. For details see The House Plant Expert, page 174.

MUSA   Banana
Minimum temperature: 55°F

The Banana appears in the Ornamentals rather than the Fruit section because it is generally grown for its exotic shape and flowers rather than for fruit production, although there is one variety (**M. cavendishii**) which does produce edible bananas. **M. velutina** grows about 4 ft high and produces yellow flowers and velvety red fruit. **M. coccinea** (3–4 ft) has red and yellow blooms.

MYRTUS Myrtle
Minimum temperature: 45°F

A rather tender plant outdoors but an easy-to-grow one in the greenhouse or conservatory. **M. communis** will reach about 3 ft high in a tub and ¾ in. fragrant flowers are borne in summer — each bloom is white and has a central boss of yellow stamens. The leaves are glossy and aromatic. **'Variegata'** has white-edged leaves.

NANDINA Heavenly Bamboo
Minimum temperature: 35°F

A hardy Oriental plant which changes colour with the seasons. **N. domestica** is a 4–5 ft shrub with pointed leaflets which are coppery in spring, green in summer and red in autumn. Clusters of tiny white flowers appear in summer and are followed by red berries.

NERIUM Oleander
Minimum temperature: 45°F

A common sight in sub-tropical gardens and a useful tub plant for the conservatory. **N. oleander** is a spreading shrub which grows about 6 ft high, its long stems clothed with 6 in. Willow-like leaves. In summer the clusters of 2 in. wide flowers appear — white, pink, purple, red and yellow varieties are available. If possible stand the pot outdoors on sunny summer days. A word of warning — all parts of Oleander are poisonous.

OCHNA Ochna
Minimum temperature: 45°F

There is nothing special about this plant for most of the year. **O. serrulata** is a 4–5 ft shrub with leaves which are toothed and evergreen. In spring the ½ in. wide yellow flowers open, and these are followed by the unique feature of this plant — the fruits. These are glossy black berry-like drupelets which sit on recurved red calyxes. Definitely different.

OPLISMENUS Basket Grass
Minimum temperature: 45°F

This one is for the conservatory owner who wants a change from Tradescantia for ground cover or hanging baskets. The one to grow is **O. hirtellus 'Variegatus'** — the 4 in. long narrow leaves on the 3 ft trailing stems are green striped with white and pink. Small grassy flowers appear in summer.

PACHYSTACHYS Lollipop Plant
Minimum temperature: 55°F

The Lollipop Plant **P. lutea** is more popular as a house plant than a conservatory one. It is an oval-leaved bushy plant which grows about 1½ ft high and from late spring to autumn the 5 in. high flower spikes appear. Each head is made up of a series of yellow bracts with white blooms peeping through.

PALMS
Minimum temperature: 35°F or 55°F

No other plant typifies the Victorian conservatory more than the Palm and the various types still have an important part to play in modern day ones. You will need to spray the leaves occasionally and you will need to shade them from hot summer sun. Among the easiest to grow is the hardy **Chamaerops humilis** (European Fan Palm) and the traditional 'Palm Court' types such as **Kentia** and **Howea**. **Neanthe bella** is the popular dwarf Parlour Palm. The Fishtail Palm **Caryota mitis** needs warm house conditions. See The House Plant Expert pages 180–182 for details.

PANDANUS Screw Pine
Minimum temperature: 55°F

A large specimen in a conservatory can look impressive, but this Palm-like plant is not a good choice. The long leaves which spiral round the stem have sharp saw-toothed edges — painful indeed if you bump into one. **P. veitchii** grows to 4 ft x 4 ft — the variety **'Compacta'** has smaller leaves.

Myrtus communis

Nerium oleander

Ochna serrulata

Pachystachys lutea

Passiflora quadrangularis

Pellionia pulchra

Pentas lanceolata

Pilea cadierei

PASSIFLORA   Passion Flower
Minimum temperature: 35°F or 55°F

Large and often colourful flowers are borne by this rampant climber — all summer long the 10-petalled ornate blooms appear on the stems. The most popular species is the near-hardy Blue Passion Flower (**P. caerulea**) with deeply lobed leaves and 3 in. wide flowers. **P. edulis** and **P. ligularis** bear edible fruit if grown in a warm conservatory. The showiest species with the largest fruit is **P. quadrangularis**, but this one needs near-tropical conditions. Passiflora should be cut back by a third in spring — shorten side shoots.

PELARGONIUM   Geranium
Minimum temperature: 45°F or 55°F

The well-known Geranium — the ever-popular Zonal types, the frilly large-flowered Regal ones and the trailing Ivy-leaved varieties. All sorts of flower and leaf colours are available, and a floral display can be obtained all year round if a minimum of 55°F can be maintained. Pinch back young plants to induce bushiness. Repot only when it is essential. Provide plenty of fresh air and not much air humidity. Remove dead flowers and cut back unnecessary stems in late autumn. Keep the compost almost dry if the minimum temperature is in the 35°–45°F range.

PELLIONIA   Pellionia
Minimum temperature: 55°F

A ground cover plant for the warm house with moist air. **P. daveauana** (Watermelon Pellionia) has oval dark green leaves with a pale centre — the Satin Pellionia (**P. pulchra**) bears foliage which has prominent dark veins above and is purple below. Stem cuttings root easily.

PENTAS   Egyptian Star Cluster
Minimum temperature: 55°F

An easy plant to grow but one which will become straggly if you fail to cut it back after the flowers have faded. Autumn and winter is the usual blooming period for **P. lanceolata** (**P. carnea**) — each 3–4 in. flower-head is made up of numerous starry blooms. White, pink, red and mauve varieties are available. Repot in spring. Take stem cuttings in late spring or summer.

PEPEROMIA   Pepper Elder
Minimum temperature: 55°F

Peperomias are generally thought of as house plants as they do not need the moist air of the conservatory. Numerous types are available — trailing (**P. scandens 'Variegata'** etc), bushy (**P. caperata** and **P. hederaefolia** are the popular ones) and upright (**P. magnoliaefolia** etc). They are grown for their foliage, which may be fleshy, quilted, corrugated, smooth or hairy, green or variegated. The 'rat-tail' flower-heads which may appear are not particularly decorative. Take care not to overwater.

PHILODENDRON   Philodendron
Minimum temperature: 55°F

The small and easy-to-grow Philodendron **P. scandens** (Sweetheart Plant) is popular in the home, but most Philodendrons need the space and moist air provided by a conservatory. All are grown for their showy and sometimes spectacular leaves. There are bold climbers with leaves which may be green or red, smooth or velvety, arrow-shaped or palm-like. Repot every 2–3 years. The non-climbers are large, impressive plants with deeply divided leaves. See pages 189–190 in The House Plant Expert for details.

PILEA   Pilea
Minimum temperature: 55°F

Pileas are small bushy plants grown for their colourful leaves. Pinch out growing tips occasionally and keep away from draughts. The most popular one is the Aluminium Plant (**P. cadierei**) — a 1 ft high plant with oval quilted leaves which bear silvery patches. Others include **P. 'Norfolk'** (silver-striped bronze leaves) and **P. 'Moon Valley'** (dark-veined green leaves).

PIPER Ornamental Pepper
Minimum temperature: 55°F

This climbing plant looks like a colourful version of the well-known Philodendron scandens, but it is difficult to find a supplier. **P. ornatum** bears 4 in. long heart-shaped leaves with a puckered surface which is dappled with pink and silver. It will reach about 5 ft if provided with support and the right conditions. Frequent misting is necessary.

Piper ornatum

PISONIA Birdcatcher Tree
Minimum temperature: 55°F

At first glance **P. umbellifera 'Variegata'** is a look-alike of the variegated Rubber Plant, but there are differences. Pisonia has branched stems and the leaves are sticky — these leaves are large, oval, white edged and flecked with pink. Tiny tubular white flowers occasionally appear.

PITTOSPORUM Mock Orange
Minimum temperature: 35°F

The species to grow in the conservatory is **P. tobira**. This woody plant will grow about 4 ft high — flat-topped and covered with leathery oval leaves. In spring or summer clusters of ½ in. wide star-faced flowers appear — cream-coloured and fragrant. Choose the white-blotched variety **'Variegatum'**.

PLUMBAGO Cape Leadwort
Minimum temperature: 45°F

Clusters of sky-blue 1 in. starry flowers appear throughout the summer and autumn on this rambling climber. **P. auriculata (P. capensis)** is readily available from garden centres — you should also be able to find the white-flowering variety **'Alba'**. It will grow 6 ft or more — prune back after flowering. There is a pink non-climbing species (**P. rosea**) — stove house conditions are required.

Plumbago auriculata

PLUMERIA Frangipani
Minimum temperature: 55°F

This popular shrub of the sub-tropics can be grown in the conservatory. **P. rubra** reaches about 6 ft, and in late summer clusters of 2 in. wide flowers appear — white or pink and with a strong fragrance. The problem is that the leaves fall in winter and so the branches are bare. Keep almost dry during this dormant period. Repot every 2 years in spring.

POINSETTIA Poinsettia
Minimum temperature: 55°F

A favourite winter house plant, but a rarity in lists of recommended greenhouse plants. The latin name of 'Poinsettia' is **Euphorbia pulcherrima**. Bought-in specimens will make a fine display alongside the late-flowering Chrysanthemums — the modern varieties in white, cream, pink or red should last for months. Getting this one to bloom again is a tricky business which calls for changing the day length — see page 195 in The House Plant Expert for details.

Plumeria rubra

POLYGALA Milkwort
Minimum temperature: 45°F

Look for this one and grow it. The Pea-shaped mauve flowers of **P. myrtifolia 'Grandiflora'** appear from May right through to October and when not in bloom it is an attractive evergreen shrub growing about 3 ft high. Cut back in late winter — make sure that the compost is kept moist at all times. Take cuttings in late spring or summer in a propagator.

POLYSCIAS Polyscias
Minimum temperature: 55°F

These shrubs or trees have twisted stems and decorative foliage — a good choice where an Oriental look is sought. The popular species in America is the ferny-leaved Ming Aralia (**P. fruticosa**). It requires moist air and should be repotted every 2 years. **P. balfouriana** (Dinner Plate Aralia) is sometimes grown.

Polygala myrtifolia 'Grandiflora'

Protea cynaroides

Punica granatum 'Nana'

Pyrostegia venusta

Rhodochiton volubilis

PRIMULA   Primrose
Minimum temperature: 45°F

The most popular species of the tender types which are grown is **P. malacoides**. The fragrant small flowers are arranged in tiers on slender stalks. The flowers of **P. obconica** are large, fragrant and available in a wide range of colours, but the leaves can cause a rash on sensitive skins. **P. kewensis** is the only yellow-flowering tender Primula. Sow seed in midsummer for blooming next spring. Polyanthus (**P. variabilis**) is hardy and will thrive in a cold house. These low-growing and large-flowered Primulas should be planted in the garden when the spring display is over.

PROSTANTHERA   Mint Bush
Minimum temperature: 35°F

These Australian plants are easy to grow — the foliage is strongly aromatic and masses of cup-shaped flowers appear in spring or summer. **P. rotundifolia** is the tallest (6 ft) and bears mauve flowers in spring. **P. nivea** has white flowers and the early-summer flowering **P. mellisifolia** produces lavender blooms.

PROTEA   Protea
Minimum temperature: 45°F

Flower arrangers know this one — the large dried flower-heads are widely used in displays. Despite their exotic appearance the species of Protea need cool and not warm house conditions. **P. cynaroides** (King Protea) produces 5 in. wide pink flower-heads which are goblet-shaped. Move the pot outdoors in summer.

PSEUDERANTHEMUM   Pseuderanthemum
Minimum temperature: 55°F

Once popular but now not often listed. Pseuderanthemum is primarily grown for its brightly-coloured foliage but there are species which are planted for their display of purple-eyed flowers. **P. (Eranthemum) atropurpureum** has 5 in. long glossy leaves which are a mixture of green, cream, pink and purple. **P. reticulatum** has yellow-veined leaves and **P. sinuatum** is grown for its summer blooms.

PUNICA   Pomegranate
Minimum temperature: 45°F

The Pomegranate **P. granatum** is grown under glass as a 6 ft pot plant for its bright red tubular flowers and glossy leaves rather than for edible fruit. Unfortunately the species does not flower until it is almost 6 years old — it is better to grow the compact variety **'Nana'** (3 ft) which produces its summer flowers whilst still small. Ball-like fruit may develop.

PYROSTEGIA   Flaming Trumpets
Minimum temperature: 55°F

A plant to cover part of the roof of a large conservatory. **P. venusta** grows 10 ft high or more, climbing by means of tendrils and producing clusters of orange-red flowers from late autumn to early spring. Cut back shoots which have flowered once the display is over.

REHMANNIA   Rehmannia
Minimum temperature: 45°F

An unusual summer-flowering plant which is grown as a biennial — sow seed in May for flowering in June next year. The tufted leaves of **R. angulata** (**R. elata**) grow about 1 ft high and the spotted pale red blooms are borne along 2 ft high flower spikes. The tubular flowers are 2–3 in. long.

RHODOCHITON   Purple Bellvine
Minimum temperature: 35°F

A good climber for the frost-free house. The long leaf stalks of **R. volubilis** (**R. atrosanguineus**) curl around the supports and the stems grow about 5 ft high. In late summer the colourful 2 in. long flowers appear — each purple corolla surrounded by a pink calyx. Cut back each winter if grown as a perennial, or treat as an annual by sowing seed each spring.

RHODODENDRON   Azalea, Rhododendron
Minimum temperature: 45°F

The only two sorts of Rhododendron generally grown in the greenhouse or conservatory are both popularly known as 'Azaleas' — daintier (1–1½ ft high) and smaller-leaved than the typical garden Rhododendron. The more widely-grown are the **R. simsii** hybrids (Indian Azalea or just plain 'Azalea'). Countless pots are bought every year at Christmas to provide flowers during the holiday season. To keep in flower and to ensure blooms next year it is necessary to keep the compost wet (not just moist) and keep the plant cool and brightly lit. Move the plant outdoors from late May to late September. The other type is the Japanese Azalea **R. obtusum**. The funnel-shaped flowers are smaller than the Indian Azalea blooms. Apart from the Azaleas there are several species of dwarf Rhododendrons (e.g **R. ciliatum**) which can be grown.

Rhododendron simsii

RHOEO   Boat Lily
Minimum temperature: 55°F

An interesting plant with curious rather than attractive flowers. There is a rosette of 1 ft long strap-like leaves, green above and purple below on the species **R. discolor** — green with a broad yellow stripe on the variety **'Vittata'**. The flowers appear at intervals during the year — small white blooms in boat-shaped bracts at the base of the outer leaves.

RIVINA   Bloodberry
Minimum temperature: 55°F

You can recognise this plant by its chains of Pea-sized berries which appear in autumn and last all winter. **R. humilis** has red berries — the variety **'Aurantiaca'** has yellow ones. The bush grows about 2 ft high and the flowers are insignificant.

Rochea coccinea

ROCHEA   Crassula
Minimum temperature: 45°F

A leathery-leaved plant which is usually bought in flower. **R. coccinea** grows 1–1½ ft high. The 1 in. triangular foliage clothes the upright stems, and in summer terminal clusters of red tubular flowers appear. There are white and bicoloured (red and white) varieties.

ROSA   Rose
Minimum temperature: 45°F

Hybrid Tea or Floribunda bushes are planted in 7 in. pots in September. Leave the pots in the garden until December, then bring into the greenhouse. Prune the stems hard in January — blooms appear in April. Harden off and stand the pot outdoors in May before repotting in September.

RUELLIA   Monkey Plant
Minimum temperature: 55°F

Plants with eye-catching leaves and attractive flowers are always worth growing. **R. makoyana** is a weak-stemmed 2 ft shrub which needs support — the leaves are veined in silver and the pink trumpet-shaped flowers appear in winter and early spring.

Ruellia macrantha

SAINTPAULIA   African Violet
Minimum temperature: 55°F

The range of **S. hybrida** varieties these days is bewildering. Micro-miniatures which will grow in an egg-cup, singles and doubles, reds, pinks and corals, bushy and trailing. Study what to do and you can have African Violets in flower nearly all year round — see pages 201–203 in The House Plant Expert for details.

SALPIGLOSSIS   Painted Tongue
Minimum temperature: 45°F

Sow seed of **S. sinuata** in early spring for summer flowering or sow in autumn for an early spring display. Stake the 1–2 ft stems. The flowers are 2 in. wide trumpets in yellow, orange, red or lilac with darker feathery veins. Exotic blooms for the price of a pack of seeds — discard after flowering.

Salpiglossis sinuata

Salvia involucrata

Saxifraga sarmentosa 'Tricolor'

Schizanthus hybrida 'Hit Parade'

Scindapsus aureus 'Marble Queen'

SALVIA   Sage
Minimum temperature: 45°F

Best known as a garden annual (page 34), but there are a few perennial species which belong in a greenhouse or conservatory. **S. involucrata** grows about 3 ft high and in summer and autumn the spikes of tubular pink flowers appear. **S. leucantha** bears white flowers, **S. elegans** has red blooms. All are easy to grow. Propagate by cuttings in spring or summer.

SANCHEZIA   Sanchezia
Minimum temperature: 55°F

Obviously related to the much more popular Aphelandra (page 24). The yellow 2 in. long tubular flowers of **S. nobilis** are borne in upright clusters above the leaves in summer, and this foliage has prominent yellow veins. However, it is larger (3 ft high with 1 ft long leaves) and more difficult to grow than its well-known cousin.

SANSEVIERIA   Sansevieria
Minimum temperature: 45°F

One of the most popular of all house plants, which is occasionally used to fill up an empty space in a cool greenhouse or conservatory. The variety you see everywhere is the yellow-edged Mother-in-law's Tongue (**S. trifasciata 'Laurentii'**) but there are many others — see page 204 in The House Plant Expert for details.

SAXIFRAGA   Mother of Thousands
Minimum temperature: 45°F

A trailing house plant which forms long red runners with miniature plants at their ends. **S. sarmentosa** has green foliage with silvery veins — the leaves of the variety '**Tricolor**' are green, edged with white and pink. The species is larger (2–3 ft runners) and easier to grow than its more colourful variety.

SCHEFFLERA   Umbrella Tree
Minimum temperature: 55°F

The common name refers to the finger-like leathery leaflets which radiate like umbrella spokes from the leaf stalk. **S. actinophylla** is the popular one, growing 6–8 ft high and bearing 1 ft long leaflets. The widely-available small-leaved species **S. arboricola** is usually sold as **Heptapleurum arboricola**, a 3–6 ft tree with 3–6 in. long leaflets — there are 6–15 attached to each stalk. The leaves of '**Variegata**' have bold yellow markings.

SCHIZANTHUS   Poor Man's Orchid
Minimum temperature: 55°F

Sow seed in spring for late summer flowering or in autumn for blooming in spring. Pinch out the tips of young plants to induce bushiness. **S. hybrida** bears orchid-like yellow-eyed flowers in a wide variety of colours above the ferny foliage. A dwarf variety such as '**Hit Parade**' (1 ft) or '**Dwarf Bouquet**' is usually chosen. Discard after flowering.

SCINDAPSUS   Pothos
Minimum temperature: 55°F

A popular climber with heart-shaped variegated leaves and aerial roots which will cling to any damp surface. The one you are most likely to find is **S. aureus** — Devil's Ivy in Britain and Pothos in the U.S. The glossy leaves are splashed with yellow — there are varieties which are nearly all-yellow ('**Golden Queen**') or nearly all-white ('**Marble Queen**').

SELAGINELLA   Creeping Moss
Minimum temperature: 55°F

A favourite Victorian conservatory plant which is rarely grown these days. The trailing types are used as ground cover under ferns etc and the bushy ones (6 in.–1 ft high) can be placed at the front of the border or bench. They all have tiny leaves which need moist air — **S. kraussiana** is the most popular trailing species. Grow in compost or on damp bark.

SOLANDRA   Cup of Gold
Minimum temperature: 45°F

A vigorous climber which bears large trumpet-shaped flowers in spring and summer. **S. maxima** is the species to look for. It can grow to 10 ft and the fragrant flowers are about 8 in. long — spectacular indeed! They are cream-coloured at first but change to golden-yellow and finally to pale brown. Cut back overcrowded branches after flowering.

SOLANUM   Solanum
Minimum temperature: 45°F

There are two distinct types. **S. capsicastrum** (Winter Cherry) is a familiar sight at Christmas — small bushes with orange or red round (and poisonous) fruit. Stand outdoors in summer — repot in spring. Then there are the climbers which bloom in summer and autumn, such as **S. jasminoides** (pale blue flowers), **S. wendlandii** (blue flowers) and **S. rantonettii** (deep purple-blue flowers).

SOLLYA   Australian Bluebell
Minimum temperature: 45°F

A twining climber which is often recommended for growing through tall foliage trees or shrubs. **S. heterophylla** grows 4–6 ft high and in summer the nodding groups of ½ in. wide bell-like blooms appear. The colour is sky-blue and they are followed by purple fruits. An easy plant which is well worth trying.

SPARMANNIA   House Lime
Minimum temperature: 45°F

This tree-like plant needs space — it grows quickly and does not flower until it is several feet high. **S. africana** has large downy leaves and in early spring the clusters of golden-centred white flowers appear. Cut back after blooming has finished and repot every year. Keep the compost moist at all times.

SPATHIPHYLLUM   Peace Lily
Minimum temperature: 55°F

The Peace Lily thrives in tropical conditions, but it should do well in a warm house if grown in the shade of taller plants in summer. **S. wallisii** is a popular house plant — the Arum-like white flowers grow on 1 ft stalks above the lance-shaped leaves. It flowers in spring and again in autumn. Where space permits grow the much bolder **S. 'Mauna Loa'** which flowers nearly all year round.

STENOTAPHRUM   St Augustine Grass
Minimum temperature: 45°F

The basic species **S. secundatum** is grown as a lawn grass in Florida and other southern U.S states — the variegated form **'Variegatum'** is used as a trailing plant in the conservatory. The 6 in. linear leaves have a broad creamy-white band down the centre. An easy and undemanding plant for the edge of the staging.

STEPHANOTIS   Madagascar Jasmine
Minimum temperature: 55°F

From spring to autumn the star-shaped tubular flowers are borne in clusters — white, waxy and heavily perfumed. **S. floribunda** is a vigorous glossy-leaved climber which can reach 10 ft or more, and is recommended by many experts. But it is a difficult plant, needing steady temperatures and reasonably cool conditions during the day in winter and spring.

STRELITZIA   Bird of Paradise
Minimum temperature: 55°F

For most people this one is the most spectacular of all conservatory plants, but it is not difficult to grow. The 6 in. orange and purple flowers of **S. reginae** look like the head of a bird, standing 4 ft above the compost and surrounded by large paddle-shaped leaves. The blooms open in spring or summer and last for several weeks. New plants take 4–6 years before flowering starts. Feed and water freely in summer — water sparingly in winter.

Solandra maxima

Sparmannia africana

Stephanotis floribunda

Strelitzia reginae

Streptocarpus 'Concorde Mixed'

STREPTOCARPUS   Cape Primrose
Minimum temperature: 55°F

Many colourful varieties of **S. hybrida** have appeared in recent years, but **'Constant Nymph'** (lilac with violet veins) remains the favourite. The 2 in. wide trumpet-shaped flowers are held on slender stalks above the rosette of long strap-shaped leaves. Other types include **'Baby Blue'** (dark-striped lavender blue) and **'Royal Mixed'** (assorted colours). Sow seed in the spring — summer is the usual flowering season. A tricky plant — it needs moist air, protection from hot summer sun and freedom from draughts. Remove flowers as they fade.

STREPTOSOLEN   Marmalade Bush
Minimum temperature: 45°F

The Marmalade Bush is a rambling shrub which produces masses of funnel-shaped orange blooms in late spring. **S. jamesonii** grows 4–6 ft high and tends to become leggy with age — some form of support is necessary. Keep the compost moist at all times.

STROBILANTHES   Purple Shield
Minimum temperature: 55°F

There is just one species — **S. dyeranus**. This shrub is grown for its colourful 6 in. long leaves. When young the pointed foliage is dark green with purple patches between the veins. The underside is purple. As the leaves age, the coloured patches change to silvery-lilac. Tubular pale blue flowers appear in summer. Not an easy plant to grow.

SUCCULENTS
Minimum temperature: 45°F

The succulents are plants with fleshy leaves — cacti are a group of succulents which are different and important enough to warrant a section on their own (pages 58–59). Some of the remaining succulents have their own entry in this section, for example Sansevieria and the flowering types such as Hoya and Rochea. That still leaves hundreds of varieties which are grown in the cool greenhouse or conservatory and have the same basic needs: free-draining compost, sunshine, fresh air, adequate water in the growing season and a cool and dry resting period. See pages 212–218 of The House Plant Expert for details of **Adromischus, Aeonium, Agave, Aloe, Bryophyllum, Crassula, Cotyledon, Echeveria, Euphorbia, Faucaria, Gasteria, Graptopetalum, Haworthia, Kalanchoe, Kleinia, Orostachys, Pachyphytum, Pedilanthus, Sedum, Sempervivum** and **Senecio**. A couple of tips. Only repot succulents when it is essential and make sure that the new pot is only slightly larger than the old one. Secondly, let cuttings dry out for a few days before inserting them in the compost.

Streptosolen jamesonii

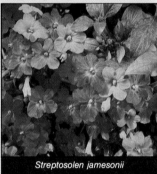

Strobilanthes dyeranus

SYNGONIUM   Goosefoot Plant
Minimum temperature: 55°F

These climbers are relatives of Philodendron (page 40). You can tell them apart by the leaf shape — the young leaves of Syngonium are arrow-shaped and with age become lobed. The popular species is **S. podophyllum** and the favourite types are the variegated species such as **'Green Gold'** and **'Emerald Gem'**.

TECOMA   Yellow Bells
Minimum temperature: 55°F

An upright shrub with fern-like leaves and pendent clusters of funnel-shaped flowers. The flowering period lasts from spring to autumn. **T. stans (Bignonia stans)** grows up to 6 ft high, but the shoots should be pruned after flowering. Water very sparingly in winter.

TECOMARIA   Cape Honeysuckle
Minimum temperature: 45°F

This sprawling plant has an untidy growth habit and benefits from some form of support. The flowers of **T. capensis** are borne in clusters and are narrow curved tubes with orange-red flared mouths. The flowering season starts in spring and may go on for 6 months or more. The variety **'Aurea'** has yellow flowers.

Tecomaria capensis

TETRANEMA   Mexican Foxglove
Minimum temperature: 55°F

The Mexican Foxglove **T. roseum** will bloom intermittently all year round if the temperature is kept above 55°F. These tubular flowers are purple with a pale throat — the clusters are borne above a rosette of oval leaves. The variety **'Album'** has white flowers.

THUNBERGIA   Clock Vine
Minimum temperature: 55°F

Black-eyed Susan (**T. alata**) is a well-known annual climber which will quickly clothe a large area and produce brown-throated flowers in summer. **T. grandiflora** is an evergreen perennial climber — 3 in. wide blue flowers open in summer. **T. fragrans**, which is not fragrant, has white flowers.

Thunbergia grandiflora

TIBOUCHINA   Glory Bush
Minimum temperature: 55°F

An excellent choice for the warm house — under such conditions it will flower from spring to autumn. These blooms are eye-catching — **T. urvilleana** bears 4 in. wide purple flowers with oddly-shaped stamens. High humidity and good light are essential — water sparingly in winter.

TRACHELOSPERMUM   Trachelospermum
Minimum temperature: 35°F

A climber which will flourish in a frost-free house — **T. asiaticum** and **T. jasminoides** are sold for growing outdoors in mild areas. The cream-coloured flowers are star-shaped, appearing above the glossy foliage in summer. Fragrance is an important feature — the perfume can fill a small greenhouse. It may be slow to establish.

Tibouchina urvilleana

TRADESCANTIA   Wandering Jew
Minimum temperature: 45°F

A group of plants with leaves which clasp the creeping or trailing stems. Tips must be pinched out regularly to maintain bushiness and stem cuttings root very easily in spring, summer or autumn. They are best known as house plants but have a part to play in the conservatory. The species and varieties of **Tradescantia** are the most popular, but there are also **Callisia**, **Zebrina** and **Setcreasea** (Purple Heart). See pages 221–222 in The House Plant Expert for details.

TWEEDIA   Tweedia
Minimum temperature: 45°F

A highly recommended scrambling shrub (2–3 ft) — **T. caerulea (Oxypetalum caerulum)** does not need warm and steamy conditions. The heart-shaped leaves are hairy and the summer and autumn flowers change colour with age, from pale blue/green to purple and finally to mauve.

Trachelospermum asiaticum

VINES
Minimum temperature: 45°F or 55°F

Vines are climbing plants which cling to the supports by means of tendrils. Their role is to clothe trellis, poles or a bare brick wall. Several are popular house plants — **Cissus antarctica**, **Rhoicissus rhomboidea** and its variety **'Ellen Danica'**. Two others belong in the conservatory — **Tetrastigma voinierianum** needs space and **Cissus discolor** needs moist air. See pages 223–224 in The House Plant Expert for details.

YUCCA   Yucca
Minimum temperature: 45°F

A false palm to provide a tropical look, although this plant demands cool conditions in winter. The 3–5 ft woody trunk is crowned by long leathery leaves. Choose **Y. elephantipes** — the Spanish Bayonet (**Y. aloifolia**) has dangerously sharp-pointed foliage. White bell-shaped flowers on tall stalks may appear after a number of years.

Tweedia caerulea

Ornamentals : Bulbs

Many of the ornamentals grown in the greenhouse or conservatory produce swollen underground parts ('bulbs') which can be used for propagation. Sometimes these storage organs are true bulbs (fleshy scales surrounding a central bud), but others are corms, tubers or rhizomes.

The dividing line between bulbs and general ornamentals is not a clear-cut one. Some bulbous plants are evergreen and are generally propagated by lifting and dividing the growing plants. They are often grouped with the general ornamentals — examples in this book are Clivia and Agapanthus.

That still leaves a large number of plants, the bulbs, which are usually grown by planting the bulb, corm, tuber etc in a suitable compost. Most of them lose their leaves during the dormant period, so they are placed on display for the flowering period and then moved out of sight.

The plants in this section are divided into two basic groups. The greenhouse bulbs are generally half hardy and cannot be grown outdoors where frost can kill the leaves or other parts of the plant. In most cases they are left in the pot when the foliage dies down — the compost is kept almost dry until growth is started again by watering. There are no general rules about the frequency of repotting these bulbs — some types benefit from an annual change of compost before being brought back into growth whereas others do best when left undisturbed for several years. There are a few greenhouse bulbs where the storage organ is lifted and stored in peat during the dormant period, and then potted up prior to the start of the growing season. Propagation of greenhouse bulbs usually involves the removal of offsets and the planting up of these small bulbs at repotting time.

The second group is made up of the hardy spring bulbs. Many of the popular bulbs which flower in the garden in late winter or spring can be used for greenhouse or conservatory display. The larger bulbs are 'forced' by keeping them cold and dark to make the roots grow, and then providing them with light and warmth for leaf and flower development. The smaller ones are not forced — they are planted in pots which are placed outdoors and then brought indoors when the flower buds are ready to open.

One final point. Always buy good quality stock — how well a bulb will flower depends largely on the way it was grown and stored.

Sprekelia

Greenhouse Bulbs

Nearly all of these plants cannot tolerate frost and are never placed outdoors in winter. Most are summer- or autumn-flowering and they usually lose their leaves during the dormant period. Depending on the variety the bulb may be left in the pot during this time or it should be removed and stored in slightly moist peat.

Hardy Spring Bulbs

These plants are better known as bulbs for garden use, but can be grown for display under glass. There are two basic growing techniques. The forcing method is used for large bulbs to make them bloom well ahead of their garden counterparts. The second method is used for smaller bulbs and is simpler than forcing, but flowering will only be a short time ahead of similar bulbs in the garden.

Greenhouse Bulbs

ACHIMENES   Hot Water Plant
Minimum temperature: 55°F during growing season

An easy-to-grow plant — trailing or bushy growing 6–12 in. high. The modern hybrids of **A. heterophylla** and other species produce masses of trumpet-shaped flowers from June to October — white, blue, purple, pink or yellow depending on the variety. Plant the small tubers ½–1 in. deep in early spring and make sure the compost never dries out when the plant is growing. Stop watering when the flowering season comes to an end and start into growth next spring by watering with tepid water. Protect the plant from direct sun in summer. Good for hanging baskets.

Achimenes heterophylla

AMARYLLIS   Belladonna Lily
Minimum temperature: 45°F during growing season

The popular 'Amaryllis' bulbs offered for sale in autumn are really Hippeastrum hybrids. The true Amaryllis is planted in October and its leaves appear in spring. It is only after the foliage dies away that the 2 ft flower-stalks appear in autumn, each one crowned by a cluster of 3 in. wide trumpet-shaped flowers. The sweet-smelling blooms last for about 6 weeks. Pink and pale red varieties of **A. belladonna** are available. Repot about every 5 years. For propagation remove offsets at repotting time and plant up in compost.

Amaryllis belladonna

BABIANA   Baboon Root
Minimum temperature: 55°F during growing season

Babiana stricta is related to the Gladiolus but it is a much smaller plant — the leaves are ribbed and hairy and the 6–12 in. flower-stalks bear clusters of 1 in. wide fragrant flowers. In its native home in S. Africa baboons collect the corms for food — hence the common name. White, blue, red and violet varieties are available. Plant the corms 2 in. deep in autumn for spring flowers — when leaves wither store corms in dry peat until planting time.

BEGONIA   Tuberous Begonia
Minimum temperature: 55°F during growing season

The most popular Tuberous Begonias are the **B. tuberhybrida** varieties with 3–6 in. wide blooms on 1 ft high fleshy stems. The female flowers are small — it is the male ones which are large and showy. A wide range of single, semi-double and double types is available in many colours and colour combinations. Examples include **'Gold Plate'** (yellow), **'Guardsman'** (red) and picotees such as **'Double Picotee'** (red-edged cream). **B. multiflora** flowers are similar in shape but they are more numerous and smaller. **B. tuberhybrida pendula** has long, drooping stems. Tuberous Begonias are raised by planting tubers in spring in boxes of moist peat. Keep at 60°–70°F and when shoots are 2 in. high transplant into 5 in. and later 8 in. pots. Flowering time is summer and autumn. Lift tubers and store in peat at the end of the season.

*Begonia pendula
'Picotee Cascade'*

BRODIAEA   Brodiaea
Minimum temperature: 45°F during growing season

Brodiaea is an uncommon bulbous plant for people who prefer delicate blooms to big showy ones. The grassy leaves are about 1 ft long and the 1–2 ft flower-stalks bear dense clusters of small flowers. Plant the corms in autumn and repot every 5–6 years. **B. laxa** bears white or blue blooms during spring, unlike **B. coronaria** which flowers in summer. **B. ida-maia** (Firecracker) is quite different — the green-edged tubular red flowers are pendent.

CANNA   Indian Shot
Minimum temperature: 55°F during growing season

Canna hybrida plants are big, bold and colourful, giving the conservatory a tropical air. The 4–5 in. wide flowers are orchid-like and are borne on 2–4 ft high stalks — there are striped, spotted and plain varieties in white, yellow, orange, pink and red. There is also a choice of leaf colour — green, bronze or purple. For yellow marked leaves and yellow flowers grow **C. variegata**. Plant the tuber-like rhizomes in spring and start into growth at 55°–65°F. Water freely and feed during the summer months. Keep cool and almost dry in winter — divide and repot in spring.

Canna hybrida

Crinum powellii

Eucharis grandiflora

Eucomis comosa

Gloriosa rothschildiana

CHLIDANTHUS   Delicate Lily
Minimum temperature: 45°F during growing season

There is just one species — **C. fragrans**. In summer the 1 ft high slender flower-stalks appear, each one topped with a small cluster of Lily-like blooms. The yellow flowers measure about 3 in. across and have a strong fragrance. The narrow grey-green leaves appear shortly after the flowers. Plant the bulbs 2 in. deep in autumn — when repotting use the small bulbs at the base for propagation.

CRINUM   Swamp Lily
Minimum temperature: 55°F during growing season

Everything about **C. powellii** is large — 6 in. bulbs, 3 ft tall flower-stalks in late summer and 6 in. wide fragrant Lily-like flowers. Pink is the usual colour but there are white and red varieties. Pot up the bulb in a large tub in spring or summer with one-third above the surface of the compost. You will need patience — the bulbs take several years to reach the flowering stage. Water liberally between spring and the end of flowering — water sparingly in winter. Repot every 3–4 years.

CYCLAMEN   Cyclamen
Minimum temperature: 45°F during growing season

The hybrids of **C. persicum** are greenhouse favourites — swept-back flowers above silver-patterned leaves. The blooms may be in bright or pastel colours — large and eye-catching or small and perfumed. Buy a plant in autumn and not midwinter, and choose one with plenty of unopened buds. It needs a cool spot (50°–60°F is ideal) away from direct sunlight. Reduce watering when flowers fade and place the pot on its side and keep dry until midsummer. Then repot using fresh compost, burying the crown to half its depth. Cyclamen can be raised from summer-sown seed — most varieties take 15–18 months to flower.

EUCHARIS   Amazon Lily
Minimum temperature: 65°F during growing season

A late summer flowering bulb which may repeat the display in early winter when conditions are favourable. The 3 in. wide fragrant bloom of **E. grandiflora** looks like a white Narcissus with a spiky trumpet — about 3–6 are borne on a 2 ft stalk. Plant in spring or autumn — water sparingly until growth starts. Repot in spring every 3–4 years.

EUCOMIS   Pineapple Lily
Minimum temperature: 45°F during growing season

E. comosa needs lots of space — the 1½–2 ft long leaves form a large rosette and the 1 ft high cylindrical flower-head bears small white blooms and a leafy crown. **E. bicolor** (purplish-green flowers, purple-spotted stalk) is smaller. Plant the bulbs early in the year — the flowers appear in midsummer and last for several weeks. The leaves die down in winter — keep the compost dry until growth starts again.

FREESIA   Freesia
Minimum temperature: 45°F during growing season

The 2 in. long tubular flowers of **F. hybrida** grow on one side of the 1–1½ ft long wiry stems — you can choose from white, yellow, blue, lilac, orange, pink or red. Fragrance is an important feature and the floral sprays are popular with flower arrangers. Plant the corms about 2 in. deep in summer and stand the pots outdoors until early autumn. Bring indoors and the flowers will begin to appear in winter. When flowers and leaves have died down, store the corms in dry peat and repot the largest ones in summer. Alternatively sow seed in early spring for autumn flowering.

GLORIOSA   Glory Lily
Minimum temperature: 55°F during growing season

This 4–6 ft high climber bears large and colourful flowers from June to August. Some form of support is necessary. **G. rothschildiana** has swept-back red petals with a yellow base — **G. superba** has a similar growth habit but with petals which change from green to orange and finally to red. Plant the tuber in a 6 in. pot in spring with the tip 1 in. below the surface — water sparingly at first. After flowering reduce and then stop watering. Store the tuber in its pot at 50°–55°F. Repot in spring. For propagation remove offsets at repotting time and plant up in compost.

HABRANTHUS   Habranthus
Minimum temperature: 45°F during growing season

An unusual bulb which looks like a miniature Hippeastrum. The most popular species is **H. tubispathus** which in early autumn produces 9 in. high flower-stalks topped by solitary funnel-shaped flowers. These blooms are yellow or coppery gold inside and grey-pink outside. The narrow leaves appear shortly after the flowers — when this foliage turns yellow stop watering and keep the pot cool but frost-free. Repot every 2–3 years in spring. **H. robustus** is a taller plant with 2 ft flower-stalks.

HAEMANTHUS   Blood Lily
Minimum temperature: 55°F during growing season

The ball-like flower-head measuring 6–8 in. across carries up to 100 tubular red flowers in spring (**H. multiflorus**) or summer (**H. katherinae**). The leaves are about 1 ft long and the flower-stalks 1–2 ft high. Plant the bulb in summer with its tip above the compost. After flowering water sparingly. The plant is evergreen — repot every 4–5 years.

Haemanthus multiflorus

HIPPEASTRUM   Amaryllis
Minimum temperature: 55°F during growing season

In autumn you will find the large bulbs on sale in garden centres, DIY shops and department stores everywhere. These varieties of **H. hybrida** (which may be labelled 'Amaryllis') are planted in a 7 in. pot with half the bulb above the surface. Midwinter planting produces spring blooms — plant prepared bulbs in autumn for earlier flowering. The 1½–2 ft high flower-stalks bear several funnel-shaped blooms which are 5–6 in. across — the strap-like leaves appear at or shortly after flowering. Colours include white, orange, pink, red and purple — the petals may be plain, streaked, veined or edged in various shades. Stop watering when the leaves turn yellow and repot every 2 years in autumn.

Hippeastrum hybrida 'Minerva'

HYMENOCALLIS   Spider Lily
Minimum temperature: 55°F during growing season

This bulb is grown for its attractive sweet-smelling blooms which appear in late spring or summer. Each flower looks rather like a Daffodil — there is a long cup (corona) with projecting stamens and 6 narrow petals at the base. **H. festalis** is the most popular species — the 1 ft flower-stalk carries about 8 white blooms and the evergreen leaves are 1–2 ft long. Plant the bulb in winter with the top above the surface — water sparingly after flowering. Repot every 2 years in spring.

Hymenocallis festalis

IXIA   Corn Lily
Minimum temperature: 45°F during growing season

Clusters of 6-petalled starry or cup-shaped flowers are borne on wiry stems in early summer. The colours are usually bright — yellow, orange, pink or red and the centre is generally dark red or brown. **I. hybrida** is available as a number of named varieties, but is usually sold as a mixture which produces a host of 1 in. flowers in various colours. Pot up the corms in autumn — dry off and store after the leaves have withered.

LACHENALIA   Cape Cowslip
Minimum temperature: 45°F during growing season

The 1 ft stems of Lachenalia bear tubular pendent flowers. The 1 in. blooms of **L. aloides** are yellow tinged with green and red — the variety **'Lutea'** has all-yellow flowers. The flower-stalks and leaves bear brown or purple blotches. Plant 6–8 bulbs in a 6 in. pot in late summer for winter flowering — the tips should be just below the surface. After flowering reduce and then stop watering until repotting in autumn. An attractive plant, but it will fail if the conditions are too warm.

LILIUM   Lily
Minimum temperature: 35°F during growing season

A number of Lily varieties can be grown successfully under glass, including the white Easter Lily (**L. longiflorum**) which flowers in summer. The Mid-Century Hybrids such as **L. 'Enchantment'** (orange-red) are popular and easy to grow — height 2–4 ft, flowers 4–5 in. across. Plant the bulb in a 6 in. pot in autumn. Cover the tip with 1½ in. of compost. Keep cool, dark and moist. When shoots appear move to a brightly lit spot for early summer flowering.

Lilium 'Enchantment'

Nerine sarniensis

Ornithogalum thyrsoides

Rechsteineria cardinalis

Sinningia speciosa

LYCORIS   Lycoris
Minimum temperature: 55°F during growing season

You will have to search for this bulb — the only one you are likely to find is the Golden Spider Lily **L. aurea**. The plant is leafless when the 1 ft high flower-stalks appear — each bloom measures about 3 in. across and is made up of narrow wavy petals. These golden-yellow flowers open in late summer. Plant the bulb in spring in a heated house — do not water after the leaves and the flowers have faded. Repot every 2–3 years.

NERINE   Nerine
Minimum temperature: 45°F during growing season

N. sarniensis is the Guernsey Lily — narrow-petalled white, orange or red flowers are tightly clustered on top of 1–1½ ft high stalks. **N. flexuosa** produces Lily-like 3 in. flowers with wavy-edged petals in pink or white. Nerines bloom in autumn and the 1 ft sword-like leaves develop as the flowers open. Plant the bulb in August with the top well above the compost. Keep in a cold frame until shoots appear — then water and bring into the greenhouse or conservatory. Repot every 3 years.

ORNITHOGALUM   Chincherinchee
Minimum temperature: 55°F during growing season

Chincherinchee (**O. thyrsoides**) bears 1 ft long fleshy strap-like leaves and in late spring the 1½ ft high stems appear. These stems are crowned by a crowded spike of 20–30 white or creamy star-shaped flowers. These blooms are long-lasting in water and so this plant is popular with flower arrangers. Plant about 6 bulbs in a 6 in. pot in autumn — reduce watering once flowering is over and repot each autumn.

OXALIS   Wood Sorrel
Minimum temperature: 45°F during growing season

Oxalis is not a particularly showy plant and has never become popular. It grows as a rounded clump of Shamrock-like leaves and bears 1 in. wide 5-petalled flowers. **O. deppei** (Lucky or Rosette Buttercup) produces red or white flowers in spring, **O. cernua** (Bermuda Buttercup) has yellow blooms and **O. bowiei** is pale purple. The leaves close at night, and so do the flowers of some species. Plant the bulbs in autumn — keep the compost moist during the growing season but water sparingly after the leaves wither.

POLIANTHES   Tuberose
Minimum temperature: 55°F during growing season

A popular conservatory plant in Victorian times but now not often seen. The outstanding feature of this tall (2–4 ft) plant is the strong fragrance of its white flowers which appear on the unbranched stems in autumn. **P. tuberosa** bears single flowers — the variety **'The Pearl'** has double blooms. Plant the bulb-like rhizome 1 in. deep in spring — do not water until the foliage appears. Water regularly during the growing season. The plant cannot be repotted after flowering — start again with fresh rhizomes.

RECHSTEINERIA   Cardinal Flower
Minimum temperature: 55°F during growing season

The Cardinal Flower (**R. cardinalis**) may be listed as **Gesneria** or **Sinningia cardinalis**. It is closely related to Gloxinia, and the treatment required is very similar. The shape of the flowers, however, is completely different. R. cardinalis bears 2 in. long tubular blooms at the top of 1 ft stems — Gloxinia produces open bells. Plant the tubers in winter for bright red summer flowers.

SINNINGIA   Gloxinia
Minimum temperature: 55°F during growing season

The bell-shaped velvety blooms of Gloxinia (**S. speciosa**) are 3 in. or more in diameter — a greenhouse and conservatory favourite for summer display. White, pink, red, blue and purple varieties can be purchased — petal edges may be smooth or ruffled. Plant the tuber in a 5 in. pot in early spring — hollow side up and the top of the tuber level with the surface. Keep warm and rather dry until leaves appear, then keep the compost moist at all times with tepid water. Do not wet the large velvety leaves. Allow to dry out when leaves turn yellow. Repot in spring.

SMITHIANTHA   Temple Bells
Minimum temperature: 55°F during growing season

The pendent bell-like flowers of Temple Bells hang down above the mottled velvety leaves. **S. zebrina** is a tall variety, growing 2–3 ft high. For a more compact plant choose a variety of **S. hybrida** — the flowers are a blend of yellow, orange and/or pink. Plant 3 rhizomes on their sides in a 5 in. pot in late winter. Keep the compost moist at all times during the growing season. Stop watering when the flowers have faded and repot in spring. Divide rhizomes at repotting time.

SPARAXIS   Harlequin Flower
Minimum temperature: 45°F during growing season

In late spring and early summer a mixture of **S. tricolor** varieties will produce a riot of colour. The 2 in. wide blooms are borne on 1–1½ ft high stalks above the strap-like foliage — with some types each star-shaped flower has a black-edged yellow throat and petals in shades of white, yellow, red and purple. **S. elegans** (white or orange flowers) grows only 6–8 in. high. Sparaxis is a useful cut flower for floral arrangements. Plant the corms in autumn — repot every 2–3 years.

SPREKELIA   Jacobean Lily
Minimum temperature: 45°F during growing season

Do grow this one if it is new to you. The 4 in. flowers of **S. formosissima** look like bright red orchids — they are borne singly in early summer on top of 1 ft high stalks. Plant in autumn with the neck of the bulb above the surface. Once the flowers have faded and the foliage has died down let the compost dry out. Keep cool until spring and then bring into growth by watering. Repot every 3 years.

VALLOTA   Scarborough Lily
Minimum temperature: 45°F during growing season

The large funnel-shaped flowers of **V. speciosa** cluster in groups of 4–10 on top of 1–2 ft high stalks in late summer. Red is the usual colour, but there are white and pink varieties. Plant in spring in a 5 in. pot, leaving the top of the bulb uncovered. Do not overwater during the growing season — let the surface dry out between waterings. The leaves are evergreen — do not repot until the clump of bulbs becomes overcrowded. Reduce watering during the winter months.

VELTHEIMIA   Forest Lily
Minimum temperature: 45°F during growing season

An easy one to recognise. The cluster of about 60 small and tubular pink and green flowers at the top of the stout flower-stalk makes the plant look like the Red Hot Poker of the herbaceous border. The 1 ft long leaves are strap-like with wavy margins. Plant the large bulb in autumn — water sparingly until the leaves appear. Flowering takes place in spring and the flower-heads last for about a month. Aftercare depends on the species. The deciduous **V. capensis** should be kept dry until the autumn — the evergreen **V. bracteatus** should be kept moist. Repot every 2–3 years.

ZANTEDESCHIA   Arum Lily
Minimum temperature: 55°F during growing season

One of the beauties of the greenhouse plant world — the Calla Lily in the U.S and **Z. aethiopica** in the catalogues. The 6–9 in. long flowers are upturned white trumpets and are borne on 3 ft stalks in spring — the stalked leaves are arrow-shaped. Other species include **Z. rehmannii** (pink) and **Z. elliottiana** (yellow). Plant the rhizome in autumn — water sparingly at first and then liberally when growth starts. Reduce watering after flowering — start into growth again by more liberal watering in autumn.

ZEPHYRANTHES   Zephyr Lily
Minimum temperature: 45°F during growing season

The Zephyr Lily is a dainty and compact plant — **Z. grandiflora** produces 6 in. flower-stalks in early summer, each bearing a Crocus-like bloom. **Z. candida** is smaller with evergreen leaves and little white flowers in autumn, but there are hybrids with flowers up to 4–5 in. wide. Plant about 6 bulbs in a 5 in. pot in early spring. Stop watering deciduous types when the foliage withers — start into growth again in spring by moistening the compost. Repot only when pot-bound.

Smithiantha hybrida

Vallota speciosa

Veltheimia capensis

Zantedeschia aethiopica

**ORNAMENTALS:
BULBS**

Hardy Spring Bulbs

GROWING HYACINTHS, NARCISSI & TULIPS

- **Planting:** Choose bulbs which are good-sized, disease-free and firm. For flowering at Christmas choose 'prepared' bulbs and plant in September. Bulb fibre is sometimes used as the growing medium, but if you intend to save the bulbs for garden use after blooming then choose seed and cutting compost. Place a layer of moist compost in the bottom of the pot and set the bulbs on it. They should be close together but must not touch each other nor the sides of the pot. Never force bulbs downwards into the compost. Fill up with more of this compost, pressing it firmly but not too tightly around the bulbs. When finished the tips should be above the surface and there should be about ½ in. between the top of the compost and the rim of the pot.

- **Care After Planting:** The bulbs need a 'plunging' period of complete darkness and a temperature of about 40°F. The best spot is in the garden covering the pot with about 4 in. of peat. Failing this, place the container in a black polythene bag and stand it in a shed, cellar or garage. Any warmth at this stage will lead to failure. The plunging period lasts for about 6–10 weeks. Check occasionally to make sure that the compost is still moist.

- **Care During Growth:** When the shoots are about 1–2 in. high move the pot into a shady spot in the greenhouse — under the staging is ideal. This should not be later than December 1 for prepared bulbs for Christmas flowering. Conditions should be cool but frost-free. After 7 days move the pot to a bright and then to a sunny part of the house. The leaves will now develop and in a few weeks the flower buds will appear. Now is the time to move the pot to the chosen site for flowering. Keep the compost moist at all times. Provide some support for tall-flowering types. Feed with a liquid fertilizer.

- **Care After Flowering:** Cut off flowers, not flower-stalks. Continue watering and feeding until leaves have withered. Remove bulbs and allow to dry, then remove dead foliage and store in a cool dry place. These bulbs will not provide a second display indoors — plant in the garden in autumn.

Hyacinthus orientalis

Tulipa greigii

HYACINTHUS   Hyacinth

The Dutch or Common Hyacinth (**H. orientalis**) is a favourite indoor plant as its fragrance fills the space and its leafless flower-stalks crowded with waxy flowers are eye-catching. There are scores of varieties in a wide range of colours. Basic details are height 7–12 in., flowers 1–2 in. long, planting time September–October, flowering time January–March. Roman Hyacinths (**H. orientalis albulus**) differ in a number of ways. The flowers are smaller and less tightly packed and 2 or 3 stalks are produced by each bulb. Colours are restricted to white, pink or blue. Plant in August–September for December–January flowers.

NARCISSUS   Narcissus, Daffodil

A bulb which everybody knows — 6 spreading petals and a central trumpet (corona). The 4 groups described below are generally considered to be the most reliable. **N. hybrida** Daffodil: 12–20 in. tall, trumpet longer than the petals. **N. hybrida** Narcissus: 12–24 in. tall, trumpet shorter than the petals — double varieties available. **N. cyclamineus**: 6–12 in. tall, drooping flowers with long trumpets and strongly reflexed petals. **N. tazetta**: 12–18 in. tall, several flowers per stem and a central short cup surrounded by longer petals. Plant Narcissus bulbs in August–October for flowering in January–April. The N. tazetta varieties bear bunches of flowers on each stem at Christmas or early in the New Year.

TULIPA   Tulip

Tulips are an indispensible part of the spring garden but they are sometimes disappointing in the conservatory. They do need cool conditions and it is necessary to choose the right sorts. There are several recommended groups. The most satisfactory varieties are those classed as Earlies. **T. hybrida** Single Early and Double Early: 9–16 in. tall. **T. kaufmanniana**: 6–10 in. tall, flat 'Water Lily' flowers. **T. greigii**: 8–12 in. tall, leaves streaked or mottled with brown. **T. hybrida** Darwin Tulip: 24–30 in. tall, very large flowers in April, may need support. **T. hybrida** Lily-flowered Tulip: 20–24 in. tall, pointed reflexed petals. Plant Tulip bulbs in September–October for flowering in January–April.

GROWING DWARF BULBS

- **Planting:** It is essential to choose a container with adequate drainage holes. Place a layer of crocks at the bottom and add a layer of seed and cutting compost. Plant the bulbs closely together and add more compost. The tips of the bulbs should be completely covered.

- **Care After Planting:** Place the pot in the garden.

- **Care During Growth:** Protect the shoots from slugs and mice. When the plants are fully grown and flower buds are present bring the pot inside to the site chosen for flowering. Keep the compost moist at all times — the maximum temperature should be 60°–65°F during the flowering period.

- **Care After Flowering:** Treat in the same way as Hyacinths, Narcissi & Tulips — see page 54.

CHIONODOXA Glory of the Snow

The most popular Chionodoxa is **C. luciliae** — about 10 blooms are borne on each flower-stalk — pale blue stars with a prominent white centre. Varieties include **'Alba'** (white) and **'Pink Giant'** (pink). **C. sardensis** has all-blue flowers and the largest blooms (1½ in. across) are on **C. gigantea**. Plant bulbs in September for February flowers.

Chionodoxa gigantea

CROCUS Crocus

Plant Crocus corms in September or October. The varieties of **C. chrysanthus** (**'Cream Beauty'**, **'Goldilocks'** etc) bear 3–4 in. long flowers in February — the usual colour is yellow. Some varieties can be "forced" in the same way as Hyacinths etc — see page 54. Varieties of **C. vernus** have larger flowers, bloom a little later and are usually white, blue or purple. Popular ones include **'Joan of Arc'** and **'Vanguard'**.

ERANTHIS Winter Aconite

For something different plant tubers of Eranthis in pots or bowls in September. In January the 3 in. high flower-stalks appear, each one topped with a bright yellow flower bearing a frilled leafy collar. The usual species is **E. hyemalis** which has 1 in. wide Buttercup-like flowers — for larger blooms grow **E. tubergenii**.

Eranthis hyemalis

GALANTHUS Snowdrop

The Snowdrops of January are neither large nor colourful, but they are a much-loved indicator that a new floral year has started. Plant the bulbs in September. The usual species is **G. nivalis** — 4–6 in. high with 1 in. pendent flowers. For bolder flowers and 10 in. stalks choose **G. elwesii**.

IRIS Iris

Dwarf bulbous Irises produce 3 in. wide blooms on 4–6 in. flower-stalks in January or February following planting in September or October. Choose from **I. histrioides 'Major'** (deep blue, with white and yellow centres), **I. reticulata** (purple, yellow centres — fragrant) and **I. danfordiae** (yellow — fragrant). For the earliest blooms grow I. histrioides 'Major'.

Iris histrioides 'Major'

MUSCARI Grape Hyacinth

There is nothing spectacular about this old favourite — just lots of tiny, bell-like blooms clustered at the top of each flower spike. The usual choice is **M. armeniacum** (9 in., white-edged blue flowers) — for sky-blue flowers grow **M. botryoides**. **M. comosus 'Plumosum'** has feathery blooms. Plant bulbs in September for January–March flowers.

SCILLA Bluebell

The popular Siberian Bluebell **S. siberica** (6 in. stalk, pendent ½ in. flowers) can be grown under glass — rich blue, sky-blue and white varieties are available. Other suitable Bluebells are the dwarf and early-blooming **S. tubergeniana**, **S. adlamii** and **S. violacea**. Plant Scilla bulbs in September–October for January–March flowers.

Ornamentals : Alpines

It may seem strange that alpines from the high mountains should need the cosseted environment of a greenhouse. The reason is simple — some of the more delicate varieties can survive quite happily under a winter blanket of snow away from icy winds, rain and frost, but in our 'milder' climate the roots may quickly rot. There are added benefits under glass — the foliage and flowers are protected from spring winds and rain, and the plants are raised closer to eye-level.

A custom-made alpine house is very expensive — the usual action is to buy a standard small green-house and have extra ventilators fitted to the roof and sides. Good ventilation is vital — doors and windows should be left open for most of the year. Fill pots with J.I. No.1 or a peat-based compost with added grit — cover the surface with shingle, grit or coarse sand. Water thoroughly during the growing season but quite sparingly in winter.

Root systems are shallow, so pans and half pots are frequently used. These should be plunged in sharp sand or grit — this will help to keep the compost moist and at an even temperature. Shade the glass when the air temperature approaches 90° F. The pots can be moved outdoors during the summer months.

The extra ventilation needed in the alpine house makes it unsuitable for most greenhouse plants, but many small bulbs, *bonsai* trees and dwarf conifers can be grown for added variety. The robust favourites from the outdoor rockery can be grown, but it is much more usual to base an alpine collection on the more delicate types which require protection. Some of them are listed here.

Androsace hirtella

Campanula raineri

ANDROSACE   Rock Jasmine

Specialist catalogues list many varieties and a few can be grown outdoors. The alpine house ones all bear tiny, Primrose-like blooms on 1–4 in. flower-stalks above cushions or mats of small leaves. Examples include **A. ciliata** (pink flowers, early summer), **A. cylindrica** (white flowers, spring), **A. hirtella** (white flowers, spring) and **A. vandellii** (white flowers, spring, silvery leaves).

CAMPANULA   Bellflower

A favourite rockery plant — blue or white bells or stars in June and July. Some are easy and reliable in the open garden, but there are tender dwarfs which need the protection of a greenhouse. **C. lasiocarpa** (3 in.) produces solitary blue bells in summer — **C. piperi** (3 in.) is a showier plant with large blue petals and red anthers. **C. raineri** (3 in.) bears large flat blue blooms and for something different there is **C. vidalii** (9 in.) which has orange-marked white blooms.

DRABA   Whitlow Grass

No more than a couple of inches high, the mounds of tiny leaves bear clusters of white or yellow flowers on thread-like stalks in spring. **D. bryoides** produces dense cushions of tiny leaves and masses of yellow flowers — for a wider-spreading species grow **D. mollissima** which forms large rosettes and bright yellow flowers. Propagate by sowing seed under glass.

GENTIANA   Gentian

A large genus — the bright blue trumpet-like species are perhaps the best-loved of all rock plants. However, do not be tempted to grow these attractive plants in a heated greenhouse or conservatory as both winter warmth and inadequate ventilation cannot be tolerated. **G. verna** is one of these garden favourites which flowers in the spring and can be grown under glass — amongst the alpine house Gentians are **G. saxosa** (white, late summer, 2 in.), **G. brachyphylla** (bright blue, early summer, 2 in.) and **G. bavarica** (bright blue, spring, 3 in.).

LEWISIA   Lewisia

Lewisia is one of the most colourful of all rock plants — flowers are in pink, peach, orange or white with petals which are often striped. Buy one of the showy hybrids of **L. cotyledon** — height 1 ft, spread 9 in., flowering period May–June. Even more attractive is **L. tweedyi** which bears 2½ in. wide apricot blooms in April and May. To propagate sow seed under glass in early spring.

Primula allionii

OMPHALODES   Omphalodes

The flowers of Omphalodes are borne in loose clusters above the foliage, each one looking like a blue or white Forget-me-not. One of them (**O. verna** or Blue-eyed Mary) is robust enough to be grown outdoors and become invasive, but **O. luciliae** is fussy enough to need alpine house conditions. The sky-blue flowers are borne above the blue-grey foliage in May–July.

PRIMULA   Rockery Primrose

Hundreds of species and varieties are dwarf enough to be grown in the rockery or alpine house. There is a basal rosette of leaves and Primrose-shaped blooms which may be pendent or upright. Under-glass examples include **P. allionii** (white, pink or red stalkless flowers, spring, 2 in.), **P. marginata** (mauve or blue flowers, early spring, 3 in.) and **P. sonchifolia** (red-eyed purple or blue flowers, early spring, 4 in.). Some Primulas are rather delicate and need greenhouse protection from winter rain — an example is the early-flowering **P. edgeworthii**.

Ranunculus asiaticus

RANUNCULUS   Dwarf Buttercup

There are a number of Dwarf Buttercups which can be grown in the rock garden. Despite being closely related to some rampant weeds, a few are hard to grow and need the protection of an alpine house. **R. crenatus** is a May-flowering white Buttercup. **R. asiaticus** (yellow or white flowers, summer, 1 ft) needs protection as the compost must be kept dry in winter — **R. calandrinioides** is grown indoors as it flowers in winter.

RHODOHYPOXIS   Rhodohypoxis

A South African rockery plant which has none of the hardiness found in some of the popular plants which have come from the European Alps. Use lime-free gritty compost and grow a variety of **R. baurii** — height 2 in., spread 3 in., flowering period April–September. White, pink, rose and purple types are available. Tufts of narrow leaves are produced by the corm-like roots. Divide clumps in autumn.

Saxifraga 'Cranbourne'

SAXIFRAGA   Saxifrage

A very large genus, many of which are popular plants for the rockery. There are several groups — Encrusted, Mossy etc, but the favourite greenhouse group are the Kabschia or Cushion Saxifrages which are mounds of small rosettes of lime-encrusted leaves — the foliage colour may be silver, grey or green. The flowering period is February–April. Examples are **S. apiculata** (yellow), **S. burseriana** (white), **S. 'Cranbourne'** (pink) and **S. 'Jenkinsae'** (pale pink).

SOLDANELLA   Snowbell

Soldanella is grown under glass as it needs protection from winter rain. In spring dainty bell-like flowers with deeply fringed margins droop gracefully from the tops of the upright flower-stalks. Lavender-blue is the usual colour but other hues are available. **S. minima** (mauve, 2 in.) is the baby of the genus — others include **S. montana** (blue, 6 in.) and **S. villosa** (violet, 10 in.). Propagate by dividing up clumps in summer.

Soldanella montana

Ornamentals : Cacti

The cacti are a vast family of succulent plants with a wide range of sizes, shapes and flower types, but they all have a few features in common. Virtually all are leafless and on the stems there are woolly or bristly cushions (areoles). From these there may be outgrowths such as spines, hairs or hooks.

There are two reasons why some people decide to devote the whole of a greenhouse to a collection of cacti and other succulents. Firstly there is the fascination for the strange shapes and colourful flowers — some species of cacti may take a long time to reach the flowering stage but given proper treatment will then bloom year after year. The second reason for choosing cacti is a purely practical one — they do not demand the same degree of attention as other ornamentals. There is no need to create a moist atmosphere and little or no watering is required between November and March. All they want is a lot of light, frost-free conditions, a gritty compost and ventilation when the temperature reaches 70° F. They will tolerate neglect, so there are no worries when you have to be away for a few days, but for proper development and regular flowering you do have to treat them properly. This calls for watering thoroughly in summer each time the compost starts to dry out.

The above remarks apply to the desert cacti, which include nearly all the species in the family. The forest, jungle or orchid cacti (Epiphyllum, Zygocactus and Rhipsalidopsis) grow on trees in their natural home in the forests of tropical America. They have their own special and somewhat fussy needs — see pages 108–109 in The House Plant Expert for details.

Aporocactus flagelliformis

Cereus peruvianus

APOROCACTUS Rat-tail Cactus

The popular species is **A. flagelliformis**, reputed to be the easiest cactus to grow and bring into flower. It is a plant for a pedestal or hanging basket — the ½ in. wide cylindrical stems hang down and grow several inches each year. In spring the 3 in. long tubular flowers appear — they open during the day and close at night **A. mallisonii (Heliaporus smithii)** is similar but the stems are thicker, the spines longer and the flowers larger.

CEPHALOCEREUS Old Man Cactus

This genus has been grown as an ornamental in Britain for over 100 years. It produces a columnar stem — 50 ft high in the wild but reaching only 1–1½ ft in the conservatory. **C. senilis** has about 30 shallow ribs and thin spines — it is grown for the dense covering of long silvery hairs which gives the plant its common name. The Golden Old Man Cactus **C. chrysacanthus** bears prominent golden spines. The pink flowers of Cephalocereus rarely appear on conservatory plants.

CEREUS Cereus

The Column Cactus **C. peruvianus** is an old favourite. The stem reaches 2–3 ft in time and its prominent ribs bear brown spines. In summer the 6 in. long funnel-shaped flowers appear on mature specimens — these slightly fragrant blooms open at night. **C. jamacaru** is quite similar, but the spines are yellow and the white, night-opening flowers are even longer. The Rock Cactus **C. peruvianus 'Monstrosus'** is a slow-growing oddity with distorted branched stems.

ECHINOCACTUS   Barrel Cactus

Echinocactus is a round ribbed ball with sharp spines. It is slow-growing, taking about 10 years to reach a diameter of 9 in. The Golden Barrel Cactus **E. grusonii** has yellow spines and can form a 3 ft wide globe in time. It takes about 15 years to reach the flowering stage, so the yellow blooms are rare under glass. For an even larger specimen grow the Large Barrel Cactus **E. ingens**.

ECHINOPSIS   Sea Urchin Cactus

You can choose a globular or columnar species of this fast-growing genus — the ribs are prominent and the spines are sharp. Nothing special, but the flowers are. The 4–6 in. long night-opening blooms are borne on long stalks in summer. **E. eyriesii** is ball-like and has white, scented blooms and short brown spines — **E. rhodotricha** is oval and bears 1 in. spines and scentless blooms. **E. aurea** produces yellow flowers. Echinopsis is a near-hardy plant which can be grown in a cold house.

Lobivia hertrichiana

LOBIVIA   Lobivia

Lobivia is often described as a beginner's cactus — it is easy to care for, remains compact (3–6 in. high) and readily produces white, red, pink, yellow or orange flowers from late spring to early autumn. Each bloom lasts for only a day. Several species are available. The oval **L. famatimensis** (Sunset Cactus) is covered with spreading yellow spines and bears large golden flowers. Both **L. aurea** (Golden Lily Cactus) and **L. hertrichiana** are ball-shaped.

MAMMILLARIA   Pin Cushion Cactus

Any large collection of cacti will contain several species of this large genus. Some are very easy — others are a challenge even for the expert. The standard pattern is a globe bearing spine-topped tubercles instead of ribs with a ring of spring or summer flowers near the top of the ball. These flowers often produce fruits. The favourite species is **M. bocasana** with silky hairs, hooked spines and white flowers. Others include **M. rhodantha** (magenta flowers), **M. zeilmanniana** (purple) and **M. hahniana** (pink).

Mammillaria hahniana

OPUNTIA   Prickly Pear

The species grown as indoor plants are generally made up of flattened pads which bear yellow flowers along the edges and then edible fruit. Don't expect to harvest prickly pears from your greenhouse or conservatory. The popular one is **O. microdasys** (Bunny Ears) which grows 1 ft high with golden bristles and yellow flowers. The variety **'Albinospina'** has white bristles. **O. bergeriana** is the freest-flowering species — **O. cylindrica** is a columnar plant which looks nothing like a Prickly Pear.

OREOCEREUS   Old Man of the Andes

You will find the popular species labelled as **O. celsianus**, **Borzicactus celsianus** or **Pilocereus celsianus**. The oval columnar stem will reach 3 ft in time and branches arise from the base. There are prominent yellow spines which turn red with age, and the key feature is the covering of long white hairs which gives the plant its common name. In summer the 3 in. long red flowers appear. **O. trollii** is a smaller and less common species.

Opuntia microdasys 'Albinospina'

PARODIA   Tom Thumb Cactus

Like Mammillarias, the Parodias are small globular cacti which are tubercled rather than ribbed and which flower from an early age. The spines are often attractively coloured. The red-flowering one is **P. sanguiniflora** — the yellow-flowering types are **P. aureispina** (Golden Tom Thumb Cactus) which bears hooked spines and **P. chrysacanthion** which has bristle-like spines.

REBUTIA   Crown Cactus

Rebutia is another favourite as it is easy to grow and begins to flower when only one year old. It can be confused with Mammillaria as the ball-like stems are covered with tubercles. There is a basic difference — the long-tubed funnel-like flowers are borne near the base and not as a ring around the top. **R. miniscula** bears orange or pink flowers in early summer. The dwarf is **R. pygmaea** (less than 1 in. high) and the giant is **R. senilis** (4 in. high).

Parodia aureispina

Ornamentals : Ferns

There has been a revival of interest in ferns as more types have become available at garden centres, led by the varieties of Boston Fern which have become popular house plants. This increased interest, however, cannot match the popularity enjoyed by these non-flowering plants in Victorian times — they were grown in large numbers and variety in every conservatory. Today we generally use a few ferns as background plants between flowering ones, although large specimens are often displayed on their own in pots or hanging baskets.

For the serious fern enthusiast it is a good idea to have a greenhouse devoted to this large group, if money and space allow. The ferns have their own special needs — high humidity, protection from direct sunlight and a compost which is kept moist at all times during the growing season. An east- or north-facing lean-to is ideal.

Temperature requirement depends on the species you have chosen to grow. Some will thrive in a cold house whereas others need near-tropical conditions. A cool house kept in the 50°–80°F range is satisfactory for almost all the popular types. High air humidity is vital for most ferns — this calls for damping down the floor of the house each day in warm weather if tropical or filmy-leaved types are grown.

Repot in spring when the roots fill the pot — young specimens will probably require annual repotting. Do not bury the crown of the plant. Rhizome-bearing types can be propagated by being cut into 2 or 3 pieces at repotting time. Specialist suppliers offer scores of different ferns — described here are some of the more popular ones.

Adiantum raddianum

Asplenium nidus

ADIANTUM   Maidenhair Fern
Minimum temperature: 45°F

The Maidenhair Ferns bear filmy leaflets on wiry stems. They are as delicate as they look — constantly moist air and warmth when actively growing are vital. **A. raddianum** is one of the more robust types — it grows about 1 ft high with black stems and fan-shaped leaves. The variety **'Fragrantissimum'** has larger leaflets. **A. capillus-veneris** is the species which grows wild.

ASPLENIUM   Asplenium
Minimum temperature: 55°F

There are 2 basic types which look nothing like each other. **A. nidus** is the well-known Bird's Nest Fern — 2 ft long spear-like leaves surround the fibrous 'nest' at the centre. The other type is the Mother Fern with feathery fronds which bear numerous tiny plantlets when mature — **A. bulbiferum** is the usual one. All Aspleniums need shade and a moist atmosphere.

BLECHNUM   Blechnum
Minimum temperature: 45°F

The popular species is **B. gibbum**, a large fern which has a crown of palm-like stiff fronds. With age a short trunk is formed, so this plant needs space — a mature specimen will be 3 ft high with a 3–5 ft spread. **B. brasiliense** has even larger fronds, reaching 3–4 ft, and needs a warm or stove house if it is to flourish.

DAVALLIA   Hare's Foot Fern
Minimum temperature: 45°F

The 'hare's foot' is a furry creeping rhizome which grows over the surface of the compost and down the side of the pot. The fronds are carried on wiry stems and are made up of tiny leaflets. The most popular species is **D. canariensis** with Carrot-like foliage — it will succeed more than most ferns in a rather dry atmosphere.

DICKSONIA   Tree Fern
Minimum temperature: 35°F

Dicksonia is the most widely available tree fern. **D. antarctica** will grow outdoors in mild areas — in a large conservatory the trunk will slowly reach 10 ft or more with 5–6 ft feathery fronds. Not an easy plant to care for — the thick trunk has to be sprayed at least once a day in summer. The trunk of **D. fibrosa** is covered with yellow fibrous roots.

NEPHROLEPIS   Boston Fern
Minimum temperature: 45°F

In Victorian times it was the stiff-leaved **N. exaltata** and **N. cordifolia** which were popular. Today they have been largely replaced by a mutation with gracefully drooping fronds — **N. exaltata 'Bostoniensis'** or Boston Fern. There are scores of different types, such as **'Fluffy Ruffles'** with feathery leaflets and **'Whitmanii'** with lacy leaflets. All the Boston Ferns are easy to grow and make excellent hanging basket plants.

Nephrolepis exaltata 'Bostoniensis'

PELLAEA   Button Fern
Minimum temperature: 45°F

The Button Fern **P. rotundifolia** has a creeping rootstock which produces 1 ft long arching fronds — these fronds are made up of round, leathery leaflets. This low-growing fern can be used for ground cover or in a hanging basket — it will tolerate dry air much better than most other ferns.

Pellaea rotundifolia

PLATYCERIUM   Stag's Horn Fern
Minimum temperature: 45°F

The Stag's Horn Fern (**P. bifurcatum**) bears large and spectacular fronds — the sterile frond is flat and clasping and the 3 ft long fertile fronds which bear spores are antler-like and spreading. Grow it in a shallow pot or cover the root ball with sphagnum moss and attach to a piece of log or cork with plastic-coated wire. Once a week immerse the plant and plaque in water for a few minutes.

POLYPODIUM   Hare's Foot Fern
Minimum temperature: 55°F

This Hare's Foot Fern has a thick creeping rhizome like Davallia, and it will also grow in dry air. It is, however, a much larger plant — **P. aureum** (**Phlebodium aureum**) bears 2 ft long deeply-divided fronds. The best variety is **'Mandaianum'** which has bluish-green leaflets. A novel way of growing Polypodium is on old logs which are kept moist.

Platycerium bifurcatum

POLYSTICHUM   Polystichum
Minimum temperature: 45°F

A genus with several species which bear little similarity to each other. The most popular one is **P.** (**Cyrtomium**) **falcatum 'Rochfordianum'** — the fronds are made up of glossy Holly-shaped leaflets. This one does not mind dry air — neither does the Tsus-sima Holly Fern (**P. tsus-simense**) which has arching feathery fronds. **P. auriculatum** needs a humid atmosphere and bears upright and stiff herringbone-like fronds.

PTERIS   Table Fern
Minimum temperature: 45°F

Most types of Pteris are easy to grow, producing handsome fronds in a range of shapes and sizes. The most popular types are varieties of **P. cretica** which are available in an assortment of leaflet colours and forms. **P. ensiformis 'Victoriae'** (silver band along the midrib) is the prettiest Table Fern.

Pteris ensiformis 'Victoriae'

Ornamentals : Orchids

Everyone is fascinated by these plants and some greenhouse owners devote the whole area to an orchid collection. If you plan to grow a number of orchids then do read a book on the subject — they are pricey and each genus has its own special needs. Most conservatory orchids have a thickened stem-base (pseudo-bulb) which is a storage organ. From it arise both leaves and flower-stalks. About half of the species are epiphytes, which means that they live on the bark of trees in the wild. These types can be grown wired on to dead tree branches or in pots in the conservatory.

There are a number of general rules. Orchids need moist air at all times and so the pots should be stood on moist gravel. Good light is essential but they must be screened from warm direct sunlight by means of roller blinds. Good ventilation is necessary, but you must avoid draughts. The pots can be stood outdoors on warm and sunny days. Keep the compost moist — reduce watering in winter.

You cannot generalise about the temperature requirements for orchids. One or two, such as Pleione and Bletilla, die down in winter and can be grown in a cold house if it is kept frost-free. Many can be grown in a cool house but some need warm house conditions and the tropical orchids require a stove house. As a general rule orchids thrive best when there is a drop in temperature at night of about 10°F.

Do not worry if a few roots grow outside the pot — repot only when growth begins to suffer. Buy an orchid compost for this purpose. Listed here are some popular genera — choose ones which are suitable for your skill and the night temperature of the house in winter.

Vuylstekeara

Cattleya bowringiana

Coelogyne cristata

CATTLEYA   Corsage Orchid
Minimum temperature: 55°F

A popular orchid with waxy, beautiful flowers which measure 4–6 in. across. The flower-stalk (1–1½ ft high) bears 3–16 blooms, depending on the species. **C. bowringiana** (Cluster Cattleya) produces rosy-purple blooms in autumn. **C. intermedia** is a summer-flowering species with cream and purple flowers. High humidity is needed for all Cattleya varieties.

COELOGYNE   Coelogyne
Minimum temperature: 45°F

The 2–4 in. wide flowers are fragrant — plants with pendent blooms should be grown in a hanging basket. The easiest one to grow is **C. cristata**. Orange-lipped white flowers with wavy petals appear in winter and spring on pendulous flower-heads. **C. nitida** has upright stalks with brown-lipped white flowers in winter.

CYMBIDIUM   Cymbidium
Minimum temperature: 45°F

The first rule is to choose one of the dwarf hybrids rather than a species Cymbidium which may have leaves 1–2 ft long. This is often regarded as a beginner's orchid and is quite easy to grow if you give it a short resting period in autumn by keeping the compost rather dry. The prominent lip and the petals are generally different colours.

DENDROBIUM   Dendrobium
Minimum temperature: 45°F

A very large and highly varied genus — there are dwarfs and giants, prominently lipped and almost lipless blooms, and a wide range of flower colours. When buying a Dendrobium it is necessary to check whether it is a deciduous or evergreen variety — the deciduous ones need a cool period with almost dry compost between the end of flowering and the start of the growing season.

LYCASTE   Lycaste
Minimum temperature: 55°F

This deciduous orchid produces a number of flower-stalks, each one crowned by a single bloom — the flowering period may continue for a month or more. **L. aromatica** is a popular spring-flowering species — the highly fragrant blooms are about 2 in. across. One problem is that the flower-stalks are only about 6 in. high and are dwarfed by the tall leaves.

Odontoglossum grande

MILTONIA   Pansy Orchid
Minimum temperature: 55°F

The 2–4 in. wide flowers are Pansy-like and velvety. They are noted for their free-flowering nature and protracted flowering period, but they are not easy plants to grow as they are sensitive to sudden changes in temperature. Regular repotting every 2 years is required. Choose a named hybrid rather than a species Miltonia — they are easier to grow.

ODONTOGLOSSUM   Odontoglossum
Minimum temperature: 45°F

The arching sprays carry several blooms which are 6–7 in. across. These appear in autumn and winter and are quite spectacular. The most popular variety **O. grande** (Tiger Orchid) is quite easy to grow with good light, high humidity and a short rest in winter. The brown-banded yellow petals surround the creamy lip.

Paphiopedilum insigne

PAPHIOPEDILUM   Slipper Orchid
Minimum temperature: 55°F

The flowers measure 2–4 in. across — they are easy to recognise by the lip which is modified into a prominent pouch. It is one of the easier ones to grow and does not need a rest period. Paphiopedilum does not produce a pseudobulb and the flowers last for a month or two. Many species and hybrids are available.

PHALAENOPSIS   Moth Orchid
Minimum temperature: 55°F

The Moth Orchid is a common sight nowadays in the House Plant section of garden centres. Long arching stalks bear numerous flat-faced flowers, each one about 2 in. across. It needs warm conditions and high humidity. Phalaenopsis does not need a resting period so keep the compost moist at all times — a well-grown hybrid can stay in flower almost all year round.

Phalaenopsis 'Cooks Pink'

VANDA   Vanda
Minimum temperature: 55°F or 65°F

Vanda is not difficult to grow if you can satisfy its need for warm nights. The long stalks bear numerous flat-faced flowers, waxy and fragrant with a small lip. Many colours are available — a popular species is the blue **V. rothschildiana** with 10–20 blooms per stem in autumn and the ability to thrive even when night temperatures drop to 55°F.

VUYLSTEKEARA   Vuylstekeara
Minimum temperature: 45°F

This genus does not occur in nature — it is a man-made hybrid of Odontoglossum, Miltonia and Cochlioda. It is a compact plant which produces long arching sprays of flowers in winter and spring. These blooms are about 4 in. across and look quite similar to the parent Odontoglossum — the lip is wavy-edged and the usual petal colour is red.

Vanda rothschildiana

Bedding Plants

A bedding plant is generally an annual or occasionally a biennial or perennial which is raised under glass or in a nursery bed outdoors and then planted out in the garden as a temporary occupant to provide a colourful display. Until quite recently most bedding plants were set out in beds or borders — in large numbers of one type as groundwork plants or as individual tall plants (dot plants) in the case of varieties with showy leaves or flowers. These days, however, about 60 per cent of bedding plants are used in containers and hanging baskets rather than in the traditional bed or border.

Most people buy their summer bedding plants as seedlings or rooted cuttings in flimsy plastic strips or pots, or in rigid white cellular trays — the old wooden tray is now largely a thing of the past. If you have a cool greenhouse it is quite a simple job to raise your own. Begonias are raised from tubers — Pelargonium, Fuchsia, Dahlia, Heliotrope and Canna are propagated from cuttings. The rest are reproduced from seed.

Growing your own has several advantages. You can choose from a vast selection of varieties rather than the standard range of favourites offered for sale as seedlings in spring. You will save money, and this can be considerable if you have a large area to cover, and you will also be able to ensure that the plants are in peak condition at transplanting time.

There is a problem — germination generally calls for a higher temperature than is required for the growth of seedlings. This means that sowing seed calls for additional warmth — you can heat part of the greenhouse to 65°F or instal a heated propagator. Sow between late January and mid April — the hardiest types and slow growers are sown first. Follow the rules set out on page 89 and harden off for 2–3 weeks before planting out half hardy types in late May–early June.

Where this is not practical there is nowadays an excellent compromise between seed sowing and buying expensive plants in trays ready for bedding out. You can buy tiny seedlings in trays or small seedlings as plugs which are then pricked out or potted on and kept in a cool greenhouse until transplanting time arrives.

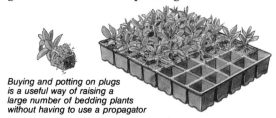

Buying and potting on plugs is a useful way of raising a large number of bedding plants without having to use a propagator

Summer Bedding Plants

Latin name	Common name	Spacing	Height	Flowering season	Colours available
AGERATUM	Floss Flower	6–9 in.	6 in.–1½ ft	Mid June–end October	
ALYSSUM	Sweet Alyssum	9 in.	3–6 in.	Mid June–end September	
AMARANTHUS	Love-lies-bleeding	9 in.–2½ ft	1–4 ft	Mid June–mid October	
ANTIRRHINUM	Snapdragon	6 in.–1½ ft	4 in.–3 ft	Mid June–end October	
BEGONIA	Tuberous Begonia	9 in.–1 ft	9 in.–1½ ft	Mid June–end September	
BEGONIA	Wax Begonia	6 in.–1 ft	4 in.–1 ft	Mid June–mid October	
CALCEOLARIA	Slipper Flower	9 in.	8–15 in.	Early June–mid October	
CALENDULA	Pot Marigold	9 in.–1 ft	9 in.–2 ft	Mid May–mid September	
CALLISTEPHUS	China Aster	9 in.–1½ ft	6 in.–3 ft	Mid July–mid October	
CAMPANULA	Canterbury Bell	6 in.–1 ft	1½–2½ ft	Early May–end July	
CANNA	Indian Shot	Dot plant	2–4 ft	Mid July–mid October	
CELOSIA	Celosia	9 in.–1½ ft	9 in.–2½ ft	Early July–end September	

Latin name	Common name	Spacing	Height	Flowering season	Colours available
CENTAUREA	Cornflower	9 in.–1 ft	1–3 ft	Early June–end September	
CHRYSANTHEMUM	Annual Chrysanthemum	9 in.–2 ft	9 in.–3 ft	Early June–mid October	
COSMOS	Cosmea	1–1½ ft	1–3 ft	Early July–end October	
CUPHEA	Cigar Plant	1 ft	1 ft	Mid July–end September	
DAHLIA	Bedding Dahlia	1 ft	1–2 ft	Early July–end October	
DIANTHUS	Annual Carnation	9 in.–1 ft	9 in.–2 ft	Early July–mid October	
DIANTHUS	Indian Pink	6–9 in.	6 in.–1 ft	Mid June–end October	
DIANTHUS	Sweet William	9 in.–1 ft	6 in.–2 ft	End May–end July	
FUCHSIA	Fuchsia	1½ ft	1–2 ft	Early July–mid October	
GODETIA	Godetia	9 in.–1 ft	9 in.–2 ft	Early July–mid September	
HELIOTROPIUM	Heliotrope	1 ft	1–1½ ft	Mid June–end September	
IBERIS	Candytuft	9 in.	6 in.–1½ ft	Mid May–mid September	
IMPATIENS	Busy Lizzie	6–9 in.	6 in.–1½ ft	Mid June–mid October	
LATHYRUS	Sweet Pea	6 in.–1 ft	6 in.–8 ft	Mid June–mid September	
LOBELIA	Lobelia	6 in.	4–6 in.	Mid June–mid October	
MATTHIOLA	Ten Week Stock	9 in.–1 ft	1–2½ ft	Mid June–mid August	
MIMULUS	Monkey Flower	9 in.	6 in.–1 ft	Early June–mid October	
NEMESIA	Nemesia	6 in.	9 in.–1 ft	Early June–end September	
NICOTIANA	Tobacco Plant	9 in.–1½ ft	9 in.–3 ft	Mid June–mid October	
PELARGONIUM	Ivy-leaved Pelargonium	9 in.–1 ft	6 in.–4 ft	Mid June–end October	
PELARGONIUM	Zonal Pelargonium	9 in.–1 ft	9 in.–2 ft	Mid June–end October	
PENSTEMON	Penstemon	9 in.–1½ ft	1–2½ ft	Early August–mid October	
PETUNIA	Petunia	9 in.–1 ft	6 in.–1½ ft	Mid June–mid October	
PHLOX	Annual Phlox	6 in.–1 ft	4 in.–1½ ft	Mid June–end September	
SALVIA	Sage	9 in.–1½ ft	6 in.–3 ft	Mid June–end October	
TAGETES	French Marigold	6–9 in.	6 in.–1 ft	Mid June–end October	
TAGETES	African Marigold	1–1½ ft	1–3 ft	Mid June–end October	
VERBENA	Verbena	1 ft	6 in.–1½ ft	Mid June–mid October	
VIOLA	Pansy, Viola	6 in.–1 ft	6–9 in.	Early June–end October	
ZINNIA	Zinnia	6 in.–1½ ft	6 in.–2½ ft	Early July–mid October	

Garden Perennials and Shrubs

Your greenhouse should be more than just a production unit for Tomatoes and Cucumbers and a display unit for a selection of ornamentals. It should also serve as a supply point for many of the plants you grow in the garden.

This concept is not a novel one — many owners put their greenhouse to this use for raising garden plants in the early part of the year. It involves sowing seeds for bedding plants (pages 64–65) or vegetables (page 78) which are then planted out in good soil conditions about 6 weeks after sowing if the variety is a hardy one or when all danger of frost has passed if the plants are half hardy. For the rest of the year the house reverts to Tomatoes and pot plants.

Even a small greenhouse can supply more than this. Many shrubs and herbaceous border plants can be raised from seed, and even more can be propagated from cuttings between spring and early autumn.

This section describes how your greenhouse can be used to give woody and herbaceous perennials their start in life before being moved to the garden. It can also be used as a place of refuge to which frost-sensitive perennials can be brought before the onset of winter, in order to escape from the sub-zero temperatures outdoors during the coldest months.

Propagating Dahlias

Dahlias are a basic feature of the late summer garden. The giant varieties with blooms more than 10 in. across are the stars of the show, but you can buy small and miniature varieties which produce much smaller blooms on compact plants. The advantage of propagating from cuttings rather than seed is that the progeny will be true to type — the disadvantage is that some diseases may be transmitted. For this reason you should begin with healthy stock.

After the first frosts have blackened the foliage gently lift the roots, taking care not to damage the tubers. Shake off any excess soil and cut back the stems to about 6 in. — label each plant and stand the tubers upside down for a few days to drain off excess moisture. Next, place them on a layer of peat in deep boxes and cover the tubers (not the crowns) with more peat. Store the boxes under the staging until February.

Now it is time to start them into growth. Plant the clumps in a moist peat/sand mixture or in seed compost and place in a brightly-lit spot. Sever and trim the new shoots when they are about 3 in. high — use them as cuttings for potting up. Plant up the rooted cuttings in late May in southern districts — waiting until early June in the North.

For most gardeners the Dahlia round is much simpler. It consists of replanting in mid April–mid May the old tubers which have been stored in the greenhouse or garage, rather than using home-grown rooted cuttings as described above. Only use tubers which have not been used for producing cuttings, and every couple of years divide up the tuber clumps carefully, making sure that each division has a piece of stem with swollen tubers attached.

For earlier flowering it is a better plan to pot up each tuber clump in a moist peat/sand mixture in March and stand the pots in a well-lit spot. When shoots have formed at the crown, cut the clump into planting pieces each with at least one good-sized tuber and stout shoot. Pot these up in potting compost. Plant out as for rooted cuttings in late May or early June.

Propagating Chrysanthemums

The Annual Chrysanthemum is a colourful hardy plant raised quite easily from seed, and amongst the herbaceous border plants you will find the Shasta Daisy. But these are unimportant relatives of the universally popular late summer- and autumn-flowering plants which are raised afresh each year from cuttings.

In November lift the roots carefully and shake off the soil. Cut back the stems to about 4 in., trim off any leaves and label each plant. These prepared roots (stools) should be closely packed into boxes and surrounded by peat. Place these boxes under the staging and keep them cool and fairly dry.

Bring them into growth by increasing the watering in January and use the new shoots as cuttings in February or March. These cuttings should be 2–3 in. long and they should be taken from the base and not the sides of the stems. Root these cuttings at 50°–60°F and then transfer them to 3 in. pots.

After hardening off plant out the rooted cuttings in early May. Water the pots thoroughly the day before and use a trowel to dig a hole which is wider but only slightly deeper than the soil ball of the cutting. Never plant Chrysanthemums too deeply.

Propagating Border Perennials

The border plants in nearly all gardens have been bought, provided by friends or derived by dividing clumps in autumn or spring. You can, however, raise most of them in the greenhouse, starting from seed, stem cuttings or root cuttings.

Seed sowing allows you to raise scores of plants which are not already in your garden. Use the technique described on page 89 — spring sowing should produce plants ready for putting into the border in the autumn. Some experts recommend sowing in early summer and then planting out in spring so that the first winter is spent protected under glass. Border perennials which can be raised from seed include Acanthus, Alstroemeria, Centranthus, Coreopsis, Delphinium, Dianthus, Gaillardia, Geum, Helianthus, Limonium, Linum, Lupin, Meconopsis, Platycodon, Primula and Salvia.

One of the problems of raising border plants from seed is that many named varieties cannot be propagated in this way. Cuttings are the answer — follow the rules laid down on page 88 and use The Flower Expert as your guide to timing. Young spring shoots, 2–3 in. high, often make ideal cuttings.

Stem cuttings must be provided with some form of transparent cover to maintain a well-lit environment and moist atmosphere — root cuttings are easier because they are simply planted in a multipurpose compost and left to produce roots and shoots. Use pieces of root 1–2 in. long. Insert into the moist compost vertically and the right way up for half their length, then cover them completely with a layer of sharp sand. Water in and transplant into individual pots when new growth appears. Use for Anchusa, Centaurea, Gaillardia, Macleaya, Phlox, Oriental Poppy and Verbascum.

Propagating Shrubs

Many shrubs can be raised in the greenhouse, but you will have to wait 1–4 years before the new plant is at the stage at which you will find it at the garden centre.

Do not begin from seed unless recommended to do so in the textbook. The most important method of propagating shrubs is to strike semi-ripe cuttings in July or August. Sturdy side shoots are usually chosen, and the cutting should be soft and green at the top but somewhat woody and stiff at the base. The cuttings must be planted quickly and not left to dry out, and some form of glass or plastic cover will be required. Many popular garden shrubs can be propagated in this way — see The Tree & Shrub Expert for details. Taking cuttings of conifers is more difficult — tackle this job in September or October. Rooting will take several months — harden off and plant out the rooted cuttings in spring.

Protecting Half hardy Perennials & Shrubs

During September and October bring into the greenhouse the tubs or pots of frost-sensitive plants which have stood in the garden to provide a display during the summer months. Included here are Citrus trees, Heliotrope, Agapanthus etc, but the most popular ones by far are Pelargonium and Fuchsia.

Pot up Pelargoniums which were bedded out during the summer — do this before the first frosts. Keep these pots at a minimum temperature of 35°F, ventilate wherever practical and let the compost remain almost dry. Cut away most of the top growth. The rules for Fuchsias are rather different — a minimum temperature of 42°–45°F is required and the compost should be kept slightly moist. In both cases the plants should be brought back into growth in February by watering and placing them in a well-lit spot. After hardening off place the plants outdoors when the danger of frost has passed.

Tomatoes

In most greenhouses you will find Tomatoes growing on the south-facing side during the summer months. It is extremely satisfying to pick succulent fruit from June until October, and the flavour is outstanding if you have chosen the variety with care.

It is still a little surprising that we have an irrepressible urge to grow them. The plants need constant care — in summer it is necessary to water growing bags or pots every day. A wide range of pests and diseases find the Tomato an ideal host and so spraying is often necessary. Added to these points is the fact that you can now buy really tasty varieties such as Gardener's Delight in the shops.

Perhaps the key is the fascination of watching tiny green pinheads swell into bright red fruits, plus the constant need we have in most house-holds for both raw and cooked Tomatoes.

If you have never grown Tomatoes before then there are a few general points you will have to know. Seed needs a temperature of about 65°F in order to ensure satisfactory germination, so if you do not have a propagator you will have to buy seedlings. Bought-in or home-grown seedlings must be at just the right stage when planting out — read the 'Planting' section carefully. A surprisingly large amount of water will be needed by the plant when it is in full fruit — a gallon or even more may be necessary each day. The yield you can expect is 7–8 lb per plant — more if you are skilled and choose the right variety but much less if you make one or more basic mistakes.

Fruit Types

ORDINARY varieties (O)

This group of red salad Tomatoes contains the traditional-sized fruiting varieties and includes several old favourites which are grown for reliability (Moneymaker), flavour (Ailsa Craig) or earliness (Harbinger).

F₁ HYBRID varieties (F₁)

This group bears fruit which is similar in appearance to the Ordinary varieties, but these modern crosses have two important advantages — they are generally heavier yielding and also have a high degree of disease resistance.

BEEFSTEAK varieties (B)

This group produces the large and meaty Tomatoes which are so popular in the U.S and on the Continent. They are excellent for sandwiches but not for frying. There are two types which are grown under glass — the true 'Beefsteak' hybrids such as Dombito and the giant hybrids such as Big Boy. Stop the plants when the fourth truss has set and provide support for the fruit if necessary.

CHERRY varieties (C)

The Cherry- or bite-sized Tomato is much smaller than the fruit from an Ordinary variety, but the flavour is outstanding. The long trusses bear a remarkable number of fruits, but total yield is generally lower than the crop from an Ordinary type of Tomato.

NOVELTY varieties (N)

There are yellow fruits, striped ones and Tomatoes which are Plum-shaped. Some catalogues sing the praises of yellow Tomatoes, but it is hard to tell when they are ripe and they remain unpopular. The first Tomatoes sent to Europe from America were gold-coloured and not red, but that was long ago.

Growth Types

CORDON varieties (C)

The standard greenhouse varieties are Cordon (single-stemmed) plants which require support using a cane, wire or string. Side shoots will have to be regularly removed and the plant will grow to 6 ft or more if it is not stopped by pinching out the growing point. It is unfortunate that most gardeners refuse to be adventurous — each year they plant Alicante, Ailsa Craig or Moneymaker, but there are so many exciting new varieties to try.

BUSH varieties (B)

Where height is a problem grow a Bush type instead of a Cordon. The 1–3 ft high plant needs little or no training, de-shooting or stopping, but growth is rather untidy. Put down black polythene to stop ground-level fruits from rotting.

Varieties

	Growth Type	Fruit Type
AILSA CRAIG Generally considered to be the best-flavoured variety in the Ordinary group. A heavy cropper with fruits which are medium-sized and brightly coloured. Listed in most catalogues.	C	O
ALICANTE A heavy cropping and reliable variety. Very popular for many years, especially with beginners. It is resistant to greenback and the flavour is good.	C	O
BIG BOY One of the older Beefsteak Tomatoes — still widely available and capable of producing fruits weighing 1 lb or more. Dombito is a better choice these days.	C	B
BLIZZARD An early variety. The yields are well above average and so is the length of the cropping season. Fruits stay firm for a long time but flavour is not outstanding.	C	F_1
CHERRY WONDER A new star amongst Cherry varieties — it is claimed that this one is even tastier than Gardener's Delight. High yields, bright red, greenback-resistant.	C	C
DOMBITO One of the best Beefsteaks you can buy. This Dutch-bred variety starts to crop early in the season and the crop of ½ lb fruits is heavy. Good disease resistance.	C	B
GARDENER'S DELIGHT The favourite Cherry Tomato. The trusses are long and heavy, and the 1 in. wide deep red fruits have a sweet and tangy flavour. You can expect about 6 lb per plant.	C	C
GOLDEN BOY This variety is basically a Beefsteak Tomato but the skin is yellow. The fruits are large and globe-shaped and the texture is meaty. Not widely available.	C	N
GOLDEN SUNRISE The most popular choice for the gardener who wants a yellow Tomato. The fruit is medium-sized with a distinctive taste. Yields are not heavy.	C	N
GRENADIER A heavy cropper which produces fairly large fruits. They have good keeping qualities and are free from greenback. The plants are resistant to leaf mould.	C	F_1
HARBINGER The earliest of the Ordinary varieties listed here. There are no other outstanding virtues but the flavour is good. Now more difficult to find than other old favourites.	C	O
IDA An early and heavy-cropping variety which is highly recommended for cold houses. Growth is compact, the fruit is medium-sized and disease resistance is very good.	C	F_1

TOMATOES

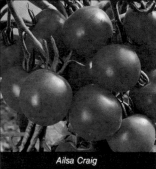
Ailsa Craig

Big Boy

Gardener's Delight

Golden Sunrise

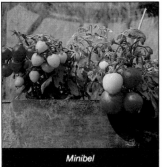

Minibel

Moneymaker

Sweet 100

Tigerella

Varieties continued

Variety	Description	Growth Type	Fruit Type
MINIBEL	The one to choose if space is strictly limited. This miniature Bush variety can be grown in a 6 in. pot and will produce masses of bite-sized deep red fruits.	B	C
MIRABELLE	This one is the yellow equivalent of Gardener's Delight. The Cherry-type Tomatoes are golden-yellow and are borne in very large trusses. The flavour is sweet.	C	N
MONEYCROSS	If you are a Moneymaker fan it is wise to choose this one for a change. It is earlier, produces heavier crops and is resistant to leaf mould.	C	O
MONEYMAKER	One of the most popular varieties for the amateur. It is early, reliable and the yields are reasonably heavy, but the 2 in. fruits have a bland flavour.	C	O
RED ALERT	An outdoor Bush variety which can be grown in a cold house. The 1 in. fruits are deep red and are claimed to have a better flavour than other Bush types.	B	O
SAN MARZANO	The popular 'Italian' Tomato, sometimes listed as Marzano Red Plum. Distinctly egg-shaped with firm flesh — use for soups, ketchups, spaghetti sauce etc.	C	N
SHIRLEY	The new star — one of the best Tomatoes you can grow. Heavy yields, early cropping, good disease resistance and unaffected by short cold spells. Better than average flavour.	C	F_1
SONATINE	A variety which is popular with professional growers but not widely available for the amateur. It crops early and sets readily — disease resistance is outstanding.	C	F_1
SWEET 100	An F_1 hybrid Cherry variety to challenge the top spot held by Gardener's Delight. The outstanding feature is the truss which may carry up to 100 bite-sized fruits.	C	C
TIGERELLA	Fun, of course, as the red fruits bear yellow vertical stripes when mature. More than a novelty — yields are good and the flavour is better than average.	C	N
TOTEM	This compact variety was bred for outdoor cultivation but can be grown in the cold house. The medium-sized fruits are borne in large trusses — staking may be necessary.	B	F_1
TUMBLER	Many greenhouses are dominated by Tomatoes, but this hanging basket variety can be tucked away in a corner. Cherry-sized fruits are borne on pendent stems.	B	C

Growing methods

There are four basic methods of growing Tomatoes in the greenhouse. Despite claims to the contrary, there is not much difference in yield between the various methods. Growing in fresh border soil tends to give the heaviest crops and plants grown in pots sometimes give the lightest, but differences between varieties and cultural practices are much more important in determining total yield.

Yields obtained using the various methods may not be very different but their relative popularities certainly are. About half the greenhouse Tomatoes are now cultivated in growing bags, with border soil and pots taking an approximately equal share of the remainder. The fourth method, ring culture, has been around for many years but is rarely used.

BORDER SOIL

Growing in the border soil has two distinct advantages. It saves money — there are no containers and bags of compost to buy. It also saves work — if the soil is enriched with organic matter there should be no need to water more than twice a week even when the plants are in full growth in summer. Dig in well-rotted compost and then rake in Growmore just before planting — do not plant until the soil temperature is at least 55°F. This method is not always practical — the trend these days is to have a solid base to the greenhouse. There is also one major drawback where border soil is used — after a few years of growing Tomatoes there is a build-up of soil pests and root diseases. The answer is to change the soil or go over to growing bags.

POTS

Pot culture is the traditional alternative to growing Tomatoes in the border of the greenhouse. The procedure is quite straightforward — a suitable container is filled with a suitable compost. Popular containers are 2 gallon polythene buckets with holes at the base and 10 or 12 in. clay or plastic pots. The most popular compost is peat-based potting or multipurpose compost, but you can use a soil-based J.I. compost or one based on coir (Coconut fibre). As a general rule soil composts need less watering than peat-based ones, but drainage is sometimes poor. Coir will need more frequent watering than peat. With all composts watering will be necessary at least once a day in summer. Stand the pots about 2 ft apart.

RING CULTURE

A clever idea but this method has never become popular. A 6–8 in. deep trench is dug and then lined with plastic sheeting. This trough is filled with fine gravel and on top of this the 'rings' are stood at 2 ft intervals. Each ring consists of a 9 or 10 in. wide whalehide pot. The ring has no bottom, so it is necessary to stand it on a board when filling with compost — the usual choice is a peat-based potting compost or soil-based J.I. No.2 compost. You will need about 12 lb of soil-based compost to fill the ring. The gravel is kept watered and a liquid feed is applied at weekly intervals to the rings. If the base of the greenhouse is paved or concrete, create a raised bed with boards and then line with plastic before filling with gravel.

GROWING BAGS

Growing bags are available at garden centres and DIY stores everywhere and have become by far the most popular Tomato growing method with both the professional nurseryman and amateur gardener. At first they were quite expensive but prices have fallen steadily over the years. Place each bag on a firm and level surface, and plant with 2, 3 or 4 seedlings, according to the manufacturer's instructions. Support can be a problem. Driving a cane through the bottom of the bag is not the answer — buy a metal frame designed for the purpose. Carefully read the watering and feeding recommendations and follow them — disappointing results are usually due to failing to master the watering technique.

Sowing

- If you need a large number of plants, then follow the conventional technique of sowing thinly in trays or pans filled with seed compost or multicompost — see page 89 for details. Cover lightly with compost — keep moist but not wet at 60°–65°F. Germination will take place in about 7 days. When the seedlings have formed a pair of true leaves pot them on into 3 in. peat pots filled with potting compost.
- If only a few plants are required, it is easier to sow a couple of seeds in 3 in. peat pots of compost, removing the weaker seedling after germination.
- Keep the pots at 60°–65°F — water little and often.

Planting

- Plant seedlings when they are about 8 in. tall and the flowers of the first truss are just beginning to open. Choose shop-bought seedlings with care — avoid lanky stems, yellow or distorted leaves and any sign of abnormal growth. Water the pots thoroughly before planting out into growing bags, border soil or pots. Plant 1½–2 ft apart in the border.

TOMATOES

Caring for the Crop

1 Tie the stem loosely to a stout cane or wind it clockwise up a well-anchored but slack length of rough twine. Be careful not to damage the stem during this operation — you will find it easier to turn the string around the plant.

2 Side shoots will appear where the leaf stalks join the stem. De-shooting is necessary — this calls for snapping them off when they are about 1 in. long. Do this job cleanly — do not leave broken stumps. You will find it easier to achieve this at the start of the day rather than in the afternoon.

3 Water regularly to keep the soil constantly moist at all times. Too little or too infrequently will result in poor and damaged fruit — too much or too frequently will result in rotten roots and stems. Be guided by the conditions and the growth stage — a plant in full fruit may need watering 2 or 3 times a day in midsummer.

4 Feeding can begin when the first fruits have set and should be continued according to the maker's instructions until the last truss has set. Use a liquid and not a powder nor granular fertilizer.

5 Remove the leaves below the first truss when the plants are about 4 ft high. This de-leafing process below fruit trusses can be continued as the season progresses, but only if the leaves are yellow, damaged or diseased. Never overdo this de-leafing operation. Use a sharp knife to remove the unwanted foliage.

6 Mist the flowers at midday and tap the supports occasionally to aid pollen dispersion and fruit set.

7 Try to avoid wide fluctuations in temperature — aim to keep the maximum below 80°F. Ventilation is essential in summer — open up when the temperature exceeds 70°F. Shade with blinds or by painting on a shading compound in order to keep down the temperature and to protect the fruit from scorch and other problems.

8 Remove the tip at 2 leaves above the top truss once the plant has reached the top of the house or when 7 trusses have set.

Calendar

	Recommended time for sowing		Recommended time for planting
Expected time for cold house harvesting		Expected time for start of heated house harvesting	

Harvesting

- Pick the fruit when they are ripe and fully coloured. Hold the Tomato in your palm and with your thumb break off the fruit at the knuckle (swelling on the flower-stalk). Do not leave fruit on the plant after they are fully ripe — flavour declines with age.

- Finish picking between late September and mid October, depending on the season and locality. Unripe fruit should be placed as a layer in a tray which is then put in a drawer. Next to the tray set a couple of ripe Apples which will generate the fruit-ripening gas ethylene.

Tomato seed is sown in a propagator — a temperature of at least 60°-65°F is necessary for satisfactory germination. This is done in late December for planting out in a heated house (minimum 50°-55°F) in late February or early March for a May–June crop.

Most gardeners, however, grow Tomatoes in a cold house. Sow seed in a propagator in early March and plant out in late April or early May. The first fruits will be ready for picking in July.

	JAN	FEB	MAR	APR	MAY	JUN	JUL	AUG	SEP	OCT	NOV	DEC
Sowing & Planting Time (Heated greenhouse)	◻	⚘	⚘									◻
Sowing & Planting Time (Cold greenhouse)		◻	◻	⚘	⚘							
Picking Time					▤	▦	▦	▦	▦	▦		

Cucumbers

A well-grown specimen of a greenhouse Cucumber, straight and cylindrical, smooth-skinned and glistening, may reach 18 in. or more in length. A thing of beauty perhaps, but until recently it was customary for textbooks to warn the reader about the difficulties. The so-called Ordinary varieties (see overleaf) need a moister atmosphere than Tomatoes and the side shoots have to be trained along horizontal wires. Male flowers have to be removed and both pests and diseases are often a headache.

The introduction of the All-female varieties has changed the situation quite dramatically. These F_1 hybrids are as easy to grow as Tomatoes, and sometimes even easier. The fruit is borne on the axils of the leaves and main stem and not on side shoots, so training up a single support is all that is needed. Male flowers rarely if ever appear, and disease is much less of a problem.

Outdoor varieties have improved greatly during the past few years and one is tempted these days to grow this crop in the garden rather than under glass. However if you want to pick Cucumbers in June or July for midsummer salads then growing them in the greenhouse is the only answer.

Sowing

- Cucumber seed germinates quickly, but warmth (minimum 70°F) is essential. Place a single seed edgeways ½ in. deep in seed compost or multicompost in a 3 in. peat pot. This should be timed for about 4 weeks before planting.

- Germination takes place in 2–3 days — do not use seedlings which germinate after this time. Keep the compost moist. Do not allow the seedlings to become pot-bound — transfer to 5 in. pots if necessary.

Planting

- Plant seedlings when they are 8–10 in. tall and there are 2 well-formed true leaves. Choose shop-bought seedlings with care — they should be a rich green colour and the variety should be stated. Water the pots thoroughly before planting — one in a 12–15 in. pot or 2 per growing bag.

- Planting in border soil is not recommended as soil sickness soon becomes a problem. If you do decide to go ahead then plant on the top of a ridge of soil, spacing the plants 2 ft apart.

Caring for the Crop

1 The temperature after planting out should be no lower than 55°–60°F.

2 Keep the compost thoroughly moist at all times, but do be careful not to keep the compost soggy for the first 2 or 3 weeks after planting out. Little and often is the watering rule, and avoid waterlogging at all costs.

3 Adequate ventilation will be necessary, and so will regular damping down. Hose down the floor, but not the plants, to maintain the humidity of the air.

4 With Ordinary varieties it is necessary to run a series of horizontal training wires 12 in. apart up the wall and across the roof. The fruit-bearing side shoots are tied along these wires. Pinch out the growing point when the main shoot reaches the ridge. The tip of each side shoot is pinched out at 2 leaves beyond a female flower. Female flowers have a miniature Cucumber behind them — male flowers have just a thin stalk. Remember to remove all male flowers promptly — fertilized fruit is bitter. Pinch out tips of flowerless side shoots when they reach 2 ft in length.

5 Things are much simpler with All-female varieties. Horizontal training wires are not needed — merely train the stem up a stout cane or vertical wire. Twist the stem around the wire or cane every few days. Fruits are borne on the main stem, so remove all side shoots. Do take care, however, not to remove the tiny fruits at the same time. Remove all flowers from the bottom 2 ft of the stem.

6 Feed every 2 weeks with a Tomato Fertilizer once the first fruits have started to swell.

7 Apply shading material to protect the fruit from the glare of midsummer sun.

Harvesting

Cut (do not pull) when the fruit has reached a reasonable size and the sides are parallel. Use secateurs or a sharp knife. Pick regularly — cropping will cease if you allow Cucumbers to mature and turn yellow on the plant.

Types

ORDINARY varieties (O)

The traditional Cucumber for the exhibitor — long, straight and smooth. But these varieties are generally demanding — warm and moist air is necessary and so is training of the side shoots along horizontal wires.

ALL-FEMALE varieties (A-F)

These modern F$_1$ hybrids have several advantages. The tiresome job of removing male flowers is not required and the plants are much more resistant to disease. They are also easier to grow and require only a simple cane for support.

Varieties

Petita

Telegraph

Varieties	Type
BIRGIT This variety is widely grown by market gardeners and is becoming increasingly popular with amateurs. It is quite similar to Pepinex 69 but is earlier and crops are claimed to be heavier.	A-F
FEMSPOT The most handsome of the modern F$_1$ hybrids, but you will only get exhibition-quality fruits if you provide enough warmth and moisture. Disease resistance is excellent.	A-F
KYOTO A good example of the Japanese group. The outstanding feature is the ease of growth — even easier to grow than Tomatoes, according to some experts. Fruit is long and straight.	O
PEPINEX 69 The first of the All-females, formerly known as Femina. A typical representative of the group, but it needs rather warmer conditions than some newer ones such as Petita.	A-F
PETITA The fruits are only about 8 in. long but a large number are borne. It grows well under cool conditions but some male flowers are produced. Plants grow about 5 ft high.	A-F
TELEGRAPH An old Cucumber named when the telegraph was a new invention. Despite its age it is still popular and is the most reliable of the Ordinary varieties. Sometimes listed as Telegraph Improved.	O

Calendar

 Recommended time for sowing

 Recommended time for planting

Expected time for cold house harvesting

Expected time for start and end of heated house harvesting

Cucumber seed is sown in a propagator — a temperature of 70°–80°F is necessary. This is done in early March for planting out in a heated house (minimum 55°F) in April for a May–June crop.

Most Cucumbers are grown in a cold house. Sow seed in a propagator in late April and plant out in late May. The first fruits will be ready for picking in July.

	JAN	FEB	MAR	APR	MAY	JUN	JUL	AUG	SEP	OCT	NOV	DEC
Sowing & Planting Time (Heated greenhouse)				🌱								
Sowing & Planting Time (Cold greenhouse)												
Picking Time												

Vegetables

The usual reason for growing vegetables in a greenhouse is the ability to grow those types which are unpredictable outdoors and even impossible in some districts — Aubergines, Capsicums and Tomatoes are typical examples. In addition there is the satisfaction of harvesting produce before the outdoor crop is ready — early Potatoes, early Carrots and so on. There is another advantage which is important but does not appear in the standard textbooks — the ability to care for your plants without having to worry about wind, rain and snow.

A large number of ornamentals need a cool or warm greenhouse for satisfactory development, but all the popular vegetables can be grown in a cold greenhouse. So the unheated house really comes into its own for growing food crops, and with a little planning you can probably make it more productive. Early in the season there is a lot of wasted space between tall crops such as Tomatoes and Cucumbers — this can be utilised for quick-growing catch crops such as Beetroots and Carrots.

The greenhouse has another role to play in the cultivation of vegetables. It can be used to give garden-grown varieties an early start in life by sowing them in a propagator, pricking out into trays or pots and then planting outdoors in order to give them several weeks' advantage over garden-sown specimens.

Greenhouse Vegetables

The greenhouse is their permanent home, from seed sowing to harvest. Some types are too tender to be trusted outdoors, others are half hardy and need the extended growing season provided by greenhouse cultivation. Others are varieties of hardy vegetables which produce an early crop when grown under glass. One basic rule — make sure that the variety selected is recommended for greenhouse cultivation.

Garden Vegetables

The greenhouse is their nursery, from seed sowing to planting outdoors. Hardy varieties are sown from January or February onwards and planted out when the soil is suitable. Half hardy vegetables are sown about 6–8 weeks before the expected planting time.

Greenhouse Vegetables

AUBERGINE

The Aubergine or Egg Plant is one of the new wave of vegetables which were once regarded as unusual but are now available from greengrocers and supermarkets everywhere. It can be grown as easily as the Tomato. Sow seed in compost-filled peat pots in late February — sow 2 seeds per pot and nip off the weaker seedling later. Place the pots in a propagator at 70°F for germination. Keep the seedlings at 60°–65°F before planting out — singly in 9 in. pots or 3 in a growing bag in late April or early May. Remove the growing point when the plant is about 1 ft high and stake the stem. Once the fruits have started to swell the plants should be fed with a liquid Tomato fertilizer, and the lateral shoots and remaining flowers should be removed when 5 fruits have formed. Mist regularly but be careful not to overwater. Cut the fruit when it is 5–6 in. long and still shiny. Recommended varieties: **Black Prince** — Early and heavier yielding than Long Purple. **Dusky** — A modern F_1 hybrid which is resistant to mosaic virus. **Easter Egg** — Colour and size of a large hen's egg. Flavour not outstanding. **Long Purple** — The old favourite with no special advantages. **Moneymaker** — An F_1 hybrid. Early, prolific and tasty.

Aubergine — Dusky

BEETROOT

Beetroot is one of the catch crops you can grow between tall vegetables in the border soil. The seeds are sown 1 in. deep directly into the soil in February or March between the planting sites planned for Tomatoes or Cucumbers. Thin to 4 in. apart — keep the soil watered and weeded. Keep watch for aphids — spray if necessary. Pulling takes place in late May or June whilst the roots are still small. Recommended varieties: **Boltardy** — The most popular of the varieties grown under glass. Globular, deep red and bolt-resistant. **Monopoly** — Similar to Boltardy but with the advantage of being a monogerm variety (one seedling per 'seed'). **Replata** — One of the earliest of all Beetroots. Semi-globular, deep red, sweet.

Beetroot — Boltardy

Greenhouse Vegetables continued

Capsicum — Gypsy

Carrot — Early Nantes

Courgette — Gold Rush

CAPSICUM

The large Sweet Pepper is becoming increasingly popular — it requires similar conditions to the Tomato. Sow seed in compost-filled peat pots in late February — sow 2 seeds per pot and nip off the weaker seedling later. Place the pots in a propagator at 70°F for germination. Keep the seedlings at 60°–65°F before planting out — singly in 9 in. pots or 3 in a growing bag in late April or early May. Pinching out the growing point is a matter of opinion — some experts advise against it whilst others tell you to stop the plant when it is 6 in. tall. Some form of support will be necessary and so will regular misting to keep down red spider mite and to encourage fruit set. Water regularly and feed with a liquid Tomato fertilizer once the fruits have started to swell. Ventilate the house and shade the glass in sunny weather. Pick at the green or orange stage when the fruit is swollen or glossy — leaving the fruits to redden on the plant will reduce yields. Recommended varieties: **Canape** — Prolific and early, but the fruits are rather small. **Golden Bell** — The one to grow if you want a change from red Peppers. The fruits are yellow. **Gypsy** — This F₁ hybrid is an improved Canape. Very early and the large fruits are orange-red. **Rainbow** — A fun Pepper with red, yellow, purple and orange fruits. **Redskin** — Medium-sized red fruits are borne on 1 ft high stems.

CARROT

A useful catch crop. Sow between January and March for a May crop or in September for December pulling. Sow very thinly in drills 9 in. apart. Thin out the seedlings when they are large enough to handle — leave the small plants 2 in. apart. Pull as required. Grow only short-rooted varieties. Recommended varieties: **Amsterdam Forcing** — Reputed to be the earliest of all. Cylindrical with a blunt end and very little core. **Early French Frame** — A round Carrot, others include **Rondo** and **Parmex**. **Early Nantes** — Very popular, with roots which are longer and more tapered than Amsterdam Forcing.

COURGETTE

Be warned — this crop takes up a lot of floor space. Sow seed in compost-filled peat pots in April — one seed edgeways per pot ½ in. below the surface. Keep at 65°–70°F. Plant the seedlings when 6 in. high into growing bags — 2 per bag. Keep them well watered — hand pollinate the flowers with a soft brush or cotton wool ball. Feed regularly once the fruit has started to swell — cut the courgettes when they are 4–5 in. long. Serve raw in salad or cooked as a hot vegetable. Recommended varieties: **Ambassador** — One of the best F₁ hybrid Courgettes, dark green with a long cropping period. **Gold Rush** — A golden variety noted for its earliness and compact growth habit. **Zucchini** — The most popular Courgette variety.

FRENCH BEAN

Both climbing and bush French Beans can be grown under glass to provide a May or June crop. For the earliest crops sow 5 beans in an 8 in. compost-filled pot in February and then place the pot in a propagator set at 60°–65°F. As an alternative grow the plants in 3 in. peat pots and germinate in a propagator as above. After hardening off plant the potted seedlings in growing bags — 8 per bag. Support the plants with twiggy sticks — water regularly and apply a liquid feed as recommended on the label. A pod is ready for picking when it snaps easily if bent. For heavy crops you must pick regularly — this may have to be done several times a week. Watch for aphids and red spider mite. Recommended varieties: **Blue Lake** — The most popular climbing variety, its 5 ft stems producing a plentiful supply of white-seeded Pencil- (round) podded beans. **Kinghorn Wax-pod** — A yellow stringless bean renowned for its flavour. The flesh is creamy yellow. **Masterpiece** — An excellent general-purpose variety which has been a popular Flat-pod for many years. **Tendergreen** — The most popular of the stringless Pencil-podded varieties. Good for freezing. **The Prince** — A favourite Flat-pod and a good choice if you want a compact variety.

HERBS

Many herbs die down in the open garden when late autumn arrives. It is therefore a good plan to dig and pot up clumps of **Chives**, **Parsley**, **Mint**, **Rosemary**, **Marjoram**, **Basil** and **Thyme**. Alternatively cuttings can be taken in August. Pots of herbs in the winter greenhouse will need good light, cool conditions and regular watering. Ventilate during periods of settled weather. Remove dead or dying leaves and flowers promptly.

French Bean — Kinghorn Wax-pod

LETTUCE

Lettuce provides a good use for growing bags after Tomatoes or Cucumbers — plant 2 rows of 6 seedlings in each bag. The standard practice is to sow seed at 55°–60°F (not higher) in trays or seed pans and then transplant them into 3 in. peat pots. When the plants have about 5 true leaves they are transplanted into the growing bags or border soil. Sowing at fortnightly intervals will result in a regular supply for several months. The correct time for sowing depends on the variety, and do make sure the variety is recommended for greenhouse growing. Recommended varieties for late summer sowing and winter cropping: **Kwiek** — A very popular greenhouse variety which is a large butterhead. **Marmer** — Something different, an Iceberg-type of crisphead for late winter use. Recommended varieties for autumn sowing and spring cropping: **May Queen** — Red-tinged medium-sized heads. **Diamant** — A large, deep green butterhead which is resistant to mildew. With all Lettuce varieties you must water with care — do not soak unless the soil surface is dry. Watch out for slugs and mildew.

Lettuce — Marmer

MUSHROOM

These days you are spared the need to prepare your own compost and then impregnate it with spawn — you can buy a ready-to-grow plastic bucket kit. Simply follow the instructions — an expensive way to grow Mushrooms but it is no bother. Buttons should appear after about a month — harvest by gently pulling and twisting. Fill the hole with the compost after you have removed a Mushroom.

MUSTARD & CRESS

The old favourite for salads, garnishing and sandwiches — useful green stuff to grow all year round. Place several sheets of paper towelling at the bottom of a shallow plastic tray. Dampen thoroughly and then pour off excess water. Sow Cress evenly and thickly — 3 days later sow Mustard over the emerging Cress seedlings. Keep constantly moist — harvest after about 14 days when seedlings are about 2 in. high.

Okra — Clemson's Spineless

OKRA

Grow in the same way as Aubergine (see page 75). Germination may take a few weeks — speed it up by soaking the seed for a day before sowing. The soft young pods are cut from June onwards — do not leave them to become hard and stringy. Keep watch for whitefly and red spider mite. Recommended varieties: **Long Green** — A reliable variety, but there are not many suppliers. **Clemson's Spineless** — The most popular greenhouse Okra with pale green ribless pods.

ONION

Another use for old growing bags. Grow Spring Onions by sprinkling seed thinly along rows — sow in September for an April crop or in February for pulling in June. Space rows 6–8 in. apart — use the thinnings for cooking and the mature plants for salads. Recommended varieties: **White Lisbon** — By far the most popular Spring Onion. The bulb is silvery white and the tops are crisp. **Ishikura** — A new type of Spring Onion. The long straight stems do not form bulbs. There is just a long white base. **Santa Claus** — Rather like Ishikura, but with the novelty of the base turning red.

Onion — White Lisbon

POTATO

Early Potatoes are easy to grow in a cold greenhouse — plant sprouted seed Potatoes in January for a May crop or in August to harvest on Christmas Day. Plant in a 10 in. pot (1 tuber per pot) or in a growing bag (2 per bag). Harvest by gathering the required number of Potatoes from the top part of the container — repeat several times before lifting and disposing of the plant. Recommended varieties: **Maris Bard** — Oval. White and waxy flesh. One of the earliest. **Epicure** — Round. White flesh with deep eyes. **Foremost** — Oval. Yellow and waxy flesh. Yields are not heavy. **Pentland Javelin** — Oval. White and waxy flesh. Later than other recommended varieties.

RADISH

A useful vegetable for growing between other plants or in odd corners at almost any time of the year, although the most popular times for sowing are February–May and again in the autumn. This crop is quick growing and takes up little room — sowing to harvest may take as little as 3 weeks. Sow ½ in. deep in rows 6 in. apart — sow thinly and no thinning should be required. Recommended varieties: **Cherry Belle** — Round, all-red. Mild and crisp. **French Breakfast** — Cylindrical, red and white. Very popular. **Large White Icicle** — Long cylindrical, white. Mild and crisp.

Radish — French Breakfast

Garden Vegetables

All sorts of vegetables can be started off in the greenhouse to give them an early start in the garden. Seed is germinated in a heated propagator or on the windowsill of a heated room if a propagator is not available. The seedlings are then grown on in the greenhouse until the time for planting outdoors arrives. Basic rules include sowing thinly, pricking out promptly and hardening off thoroughly.

Follow the rules set out on page 89. Use trays for small seeds and then prick out into trays filled with compost — a better alternative is to transplant the seedlings into peat blocks or small peat pots which avoid root disturbance at planting time. Large seeds are spaced out about 2 in. apart in trays or they can be sown into pots.

If possible cover the soil with cloches for 2 weeks before planting and for some time after planting. This will get the crop off to a flying start.

FORCING

The use of the greenhouse for the vegetables described on the left is to give them a good start in life. The use of the greenhouse for forcing is at the other end of the time scale — forcing involves bringing mature plants inside the house for the final stage before cropping.

Vegetable	When to sow	When to plant
AUBERGINE	March–April	B
BEAN, BROAD	February–March	A
BEAN, FRENCH	April	B
BEAN, RUNNER	April	B
BEETROOT	February–March	A
BROCCOLI	April	A
BRUSSELS SPROUT	February–March	A
CABBAGE, SPRING	July–August	A
CABBAGE, SUMMER	February–March	A
CABBAGE, WINTER	April	A
CABBAGE, SAVOY	April	A
CAPSICUM	April	B
CARROT	February	A
CAULIFLOWER	January–March	A
CELERIAC	March	B
CELERY	April	B
CHICORY	April	A
COURGETTE	April	B
CUCUMBER	April	B
ENDIVE	January–July	A
KOHL RABI	February	A
LEEK	February–March	A
LETTUCE	January–July	A
MARROW	April	B
ONION	February–March	A
PARSNIP	February	A
PEA	February–May	A
SALSIFY	March	A
SPINACH	February	A
SWEDE	March	A
SWEET CORN	April	B
TOMATO	March–April	B
TURNIP	February	A
Plant about 4–6 weeks after sowing. The essential requirement is good soil conditions — neither dry nor wringing wet. Seedlings are ready for planting when roots start to peep out at the bottom of the seed tray		A
Plant when the danger of frost has passed. This depends on the location — from mid May in favoured districts in the South and West to the second week in June for unfavourable areas in the North		B

RHUBARB

Dig up the crowns in November and leave them exposed to frost on the surface of the soil. After this has taken place, pack the roots closely together in a deep box, filling up the spaces in between with old compost or peat. Leave the crowns exposed. Cover the box with black polythene and place it under the staging. In about 4 weeks you will be able to pick tender sticks — harvest them as soon as they are large enough to use. When harvesting is over dispose of the crowns as they are of no further use.

CHICORY

The first stage is to lift the roots in November — discard fanged ones and roots less than 1 in. across at the crown. Cut off the tops about 1 in. above the crown and cut back roots to 6 in. Pack them horizontally in a box of sand in a cool shed. Force a few of these roots at a time in the greenhouse between November and March — do this by planting 5 in a 9 in. pot and surrounding them with damp peat or compost. Leave the crowns exposed and cover with an empty pot in which the drainage hole has been blocked. Plump leafy heads (chicons) will form. Cut them when they are about 6 in. high — this will take about 3–4 weeks.

Fruit

The first greenhouses were stove-heated structures erected each winter to protect Orange, Lemon and Fig trees. The large and permanent conservatories and tropical greenhouses of the rich Victorians contained Bananas, Pineapples and other exotic fruits.

Times have changed. Today's cold and cool houses are more often used for vegetables such as Tomatoes and various ornamentals such as Chrysanthemums and pot plants. Unfortunately Peaches and Grapes have given fruit a bad image for the owner of a small structure. These vigorous plants are excellent against the wall of a large lean-to but have no place in an 8 ft x 6 ft greenhouse. Even here, however, there is a place for some fruit — a few pots of Strawberries for picking in April and a growing bag with Melons to produce fruits in July.

The temperature as well as the size of the greenhouse or conservatory will dictate what you can grow. Figs and Apricots like cool conditions but Oranges need a warm house.

The length of time the plant resides in the house depends on the type of fruit you have chosen to grow. Apricot and Nectarine are permanent residents which stay for many years. Others such as Melon stay there for the whole of their lives, but this only lasts from spring to autumn. Strawberries are temporary residents, staying for only a few months in the greenhouse where they bear fruit. The least permanent are the hardy fruit trees in pots which are brought inside for only a few weeks around blossom time.

Growing plants in containers is desirable because it means that they can be moved about — some fruits welcome or require a stay out of doors. This, however, is not always recommended — Apricots, Peaches and Nectarines often fare badly in pots and are best grown in the border soil.

APRICOT

This fruit is notoriously unreliable outdoors in the South and quite unsuitable for the North. It does well in a greenhouse as the blossom is protected from frost in early spring and fruit ripening is enhanced at the end of the season. High temperatures are not needed and are a definite disadvantage in winter — during the dormant season the plants need fresh air and temperatures which get down to 35°F or even less.

The best way to grow an Apricot is in the form of a fan planted against the wall of a large lean-to. The structure should ideally face South — don't bother with Apricots if it faces North. Apricots are self-fertile, so only one plant is needed. A semi-dwarfing variety will grow about 8 ft high and 12 ft wide.

Planting time is between November and January — prepare the border soil in October. Buy a 2 or 3 year old partly-trained tree — see The Fruit Expert for details of training and maintenance pruning. During the growing season water regularly and feed occasionally. Make sure the house is well-ventilated at flowering time. Hand pollinate and thin fruit to 4–6 in. apart. Harvest in late summer when the fruit has been fully yellow for about a week and comes away from the tree with a gentle tug.

It is possible to grow Apricots in pots or large tubs but the container becomes too small after a few years and both growth and yields decline.

Apricot

FRUIT

Cape Gooseberry

Citrus reticulata

Fig — White Marseilles

Grape — Black Hamburgh

CAPE GOOSEBERRY

A rarity in the shops but you will find it in many seed catalogues. Grow it as a half hardy annual — the cultural needs are the same as Tomatoes. Take care, however — it is a vigorous and leafy plant which is quite out of place in a small greenhouse. Sow the seed in a propagator in early March and plant the seedlings in May in large pots or a growing bag. Pinch out the growing tips when 1 ft high to induce bushiness — tie the stems loosely to 4 ft canes. Feed with a high potash liquid fertilizer once the first fruits have formed and protect from whitefly. Leave the fruits to ripen on the plants in late summer — golden shiny balls within brown and papery husks.

CITRUS

There is an obvious fascination in having an Orange or Lemon tree in the greenhouse or conservatory, but if you want it to bear edible fruit then you will have to buy a variety selected for its ability to crop under glass. Plants grown from pips will not fruit until they are too large for an ordinary greenhouse. Use compost to which some sharp sand has been added — repot each spring until the plant is in a 12 in. pot. Prune to restrict size in spring and reduce watering in late autumn. For fruit to develop and ripen you will need a minimum temperature of 50°F. The Mandarin (**Citrus reticulata**) is the hardiest Orange — popular varieties include **'Satsuma'** and **'Clementine'**. Other Oranges suitable for greenhouse culture are **C. sinensis** or Sweet Orange (4 ft, spiny) and **C. aurantium** or Bitter Orange (3 ft, spiny).

The best Lemon to choose is **C. limon 'Meyer'**, which grows to form a 4 ft x 4 ft tree. If you are adventurous you can try Lime and Kumquat.

FIG

Don't plant a Fig in the border soil — it will turn into a large leafy jungle which bears little fruit. Grow it in a large pot or tub. Train it as a fan against the wall or as a dwarf bush — even a 4 ft bush will produce a worthwhile crop.

Buy a 2 or 3 year old partly-trained tree. For outdoor cultivation **Brown Turkey** is the usual choice, but under glass it is better to choose the superb-tasting **Bourjasotte Grise** or the white-fleshed **White Marseilles**. See The Fruit Expert for instructions on training and maintenance pruning. Figs are a demanding crop — fruit thinning is quite complicated and daily watering will be necessary in summer. Repot every 2 years and feed when fruit have formed. A Fig is ready for picking when the stalk weakens and the fully-coloured fruit hangs downwards. Harvested fruit will keep in a cool place for several weeks. Little attention, however, is needed when the leaves fall — stop watering and keep the compost dry over winter.

GRAPE

There is no escaping the fact that Grapes are a time-consuming crop. For the enthusiast there are stem cleaning in midwinter, spring and summer pruning, regular watering all summer long, fruit thinning in autumn and pruning of the leading shoots in early winter. All these tasks are described in The Fruit Expert, but you might like to try the following simplified routine. Yields will not be high and you will have to start again after about 4 years, but little work is involved.

Plant a 2 or 3 year old vine in a 12 in. pot in December. Put the pot outdoors and bring back in February. Push three 5 ft canes into the compost near the rim — tie the top ends together to form a wigwam. Train the stems spirally around the canes. Stop lateral branches at 2 leaves beyond each bunch of Grapes — thin these down to leave just 6 bunches per plant. In winter cut back the main stems (rods) to half their length — a cold period down to as low as 30°F is necessary between November and February each year.

The purple **Black Hamburgh** is by far the most popular greenhouse Grape and quite rightly so — it is easy to grow, early to crop and delicious to eat. But there are others you can try. **Buckland Sweetwater** is another early cropper — the fruit is pale golden and the flavour is sweet. Even better is the rather similar **Foster's Seedling**. Late croppers include the amber-fruiting **Golden Queen** and the dark purple **West's St Peter's**.

HARDY FRUIT IN POTS

The introduction of dwarfing rootstocks has made the cultivation of hardy tree fruit such as Apples and Pears in pots a practical proposition. The trees are planted in a 12–15 in. container and are moved indoors in winter and at blossom time — hand pollination is necessary. Remember that Apples and Pears are generally not self-fertile — choose a 'family tree' bearing several varieties. After petal fall the pot is stood outdoors on the terrace or in the garden. Watering every day will be necessary in a dry summer.

FRUIT

KIWI FRUIT

Once a rarity, now seen in shops everywhere. You will sometimes see this fruit recommended as a greenhouse crop, but it is really not a good idea. Kiwi Fruit is a vigorous climber with very large leaves — the dense shade would create all sorts of problems for you. It is possible to keep it in check by careful pruning, but you can make better use of your space in a small greenhouse.

Kiwi Fruit

MELON

If you can grow Cucumbers well then you should succeed with Melons. Raise the plants in exactly the same way and plant the seedlings in growing bags — 2 per bag. Leave 1 in. of the soil ball above the surface. Do not firm. Water in, but keep water off the stem. A cane will be necessary behind each plant and there should be horizontal support wires 1 ft apart. The lateral branches are trained along these wires — nip off their tips when 5 leaves have been produced. Side shoots form, and it is these side shoots which bear the flowers.

Hand pollination of the female flowers (look for a tiny 'Melon' behind the petals) is essential. Stop the stems 2 leaves beyond the developing fruit and reduce the number to leave 4–6 Melons per plant. Regular damping down and misting are desirable at most times, but should not take place during pollination time nor when the fruits start to colour. Support each fruit with a net, and pick when ripe. It is not always easy to tell when this stage has been reached. Smell the fruit — there should be a characteristic aroma. Press the end away from the stalk — it should give slightly. The fruit when lifted should part readily from the stalk.

There are four varieties which are widely available. **Sweetheart** is generally agreed to be the best one to grow — orange flesh, early and hardier than the others. The flesh of **Blenheim Orange** is a deeper orange than Sweetheart, but it needs a heated house. **Charantais** is similar to but does not have the flavour of Sweetheart. **Ogen** has sweet, pale green flesh — not as early as Sweetheart.

Melon — Ogen

NECTARINE

Nectarine is a smooth-skinned sport of Peach. It is cultivated in the same way, although yields are lower and it has a rather more delicate constitution. The varieties suitable for greenhouse cultivation include **Elruge**, **Humboldt** and **Pine Apple**.

PEACH

Like the Apricot this fruit tree benefits from the protection and warmth of a greenhouse both at blossom time and fruit-ripening time. The wall of a south-facing lean-to is the traditional place for a Peach tree, but if this is not possible you can grow a bush in a 12 in. pot for several years, after which yields will disappoint. Buy a 2 or 3 year old partly-trained tree and plant about 1 ft away from the wall. Choose one of the well-established reliable varieties such as **Peregrine**, **Duke of York**, **Rochester** or **Bellegarde**. See The Fruit Expert for details of training and maintenance pruning. High humidity is necessary during the growing season — damp down regularly. Regular watering is also necessary — in summer that may mean once or even twice a day. Hand pollinate with a soft brush and thin fruit to 6–9 in. apart. Keep watch for aphids and red spider mite.

Harvest when the flesh around the stalk is soft and the skin bears a reddish flush. During the autumn and winter keep the house cool and open up the ventilators. Don't worry if winter temperatures fall to freezing point.

Peach — Rochester

STRAWBERRY

Here is a fruit which every greenhouse owner can grow, however small the house. In August or September plant vigorous and well-rooted plants into 6 in. pots. Water regularly and bury the pots outside in well-drained ground or peat in November to protect the roots from frost.

In January bring the pots into a cool greenhouse — keep them in a well-lit spot. When the flowers open stop damping down and hand pollinate the blooms and start to feed weekly with a liquid fertilizer. Ventilate the house when the weather is warm and sunny. Resume damping down when fruit starts to swell — stop feeding when the fruits start to show colour. April is the usual time for gathering the fruit — Strawberries are ready for picking as soon as they are red all over. Nip the stalk between thumbnail and forefinger. Don't keep the same plants for forcing next year as quality deteriorates in the second year — start again with rooted runners. The No.1 choice for many years has been **Cambridge Favourite** — reliable but somewhat lacking in flavour. The other old one is **Royal Sovereign** — renowned for its flavour. **Elvira** is a modern variety which crops heavily — **Tamella** is sometimes recommended but the flavour is only fair.

Strawberry — Cambridge Favourite

CHAPTER 4

CARE

It is a common and depressing sight to see an assortment of sickly plants lining the benches or growing in the border of greenhouses and conservatories. Scorched leaves, drooping stems, rotting fruits ... the signs that something is wrong.

Growing plants under glass is more time-consuming and more challenging than growing the same number of plants outdoors — that is both the fascination of and problem with green-house gardening. Out of doors the plants rely to a large extent on the natural elements for their needs — water, warmth, humidity and so on. Under glass the plants must depend entirely on you for their requirements.

Some of these needs are obvious. Forget to water and the plants die — the first lesson we all learn. But then we discover that most plants will also suffer if we overwater them, and generally they require a winter rest period when water must be applied sparingly.

Warmth is another obvious requirement and the newest recruit to greenhouse growing knows that half hardy and tender plants must be kept frost-free. Less obvious is the fact that many plants, including exotic ones, may be harmed or even killed if the temperature gets too high in summer. And it is not just a matter of temperature — the plants must be shaded from the direct rays of the sun in midsummer.

The list goes on. Ventilation for part of the year is vital for most plants and so is moist air. Regular feeding is necessary, especially when the plant is growing in soilless compost. There are troubles to treat, plants to repot and propagate, stems to support and autumn maintenance to carry out.

This collection of things to do is no more nor less than you could expect from a hobby which is somewhat challenging but extremely rewarding. Experience is a great teacher, and it is some comfort to know that everyone makes mistakes on the road to becoming an expert greenhouse gardener.

For the beginner there are a few golden rules. Firstly, choose plants which are right for the conditions. Sounds obvious, but all too often you can find tropical plants struggling to survive in a cool greenhouse. Secondly, do the important jobs *before* they become critical — insulate before the first frosts arrive, tackle pests before they get out of hand, water before the leaves droop, shade before the plants are scorched, and so on. Next, spend a little time looking at your plants — feeling the soil, picking off dead flowers, looking under the leaves for disease etc. Also keep the place clean — hygiene is all-important. This calls for promptly getting rid of prunings, dead fruit etc. It calls for cleaning used pots, trays, sprayers and tools. Finally, read this chapter, and then read it again.

DAMPING DOWN

The traditional method of damping down has been carried out since the early days of greenhouse growing. The ritual begins as temperatures rise in late April or May — a hose pipe is used to wet the floor and benches. Once a day at first, but as often as three times a day in midsummer. On hot days the plants may be syringed with water.

As the water evaporates the temperature of the house is lowered — a basic benefit of damping down. But there are other benefits — the increase in air humidity means that water loss through the leaves is reduced, resulting in a lower requirement for frequent watering, and moisture-loving plants are able to survive. Furthermore dry-air pests such as red spider mite and thrips are kept in check and fruit set of Tomatoes is encouraged.

The problem with the traditional method is that the benefits are temporary on a hot day with all the ventilators open. Professional growers use electrically-driven humidifiers to provide a continual source of water vapour — for the amateur a continually damp area can be created by laying down capillary matting (see page 12) on the staging.

HEATING

The basic classification of greenhouses from the cultural point of view is based on the minimum temperature at which the house is maintained — see page 16. With most greenhouse and conservatory plants the comfort level for active healthy growth is 55°–75°F, but this simple statement needs to be qualified. Mature plants are more tolerant than young ones of fluctuations outside the comfort range, and germinating seeds generally need higher temperatures than seedlings and mature plants.

The minimum temperatures quoted for many of the ornamentals in Chapter 3 are in the warm or stove house range, but this is the requirement for the plants to flourish. Most types, however, will survive quite well at temperatures somewhat below the stated minimums. This tolerance is not large and it is a mistake to mix heat-demanding plants with cool-air lovers. The best way to overcome the problem if you want a mixed collection is to divide a section of the house with transparent material and then install an adequate heater in the warm section.

It is necessary to avoid as much heat loss as you can during the winter months. Keep the glass clean to ensure maximum entry of the sun's rays and try to conserve as much of this heat as possible. Seal cracks to prevent draughts and repair broken lights and ill-fitting doors. About 80 per cent of the heat is lost through the glass, so line the sides and roof with polythene sheeting — see page 13. The use of bubble plastic is especially effective — its use will maintain frost-free conditions in a draught-free cold house in many areas of the country during an average winter. Remember that plants in cold and wet soil can quickly rot or become diseased — keep the compost or soil on the dry side in a cold house in winter.

●

In the spring and summer the problem is reversed — the temperature has to be reduced to keep the plants below the overheating level. Dry heat is more dangerous than moist heat, and several interlinked methods are used to lower temperatures. Damping down the floor (page 82) and misting the plants will lower the temperature when the house is adequately ventilated. As soon as the temperatures continually remain above 75°F it is essential to apply some form of shading (see below).

KEEPING THE PLANTS HAPPY

Aim to keep a heated house at or above the minimum temperature. The day-time temperature during the growing season should be fairly constant — for most plants a night-time drop of about 10°F is beneficial. Reduce the heat of the house during the resting season.

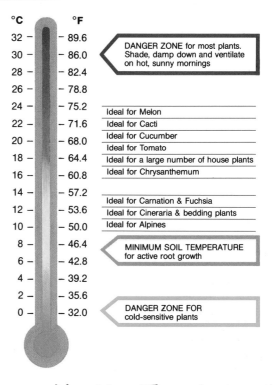

°C	°F	
32	89.6	DANGER ZONE for most plants. Shade, damp down and ventilate on hot, sunny mornings
30	86.0	
28	82.4	
26	78.8	
24	75.2	Ideal for Melon
22	71.6	Ideal for Cacti
20	68.0	Ideal for Cucumber
		Ideal for Tomato
18	64.4	Ideal for a large number of house plants
16	60.8	Ideal for Chrysanthemum
14	57.2	
12	53.6	Ideal for Carnation & Fuchsia
		Ideal for Cineraria & bedding plants
10	50.0	Ideal for Alpines
8	46.4	MINIMUM SOIL TEMPERATURE for active root growth
6	42.8	
4	39.2	
2	35.6	
0	32.0	DANGER ZONE FOR cold-sensitive plants

Heating Troubles

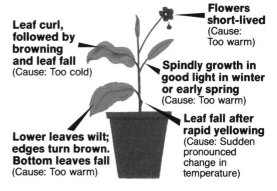

Leaf curl, followed by browning and leaf fall (Cause: Too cold)

Lower leaves wilt; edges turn brown. Bottom leaves fall (Cause: Too warm)

Flowers short-lived (Cause: Too warm)

Spindly growth in good light in winter or early spring (Cause: Too warm)

Leaf fall after rapid yellowing (Cause: Sudden pronounced change in temperature)

SHADING

In summer your greenhouse can become a death trap for plants. Many types are damaged when the temperature stays over 85°–90°F and others such as Begonia, African Violet and Gloxinia are scorched by summer sunshine. As noted on page 13 the best answer is a set of outside blinds which can be raised or lowered depending on the weather. Internal blinds screen out the harmful rays of the sun but do not reduce the internal temperature.

Most people seek a simpler form of shading. Small plants can be placed in the shade of larger ones and newspaper can be placed over seedlings, rooted cuttings and plants with delicate leaves. The usual answer is a proprietary shading paint — do not use lime wash as it is difficult to take off when no longer required. These products are painted or sprayed on to the outside of the glass (not plastic) in spring and are removed by wiping off in autumn.

WATERING

The task of watering is more time-consuming than any other aspect of greenhouse growing, and it is probably the most difficult to master. You must never allow watering to become a regular routine, such as every Sunday, Tuesday and Friday. The timing and the amount to apply depend on so many things — a partial list includes plant type, season of the year, size and type of container, temperature, compost type and air humidity. There are no firm rules, but there are a number of points for general guidance. Among the basic things to remember is that roots need air as well as water, which means that compost should be moist but not saturated. Some flowering pot plants are happy to be kept moist at all times, but others (e.g most foliage ornamentals) require a period of drying out between waterings.

WHEN TO WATER

Tapping the pot is useless — measuring water loss by estimating the weight of the pot calls for great skill. The simplest way is to look at the surface — weekly in winter, daily in summer. If the surface is dry and powdery all over, water if the plants should be kept moist at all times. With the remaining plants insert your forefinger into the compost to the full depth of your fingernail. If your fingertip remains dry then the pot needs watering. Growing bags have their own rules — these are printed on the pack. You must also be guided by the season and the weather. In summer, plants may need watering twice a day — in winter they may require water only once a fortnight. Dormant plants need hardly any water during the winter months — this is especially important for succulents. Remember that plants need much more water on a sunny day than on a cloudy one. For example, a 3 ft Tomato plant loses only ½ pint on a dull day, but this rises to 2½ pints on a sunny one. Water in the morning, especially in cool weather. Try to avoid watering when the sun is shining brightly.

THE WATER TO USE

Tap water is suitable for nearly all plants, but for delicate types it should be left to stand overnight. Do not use hard water on lime haters such as Azalea, Orchids, Cyclamen and Hydrangea. Rainwater is excellent, but it must be clean and not stagnant.

HOW TO WATER

A watering can or hose pipe is by far the commonest method. Page 12 explains the right way to water, and also gives details of automatic watering methods which make the job easier.

KEEPING THE PLANTS HAPPY

Do not make the plants beg for water by drooping their leaves and stem tips. Roots need air as well as water so do not keep the compost constantly saturated. Some plants need a partial drying-out period between waterings, others do not. Fill the space to the top of the pot and leave to drain. With growing bags follow the maker's instructions. All plants need less water during the resting period.

Watering Troubles

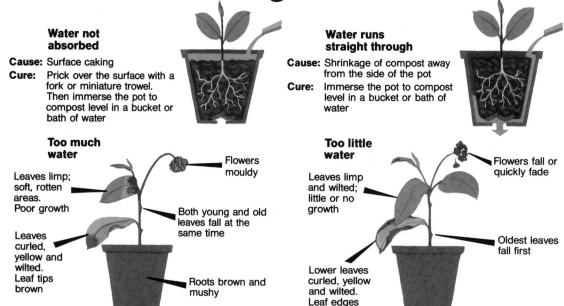

Water not absorbed

Cause: Surface caking

Cure: Prick over the surface with a fork or miniature trowel. Then immerse the pot to compost level in a bucket or bath of water

Too much water

Leaves limp; soft, rotten areas. Poor growth

Leaves curled, yellow and wilted. Leaf tips brown

Flowers mouldy

Both young and old leaves fall at the same time

Roots brown and mushy

Water runs straight through

Cause: Shrinkage of compost away from the side of the pot

Cure: Immerse the pot to compost level in a bucket or bath of water

Too little water

Leaves limp and wilted; little or no growth

Lower leaves curled, yellow and wilted. Leaf edges brown and dry

Flowers fall or quickly fade

Oldest leaves fall first

VENTILATING

The need for at least one roof ventilator and one side ventilator in even a small house was stressed on page 11. Without them you will lose the battle against plant-harming high temperatures in midsummer, but this is not the only time when ventilation is required.

In a well-stocked house ventilation will be required almost all year round. In winter the roof ventilator should be opened an inch or two for a few hours around midday if the weather is dry and above the minimum temperature of the house — do this on the side away from the wind. The purpose is to reduce air humidity and keep the atmosphere buoyant — cold, humid and stagnant air in winter is the basic cause of grey mould and other diseases. This winter ventilation is vital if you are using a paraffin, gas or oil heater.

As spring arrives the roof ventilator is opened more widely and for longer in the day but the side ventilators are still kept closed — moving cold air rapidly over foliage will damage growth. In May the situation changes — the main purpose of ventilation is to keep the temperature below 75°F. Side ventilators are now opened, and it may be necessary to open the door as well.

In high summer ventilation is not enough to keep temperatures below the plant-damaging 85°F mark. Shading is necessary and so is regular damping down. It may be necessary to leave the ventilators open all day and all night, but a change in weather can mean closing a ventilator or two at night and for part of the day.Thus daily control is often necessary, and this makes the automatic ventilator (see page 11) a boon for all greenhouse owners. An extractor fan is much less vital, but it can be a godsend in an abnormally hot summer.

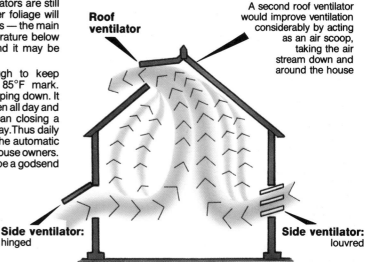

Roof ventilator

A second roof ventilator would improve ventilation considerably by acting as an air scoop, taking the air stream down and around the house

Side ventilator: hinged

Side ventilator: louvred

SUPPORTING

Few people would wish to see a conservatory filled solely with low-growing plants — many of the most attractive specimens are either climbers or tall plants with weak stems. In the greenhouse the popular vegetables and fruits such as Tomatoes, Cucumbers, Melons, Vines and Peaches all grow to a considerable height. For these situations some form of support is required.

Supports are sometimes attached either to the glazing bars, or the house wall in the case of a lean-to or conservatory. An example is the arrangement of horizontal wires used to hold Vines and fruit trees — 10 in. apart for Vines and 18 in. for fruit. Use plastic-covered straining wire or gauge 14 galvanised wire pulled taut between fixings. Make sure the arrangement is strong enough to support the plants in full fruit. Supports which are attached to the greenhouse or house wall sometimes run vertically rather than horizontally — an example is a strip of trellis work used for climbing ornamentals. Another form of vertical support is an arrangement of strings or wires attached to the glazing bars of the roof and used for Tomatoes, Cucumbers etc.

It is often necessary to use a support system which is not attached to the structure of the house. The basic example is the wooden stake or bamboo cane. In most cases it is better to insert 3 or 4 canes around the stems of a pot plant and enclose them with string or raffia rather than to use a single cane. Alternatively there is a range of circular wire supports which can be used to hold pot or border plants which grow up to 4 ft high. Tall plants in growing bags are a special case — self-supporting metal frames which stand around or over the bag are available.

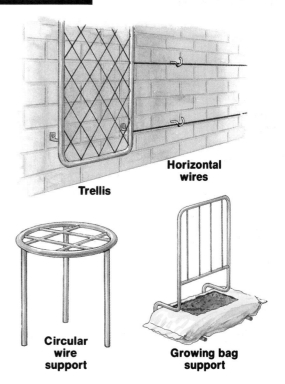

Horizontal wires

Trellis

Circular wire support

Growing bag support

POTS & POTTING

Once there were just two basic ways of growing plants under glass. Some flowers and small shrubs were kept in pots, but most flowering perennials and shrubs (Chrysanthemum, Camellia etc) and the vegetables and fruits (Tomato, Cucumber, Grape, Fig etc) were grown in the border soil. The basic rules were followed — the ground was soaked with water a couple of days before and stakes were inserted prior to and not after planting.

The problem is that soils can become 'crop sick' when the same type of plant is grown year after year. Yields diminish and disease attacks increase alarmingly. When this happens you have to choose from several courses of action. You can change the soil, of course, or you can sterilise it with a garden disinfectant. Unfortunately, both are time-consuming, inconvenient and not always successful. Alternatively you can grow more plants in pots, but the popular answer is to change over to the modern technique of growing bag cultivation.

Growing bags have revolutionised greenhouse practice. They are consistent and sterile, and are capable of giving high yields. These compost-filled plastic bolsters are excellent for vigorous plants such as Tomatoes, Cucumbers and Melons, but you must follow the instructions carefully. The rules for watering and feeding are quite different from the way one cares for plants in border soil.

Containers

CLAY POT
Advantages: Less likely to topple over. Porous — less likely to waterlog. Traditional natural appearance

PLASTIC POT
Advantages: Less likely to break if dropped. Watering is needed less often. Decorative forms available

TUB
Large decorative container in wood, plastic or fibreglass for a shrub or a collection of smaller plants. Fill bottom with gravel before adding compost — water with care if drainage holes are absent

PEAT PELLET
Useful for seed sowing and potting on. Planted directly into soil or compost — no root disturbance. Compressed — soak in water before use

POLYTHENE SLEEVE POT
Inexpensive and easily stored. Useful as a stage in the potting on process. Usually thrown away after use but can be reused

PEAT POT
Useful for potting on before transfer to garden. The pot is bio-degradable. Planted directly into soil or compost — no root disturbance

PEAT BLOCK
Compressed cube of soil-based or soilless compost made with a small hand tool. Needs careful handling — no longer popular

RAISED BED
Useful where base is paved or soil is badly drained. Make sides with 12 in. wide plastic-coated board — use brass screws. Fill with soil/peat mixture above a shallow layer of gravel

GROWING BAG
Plastic bag filled with soilless compost — drainage holes or slits are made in the sides and panels are removed from the top to create planting pockets

Growing Media

GARDEN SOIL
Soil taken straight from the garden is not suitable for filling pots. Apart from the pests and weeds it may contain the soil structure will be destroyed by regular watering. A 4:1 garden soil/peat mixture can be used for a raised bed — change every few years.

SOIL-BASED COMPOST
The introduction of the John Innes (J.I.) composts has removed the need for a wide array of mixtures. Sterilized loam and peat are blended with fertilizers, lime and sand. They have been largely replaced by soilless composts.

SOILLESS COMPOST
Because loam is difficult to obtain and its quality is variable, most modern composts are based on peat, or peat and sand. These soilless composts have several advantages over soil-based ones. Their quality does not vary and they are lighter and cleaner to handle. Perhaps the most important advantage is that the plant to be potted on was almost certainly raised in a peat-based compost, and plants do not like a change in the growing medium. Disadvantages include the difficulty of re-wetting if the compost becomes dry, and feeding must begin after a couple of months. Non-peat composts based on coir are now available.

PRICKING OUT

When a large number of seeds has been sown in a relatively small container it is essential that the seedlings are pricked out (alternative name — pricked off) into another compost-filled container in which they will have room to develop. For details see Stage 7 of Sowing Seeds on page 89.

POTTING UP

This is carried out when a seedling or rooted cutting is ready to be transferred into its first container — usually a 2½ or 3 in. plastic, clay or peat pot. The correct stage for pricked-out seedlings is when the leaves of adjacent plants start to touch each other. Potting up can be a delicate job — handle the young plant with care, make sure that some compost is transferred with the roots and fill the pot with multipurpose compost so that the plant is at the same level as it was before. There should be a ½ in. gap between the top of the compost and the rim of the pot. Water in gently.

POTTING ON

This is carried out when the roots have filled the pot and the plant is starting to become pot-bound. Learn to recognise this stage of development. Tell-tale signs are roots growing through the drainage hole, compost which dries out very quickly, and slow growth despite favourable conditions. For a final check remove the pot in the way described in Stage 2 below. If the plant is pot-bound there will be a matted mass of roots on the outside, and not much soil will be visible. If it is not pot-bound, simply replace the soil ball back into the original pot — no harm will have been done. If the plant is pot-bound it is generally necessary to pot on, following the technique shown below. The best time is spring, and choose a pot which is only slightly larger than the previous one. Potting on is often loosely referred to as 'repotting' in many articles and books (including this one!) — but Repotting is technically a rather different technique. Don't rush to pot on unless it is really necessary for the plant in question — some plants will only flower when they are pot-bound.

① A suitable sequence of pot sizes is 3 in. → 5 in. → 7 in. → 10 in. Never miss out a stage in this sequence, but stop when the desired plant size is reached. Scrub out old pots — soak clay ones overnight.

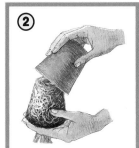

② Water the plant. One hour later remove it from the pot as shown above. If difficult to dislodge, knock the pot on the edge of a table and run a knife around the rootball. Remove old crocks. Tease out matted roots.

③ Cover drainage hole of a clay pot with crocks. Add a layer of potting compost. Place the plant on top of this layer — gradually fill surrounding space with damp potting compost. Firm compost with your thumbs.

④ Tap the pot several times on the table — leave ¾–1 in. watering space. Water carefully. Keep in the shade for a week — mist the leaves daily. Then place the plant in its growing quarters and treat normally.

REPOTTING

This technique is carried out when the plant and/or the container has reached the desired or maximum size. During the dormant season remove the plant as above and tease some of the old compost away from the rootball — a small handfork is the usual tool for this work. Trim away some of the root tips, but do not reduce the rootball size by more than 25 per cent. Pot up as described above, using the same size of pot. Wash the old pot thoroughly if it is to be reused.

TOP DRESSING

For a variety of reasons, especially with large pots and trained specimens, you may not wish or be able to disturb the plant by repotting. In this case the pot should be top dressed every spring by carefully removing the top inch of compost (2 inches for large pots). The removed material is then replaced by fresh compost.

PROPAGATING

You will miss much of the thrill of growing under glass if you don't learn the craft of propagation. Some greenhouse and conservatory plants cannot be raised at home without special skills and equipment, but a large number can be propagated quite easily in an ordinary greenhouse. There are a number of methods but two dominate all the others — striking cuttings and sowing seeds.

Cuttings using the simple polythene bag method or the electric propagator technique are the usual method for ornamentals, and seeds are the general source material for vegetables. Even with easy-to-root cuttings and seeds there are inexplicable failures, so always take more cuttings and sow more seeds than you plan to use.

There are four basic reasons for raising your own plants. You can have more specimens without having to buy them each time, you can replace ageing specimens with vigorous new ones, you can have plants which are not available from your local garden centre, and you can have the satisfaction of growing plants from scratch.

As noted earlier, sowing seeds and striking stem cuttings are the more popular but not the only ways of propagating plants for greenhouse cultivation. Begonia rex and African Violet are propagated from leaf cuttings. Strawberries are reproduced by pegging down runners, clumps of ferns are divided and small bulblets (offsets) are planted after removal from the sides of mature bulbs.

Taking Cuttings

A cutting is a small piece removed from a plant which with proper treatment can be induced to form roots and then grow into a specimen which is identical to the parent plant. Some woody plants are difficult or impossible to propagate without special equipment, whereas cuttings of some popular house plants such as Ivy and Tradescantia will form roots in a glass of water. Early summer is the time recommended for many plants, but late summer is the popular time for Fuchsia and Pelargonium. So don't guess what to do — consult guides such as The House Plant Expert, The Flower Expert and The Tree & Shrub Expert.

There are a few general rules. Plant non-succulent cuttings as soon as possible after severing from the parent plant and make sure that the compost is in close contact with the inserted part. Keep the cuttings in an enclosed environment to maintain high air humidity around the plants — Cacti, Succulents and Pelargonium are exceptions. Finally, do not keep tugging at the cutting to see if it has rooted — the appearance of new growth is the best guide.

Softwood cuttings are green at the tip and base, and are taken from early spring to midsummer. Many hardy perennials and some small shrubs are propagated in this way. Basal cuttings are shoots formed at the base of the plant and pulled away for use as softwood cuttings in spring.

Semi-ripe cuttings are green at the top and partly woody at the base — they are usually heel cuttings (see below). Midsummer to early autumn is the usual time and most shrubs and perennial climbers are propagated by this method.

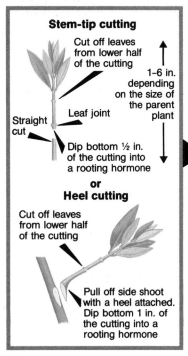

Stem-tip cutting

Cut off leaves from lower half of the cutting

1-6 in. depending on the size of the parent plant

Straight cut

Leaf joint

Dip bottom ½ in. of the cutting into a rooting hormone

or
Heel cutting

Cut off leaves from lower half of the cutting

Pull off side shoot with a heel attached. Dip bottom 1 in. of the cutting into a rooting hormone

④ Insert cutting; firm around the base with the pencil. Label if necessary

② Trim foliage of large-leaved plants by half

⑤ Water in cutting very gently

③ Make a hole in the compost with a pencil

① Fill a 5 in. pot with seed & cutting compost or multipurpose compost

Polythene bag method
(late spring-early autumn)

① Place 4 canes in the pot and drape a polythene bag over them. Secure with a rubber band. Stand pot in a bright spot, away from direct sunlight

② Leave undisturbed until new growth appears. Harden off by giving more ventilation and then lift out each rooted cutting after watering — transfer into a compost-filled 3 in. pot

or
Propagator method
(late autumn-mid spring)

① Place pots in the propagator. Keep at 65°-75°F. Shade and ventilate on hot days

② See above

Sowing Seeds

1 **SEED** You must start with good-quality seed. Buy from a reputable supplier and don't open the packet until you are ready to sow. Hard-coated seed should be shaken in a jar with coarse sand and then soaked overnight before sowing — chipping them is a risky business. Very fine seed should be mixed with dry silver sand before sowing.

2 **CONTAINER** Many types of container are suitable provided they have holes or cracks at the base for drainage. Avoid old wooden trays — disease organisms are difficult to remove by washing. Choose plastic — full trays are usually too large and a better choice is a 3½–5 in. half pot or a half tray. Large seeds can be sown into the cells of cellular trays, peat pots filled with compost or into peat pellets (Jiffy 7s).

3 **COMPOST** A peat-based seed or multipurpose compost is ideal — sterile, light and consistent. Fill the container with compost and firm gently with a piece of board — the surface should be about ½ in. below the top of the pot or tray. Sprinkle the surface with water the day before seed sowing — it should be moist but not wet when you scatter the seeds thinly over the surface. Larger seeds can be sown in rows.

4 **COVER** Do not cover very fine seed with compost — examples include Begonia, Lobelia, Petunia and Mimulus. Other seeds should be covered with compost to a depth which is twice the diameter of the seed — this compost should be applied through a sieve to form a fine and even layer. Firm gently with a board after sowing. Most but not all seeds need darkness for successful germination — put brown paper over the tray or pot and place a sheet of glass on top. Condensation is absorbed by the paper and so does not drip on to the compost below. Change the paper if necessary. Do not use brown paper for seeds which need light in order to germinate — popular examples are Antirrhinum, Alyssum, Mimulus, Impatiens, Nicotiana and Begonia.

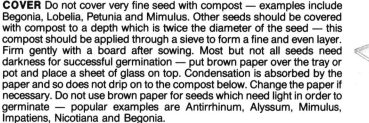

5 **WARMTH** Most seeds require a fairly warm temperature (65°–70°F) for satisfactory germination. As a general guide germination temperature is 10°F higher than the recommended minimum for the growing plant. Heating a whole greenhouse in March or April can be wasteful — a thermostatically-controlled heated propagator is a better idea. Make sure you buy one which is large enough for your future needs. For windowsill propagation you will need a centrally-heated room where the temperature can be kept in the 60°–70°F range. Raise pots or trays from the sill so that they are level with the glass.

6 **LIGHT & WATER** As soon as the seedlings break through the surface, remove the paper and prop up the sheet of glass. After a few days the glass should be removed and the container moved to a bright but sunless spot. Windowsill pots or trays should be turned every couple of days. Never let the compost dry out. The safest way to water is to use a fine sprayer which produces mist-like droplets — watering with a fine-rosed watering can or soaking the container in a basin of water can dislodge tiny plants.

7 **PRICK OUT** As soon as the first set of true leaves has opened the seedlings should be pricked out into trays, small pots or 24-cell cellular trays (Propapacks) filled with multipurpose compost. Set the seedlings so that the seed leaves are just above the surface — handle the plants by the seed leaves and not the stems. The seedlings should be set 1–1½ in. apart in pots or trays. Large seedlings such as Dahlias and Pelargoniums should be potted on into individual 3 in. pots. Keep containers in the shade for a day or two after pricking out. High temperatures are not required — 50°–55°F is satisfactory. Water as necessary — use Cheshunt Compound if damping off is a problem.

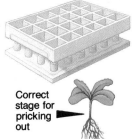

Correct stage for pricking ▶ out

8 **HARDEN OFF** When the seedlings have recovered from pricking out and potting on they can be moved to their allotted part of the greenhouse, but do shade in sunny weather until they are past the seedling stage. Seedlings destined to be transplanted outdoors must be hardened off to prepare them for life in the garden. Move the pots to the coolest part of the greenhouse and then to a cold frame. Keep the lights closed at first, then open during daylight hours. Finally, let the pots stand uncovered all the time for about 7 days before planting out.

MAINTAINING THE STRUCTURE

Virtually all of the maintenance and repair techniques set out in this chapter are designed to keep the appropriate features sound, attractive and safe for you and your family. With the greenhouse there is an additional factor — much of the maintenance is designed to keep plants in peak condition and to inhibit pests and diseases. The routine is to carry out an annual overhaul in autumn and to take immediate action at any time of the year if there is an emergency.

AUTUMN CLEANING INDOORS

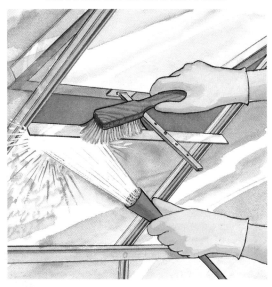

For a thorough annual cleaning, it is necessary to move out as many plants as possible — the recommended procedure is to choose a settled and reasonable day in autumn when the Tomatoes have finished cropping. Move the plants to a convenient spot outdoors — the more delicate types may have to be placed indoors.

Remove rubbish, old pots etc and then use a stiff brush to remove the dirt from the path. The next stage is washing down — for this you will need a stiff brush, scraper, sponge and a dilute warm-water solution of a disinfectant recommended for horticultural use. Scrub staging, walls and the framework — it is important to get into the crevices where insects breed. With aluminium houses the T-section bars are a hiding place for pests — these insects can be removed by rubbing down with wire wool. Use a sprayer to get into cracks and pay special attention to the glass panes (see the next page). When you have finished all surfaces should be clean and there should be no caked-on dirt — the path should have been brushed with the disinfectant solution.

Leave several hours for the disinfectant to do its work and then hose down the inside of the house. Use a long-handled brush and plain water to reach into corners so that all the disinfectant is removed. Leave the door and vents open so that the glass and framework can dry as quickly as possible — put the heater on if necessary. One safety point — it is a good idea to cover up electric points when washing down.

Make sure that all pots and trays are cleaned at this stage. When the greenhouse is dry the plants can be returned — clean the pots and remove dead and diseased leaves before they are put back in the greenhouse.

AUTUMN CLEANING OUTDOORS

Begin with the glass and framework, using water and detergent or a dilute solution of a horticultural detergent. This job is much more difficult outdoors than inside the house — you will need a long-handled mop to reach the roof sections. After washing down the glass and glazing bars it is the turn of the walls (if present) and base. Scrub brick and block walls with water and a specific cleaner — for wooden sides remove algae and moss with a proprietary moss killer.

GENERAL MAINTENANCE

There may be more to do than just cleaning the glass, framework, shelves, staging etc. Check all iron and steel fittings, hinges and screws for rust — if sound apply a thin film of oil. If corrosion is present, treat with a tannate-based rust destroyer before painting. Replace badly-rusted hinges.

Draughts are a special problem, as they are not only uncomfortable for you but they can be deadly for the plants. Check that vents and doors fit tightly — fit self-adhesive draught-proofing strips if they don't. Louvres are a common cause of draughts, so check them carefully.

Inspect the sides of the greenhouse if it is not glazed to the ground. Repoint brick walls as necessary and replace any boards which may be missing from a wooden base.

The wooden framework of the house should be inspected and the gutters will need cleaning and repairing if necessary — see the sections on the next page. Check the wires used for supporting tall plants inside the house — these generally need replacing every few years. Replace broken or cracked panes and renew damaged or missing putty or mastic.

LOOKING AFTER GLASS

It is not the unsightly nature of dirty glass which poses the real problem — it is the reduction in light intensity within the house and this can be serious during the winter and early spring months. Routine cleaning was described on the previous page, but the development of algae and the presence of encrusted dirt between overlapping panes call for special action. Use a proprietary greenhouse glass cleaner, a forceful jet of water and a thin sheet of cardboard or plastic to push between the sheets of glass if necessary.

In greenhouses containing plants, broken panes during the colder months are generally replaced without delay. They should, of course, be reglazed immediately at any time of the year as the draught can cause a great deal of harm. It is the cracked pane of glass which usually gets neglected, and this is regrettable as it can so easily blow in during a storm. See page 15 for notes on reglazing aluminium and wooden houses. Metal-framed greenhouses are reglazed in a similar way to wooden ones, but clips are used instead of glazing sprigs and you will need to buy special metal window putty.

LOOKING AFTER WOOD

If you have a greenhouse made of teak or cedar then rot should not be a worry, but a softwood house should have its framework painted with a plant-safe preservative every 2 years. If paint is cracked, strip back and reprime. Then apply undercoat and two coats of gloss paint. Open all vents and the door after treatment to speed up drying. Rot can be a serious complaint so look for the tell-tale signs — spongy wood which a steel point penetrates easily, an unusually dark colour and cracks along the grain. The trouble spots are generally around the boards at the base of the house, the lower glazing bars and the bottom of doors and vents. It is possible to repair rot with hardener and filler but it is usually more satisfactory to replace the damaged wood.

LOOKING AFTER THE DOOR

The door is a basic part of the greenhouse and is often one of the first areas to go wrong. With conventionally hung doors make sure they open easily, which calls for keeping the hinges oiled, the screws driven in tightly and a free-turning lock. Note that the lock should never be oiled if it is stiff — use instead a graphite lubricant. This smooth opening is vital because going into the greenhouse is often a one-handed job, the other one being used to carry pots, watering can or sprayer. This need for free-running is equally vital with sliding doors, and these seem to go wrong more often than ordinary ones. Clean the upper and lower tracks — dirt and small pieces of grit are common causes of jammed doors. Another cause is the presence of worn nylon wheels — replace if necessary.

LOOKING AFTER GUTTERING

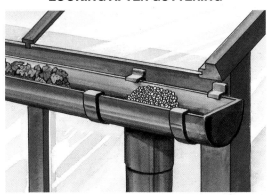

Sound guttering is essential — any overflow or leakage will pour down the glazed area and framework, leading to algal growth on the glass or transparent plastic and rot in the glazing bars. The first job is to clear leaves and other rubbish out of the gutters at least twice a year. If a filter is absent at the top of the downpipe, you should put a ball of wire netting into this spot.

Repair a sagging gutter by inserting a small wooden wedge between the gutter and bracket. The fault, however, may be the downpipe and not the guttering. If there is a leak (look for a damp patch or green slime at the back) fix a fibreglass bandage or self-adhesive flashing strip round the affected area. If the downpipe is blocked, put a bowl at the base and poke a stiff wire upwards through the shoe at the bottom to remove any lower blockage. Now work from the top of the pipe — remove any rubbish from the opening and then use a piece of hooked stout wire to lift up any debris. Finally, push a long bamboo cane down through the pipe.

FEEDING

Plants require food to remain healthy. A number of elements are involved, the main ones being nitrogen, phosphates and potash. This does not mean that plants need constant feeding — too much can be as harmful as too little. Commercial peat-based composts contain all the essential nutrients and these should last for about 6–8 weeks after planting. Feeding should then start, but how much and how often will depend on a number of factors.

Slow-growing and dormant plants need little or no food — actively-growing ones need feeding regularly. Liquid fertilizers are the best form for pot and growing bag plants — solid feeds should be confined to the border. Little and often is the golden rule — follow the manufacturer's instructions. As a general feed use a fertilizer in which nitrogen, phosphates and potash are in approximately equal proportions. Experienced gardeners, however, use more than one feed. A nitrogen-rich fertilizer is used on foliage plants and on fruiting crops when leaf and stem growth are required. The plant needs a change when the flowering and fruiting stages are reached. A high-potash feed is now called for — a tomato food is used to divert energy away from leaf production and into flower and fruit production.

Make sure that the compost is moist when feeding plants — applying fertilizer to dry compost can lead to injury. Foliar feeding is an interesting technique — dilute fertilizer is applied directly to the leaves. Make sure you use a product recommended for this purpose.

Feeding Guide

Use a compound fertilizer containing nitrogen, phosphates and potash. If there is no statement for one of them on the label then you can be sure it is missing.	
NITROGEN (N)	**The leaf maker** which promotes stem growth and foliage production. Needs to be balanced with some potash for flowering plants
PHOSPHATES (P_2O_5)	**The root maker** which stimulates active rooting in the compost. Necessary for both foliage and flowering types
POTASH (K_2O)	**The flower maker** which hardens growth so that flowering and fruiting are encouraged at the expense of leaf growth
TRACE ELEMENTS	Present in some house plant foods — derived from humus extracts or added chemicals. Shortage can result in discoloured leaves

Feeding Troubles

Cause ▶	Too little fertilizer	Too much fertilizer
Effects ▶	Slow growth — little resistance to pests and diseases	Lanky and weak growth in winter — abnormal growth in summer
	Leaves pale with 'washed-out' appearance. Lower leaves drop — weak stems	Leaves wilted with scorched edges and brown spots
	Flowers absent or small and poorly coloured	Excessive leaf production may mask floral display

LIGHTING

Most greenhouse gardeners rely solely on natural light. In summer remember that nearly all plants must be screened from the midday sun — new unfolding leaves suffer most. In winter you should keep the windows clean — removing dust can increase light intensity by 10 per cent.

It is lack of light as well as low temperatures which cause plant growth to slow down in winter. This is not just a matter of dull days — day length is also important. Most plants need illumination for 12–16 hours per day in order to maintain active growth, which is why the resting period of foliage plants is not broken by a series of sunny days in winter.

Installing lighting has several advantages in winter. The increase in the duration and intensity of light boosts seedling and young plant growth and also induces flowering in some types — African Violets can be kept in bloom almost all year round. The most important advantage, however, is that you can work in the greenhouse during the long winter evenings. The basis of a fluorescent unit is a tube or series of tubes mounted under a reflector. More practical, however, is a line of 200 watt mercury vapour lamps. Two warnings are necessary — always make sure that the lamps you choose are recommended for horticultural use, and remember that some plants require a period of short days and so may be harmed by artificially extending the day length in winter.

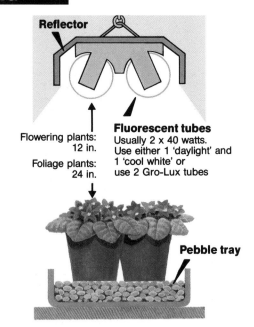

Reflector

Fluorescent tubes
Usually 2 x 40 watts. Use either 1 'daylight' and 1 'cool white' or use 2 Gro-Lux tubes

Flowering plants: 12 in.

Foliage plants: 24 in.

Pebble tray

CHAPTER 5
PLANT TROUBLES

The warm and moist conditions within a greenhouse provide a paradise for many pests and diseases. Few natural enemies are present and the breeding rate of organisms can be amazingly high. Of course there are times when you will have to spray or ignite a smoke, but a great deal can be done to prevent problems — if you follow the rules of good hygiene.

Prevent trouble before it starts

DON'T BRING TROUBLE INTO THE HOUSE
● Never use unsterilised soil. Buy a specially-prepared compost which you can be sure will be pest- and disease-free. Alternatively sterilise soil if you wish to prepare your own compost. Don't use unsterilised manures. Inspect new plants carefully and take any remedial action which may be necessary before putting them with other plants.

KEEP THE HOUSE CLEAN
● Do not leave rubbish laying about — remove dead leaves, old compost etc from benches and floor. Wash and neatly stack pots and trays after use. Cracks and woodwork can harbour pests and diseases, so clean down the house thoroughly once a year — see page 90. Use a garden disinfectant — follow the label instructions carefully.

FOLLOW GOOD GROWING PRACTICE
● Ensure that the house is properly ventilated. Dry air encourages pests such as red spider mite and thrips — saturated air encourages diseases. Water in the morning so that leaves can dry before nightfall. You can water in the early evening if the weather is warm. Do not use dirty rainwater — you can introduce pests, diseases and slime organisms in this way. Sterilise border soil annually to prevent the build-up of harmful organisms. Feed the plants regularly — potash is important.

INSPECT THE PLANTS REGULARLY
● Look for the first signs of trouble — pay special attention to the underside of leaves. Remove dead flowers and foliage promptly — take dead and dying plants out of the house. If there are problems take immediate action — see below.

Tackle trouble without delay

DO NON-SPRAYING JOBS FIRST
● Minor attacks by caterpillar and leaf miner can be controlled by hand picking. Mouldy leaves and fruits should be removed at once. Many problems are due to poor growing conditions rather than a specific pest or disease. Improve growing practice. Place a 2 in. layer of moist peat around the stems of Tomatoes and Cucumbers if damaged root action is suspected.

BUY THE RIGHT TREATMENT
● Spraying, fumigating or dusting may be necessary. Pesticides are safe to use in the way described on the label, but you must follow the instructions and precautions carefully. Make sure that the product is recommended for use under glass and for the plant in question. Cucumber, Melon, Begonia etc may appear in the 'do not spray' list.

TREAT IN THE RIGHT WAY
Do not spray or fumigate when the sun is shining. Close all ventilators before using a smoke

Take care with aerosols. Spraying too closely will cause scorch

Leaves should be dry ▶

Use a fine forceful spray. It is wise to keep all sprays off your skin. Wash off any splashes
◀ Do not spray open delicate blooms
Spray thoroughly both above and below the leaves until the leaves are covered with liquid which is just beginning to run off

FOLLOW THE AFTER-TREATMENT RULES
● Do not stay in the house after spraying. Lock the door after fumigating the house — open the ventilators and door the next day. Wash out equipment, and wash hands and face. Do not keep the spray solution to use next time. Store packs in a safe place. Do not keep unlabelled or illegible packs — throw in the dustbin after emptying liquid down an outside drain. Never store in a beer bottle or similar container.

GENERAL PESTS

APHID (Greenfly)

Small, sap-sucking insects, usually green but sometimes black, grey or orange. A wide range of ornamentals, fruit and vegetables may be attacked — the plant becomes unsightly and growth is weakened. Even worse are the viruses which aphids carry. Spray with horticultural soap.

CATERPILLAR

Caterpillars of many types can attack vegetables and ornamentals, but they are rarely a serious problem under glass. The tell-tale sign is holes in the leaves which may also be spun together. Pick off by hand — spraying with thiacloprid is not usually necessary.

EARWIG

A familiar garden insect with a dark brown body and pincer-like tail. It is not often seen as the earwig comes out of hiding at night and feeds on the leaves and lower petals of Carnations, Chrysanthemums etc. Pick them off and destroy — look under the leaves and shake the flowers.

EELWORM

Fortunately these microscopic, soil-living worms are not common green-house pests. Tomatoes and Chrysanthemums may be attacked — infested Tomato roots have corky swellings and Chrysanthemum leaves develop brown patches. Destroy affected plants immediately.

LEAF MINER

Long winding tunnels are created by small grubs which burrow into and eat the leaf tissue. Chrysanthemum foliage is often attacked in this way. Carnation fly behaves differently, producing blotches on the leaves. Pick and destroy mined leaves — spraying is not necessary.

MEALY BUG

Small pests covered with white, cottony fluff. Large clusters can occur on the stems and under the leaves of a wide variety of plants — a serious attack leads to wilting and leaf fall. Wipe off with damp cotton wool — for a severe attack spray with thiacloprid.

RED SPIDER MITE

Minute sap-sucking pests which infest the underside of leaves of many greenhouse plants when conditions are hot and dry. The upper surface of the leaf becomes mottled and white webbing is sometimes produced. Mist daily. Biological control products are available.

SCALE

Small, brown discs attached to the underside of the leaves and along the stems. These immobile adults are protected from contact sprays by their outer waxy shells. Leaving them may result in an infestation which can ruin the plant — use a systemic spray such as thiacloprid.

SLUGS

Irregular holes appear in the leaves of many plants and tell-tale slime tracks can be seen. These pests generally hide under rubbish and are attracted by decaying vegetation, so good hygiene is essential. Scatter Slug Pellets around plants in the affected area.

THRIPS

Not an important pest, but these tiny, black insects sometimes disfigure Begonias, Crotons, Fuchsias and a number of other ornamentals. They fly or jump from leaf to leaf and damaged flowers and foliage are spotted or distorted. Thrips can be controlled by spraying with thiacloprid.

VINE WEEVIL

The adult beetles attack leaves, but it is the 1 in. long grubs which do the real damage. They live in the compost and rapidly devour roots, bulbs and tubers. When plants wilt it is too late for control measures. Use a non-chemical ('biological') treatment to prevent attacks.

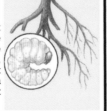

WHITEFLY

A serious and common pest. The adult flies are unsightly — the greenish larvae on the underside of the leaves suck sap and deposit sticky honeydew. Whitefly can occur in great numbers and eradication by spraying is difficult. Hang up yellow greenhouse fly catchers.

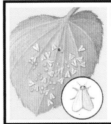

GENERAL DISEASES

ANTHRACNOSE

Sunken black spots appear on the foliage of Palms, Ficus and other susceptible ornamentals. This disease is associated with warm and moist conditions, and control is not easy. Remove and burn infected leaves, spray with a systemic fungicide and keep the plant rather dry for several weeks.

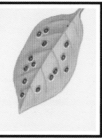

BLACK LEG

A disease of stem cuttings, especially Pelargonium. The base of the cutting turns black due to fungal invasion. The cause is overwatering or over-compaction of the compost which has prevented proper drainage. Remove the infected cuttings promptly and keep compost drier next time.

BOTRYTIS (Grey Mould)

The familiar fluffy grey mould which can cover all parts of the plant if the growing conditions are cool, humid and unventilated. All soft-leaved plants can be affected. Cut away and destroy all diseased parts — no chemical sprays are available. Reduce watering and improve ventilation.

CROWN & STEM ROT

Part of the stem turns soft and rotten — the disease is known as basal rot when the base of the plant is affected. It is nearly always fatal — throw away the plant, pot and compost. In future avoid overwatering and keep the plants a little warmer. Ventilate as recommended.

DAMPING OFF

The fungi which cause damping off attack the roots and stem base of seedlings. Shrinkage and rot occur at ground level and the plants topple over. Remove affected seedlings at once and improve ventilation. In future use sterilised compost, sow thinly and never overwater.

LEAF SPOT

Brown moist spots appear on the foliage of susceptible plants. In a bad attack the small spots enlarge and merge, killing the whole leaf. Both bacteria and fungi can cause this effect — burn infected leaves and keep the plants on the dry side for several weeks.

OEDEMA (Corky Scab)

Hard corky growths sometimes appear on the underside of leaves. This disease is not caused by fungi or bacteria — it is the plant's response to waterlogged compost coupled with low light intensity. Remove badly infected leaves, move to a better lit spot and reduce watering.

POWDERY MILDEW

A fungus disease which grows on the surface of leaves, spotting or coating them with a white powdery deposit. Unlike botrytis this disease is neither common nor fatal. Remove badly infected leaves and spray or dust with sulphur. Improve ventilation. Systemic fungicides are not available.

ROOT ROT (Tuber Rot)

A fatal disease to which Cacti, Succulents, Begonia, Palms and African Violets are particularly prone. Yellowing and wilting of the leaves are followed by plant collapse. The cause is fungal decay due to overwatering — next time make sure you follow the watering rules (page 84).

RUST

An uncommon disease which occasionally affects Chrysanthemums, Fuchsias, Carnations and Pelargoniums. Concentric rings of powdery pustules occur on the underside of the leaves. It is difficult to control — burn infected leaves and increase the ventilation.

SOOTY MOULD

A black fungus which grows on the sticky honeydew which is deposited by aphid, scale, whitefly and mealy bug. The unsightly deposit does no direct harm but it does reduce growth by shading the surface and blocking the pores. Wipe off with a damp cloth — keep pests under control.

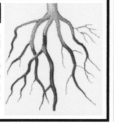

VIRUS

There is no single symptom. The growth may be severely stunted and stems are often distorted. Fruit may be misshapen and yellow spots or patches may appear on the leaves. The infection was on the plant when you bought it or was carried to it by an insect. There is no cure.

GENERAL CULTURAL DISORDERS

UPPER LEAVES FIRM AND YELLOW
Lime was present in the compost or hard water was used on lime-hating plants. Use lime-free compost.

LEAVES DULL AND LIFELESS
Usual cause is too much direct sunlight — it can also be due to red spider mite or dust on leaves.

PLANT NOT GROWING
This is normal for most plants in winter. In summer the most likely cause if the plant is not pot-bound is over-watering or too little light.

SMALL LEAVES, SPINDLY GROWTH
A common effect in winter and early spring if the plant is kept too warm. In summer the most likely cause is underfeeding or too little light.

SPOTS OR PATCHES ON LEAVES
If spots or patches are crisp and brown, underwatering is the most likely cause. If the area is soft and brown, overwatering is the probable reason. Straw-coloured patches are caused by water splashes on leaves, aerosol damage, too much direct sun or pest or disease damage. Sunken spots or blister-like ones are due to disease — see page 95.

BROWN TIPS OR EDGES ON LEAVES
If only leaf tips are affected the most likely cause is dry air. Another possible cause is bruising — people or pets touching the tips can be the culprit. If edges are yellow or brown there are numerous possible reasons, including incorrect watering, too little light, too much direct sunlight, overfeeding, too much heat or draughts. Look for other symptoms to pin-point the cause.

LEAVES CURL AND FALL
Curling followed by leaf fall is a sign of too little heat, cold draughts or overwatering.

LOWER LEAVES DRY UP AND FALL
There are three common causes — too little light, too much heat and overwatering.

LEAF FALL ON ESTABLISHED PLANTS
Rapid defoliation without a prolonged preliminary period of wilting or discoloration is generally due to a shock to the plant's system. There may have been a marked drop or rise in temperature, a sudden increase in light intensity or a prolonged cold draught. Dryness at the roots below the critical level can result in sudden leaf drop with woody specimens.

LEAF FALL ON NEW PLANTS
It is quite normal for a newly repotted plant, a new purchase or a plant moved from one spot to another to lose one or two lower leaves. Keep movement shock to a minimum by potting on into a container which is only slightly larger than the previous one and by never moving a plant from a shady spot to a very bright one without a few days in medium light.

LEAVES TURN YELLOW AND FALL
It is quite normal for an occasional lower leaf on a mature plant to turn yellow and eventually fall. When several leaves turn yellow at the same time and then fall the most likely cause is either overwatering or cold draughts.

WILTING LEAVES
The usual cause is either soil dryness (caused by under-watering) or waterlogging (caused by impeded drainage or watering too frequently). Other causes are too much sunlight, dry air, too much heat or pest damage.

FLOWER BUDS FALL
The conditions which cause leaf drop can also lead to loss of buds and flowers. The commonest causes are dry air, underwatering, too little light, moving the pot and insect damage.

FLOWERS QUICKLY FADE
For a few plants it is normal to have flowers which only last for a day or two, e.g Hibiscus. For long-lasting flower types the culprit is underwatering, dry air, too little light or too much heat.

HOLES AND TEARS IN LEAVES
There are two basic causes of torn leaves. First of all there is the effect of physical damage by pets and people — brushing against an opening leaf bud can cause a ragged margin. Secondly there is insect damage.

NO FLOWERS
If the flowering stage has been reached the most likely cause is lighting problems — too little light or wrong day length. Other possibilities are overfeeding, dry air or thrips. Some plants will only flower when pot-bound.

VARIEGATED LEAVES TURN ALL-GREEN
The simple explanation here is that the foliage is receiving too little light. The answer is to remove the all-green branch or branches if possible and move the pot to a place which receives more light.

ROTTING LEAVES AND STEMS
Rot is caused by a fungus or bacterium which attacks foliage when growing conditions are poor. The primary cause is usually overwatering (especially in winter) or leaving water on the leaves at night.

GREEN SLIME ON CLAY POT
A sure sign of watering problems — the cause is either overwatering or impeded drainage.

WHITE CRUST ON CLAY POT
There are two possible causes for this effect — use of excessively hard water or overfeeding.

TOMATO TROUBLES

BLIGHT

Brown, shrunken area appears on fruit. The affected Tomato is soon completely rotten. Infection may develop during storage.
Treatment: None. Destroy fruit.
Prevention: Protectant fungicides for preventing tomato blight under glass are no longer available.

BLOSSOM DROP

Flowers sometimes wither and break off at the knuckle. Pollination has not taken place, and the cause is usually dryness at the roots and in the air.
Treatment: None.
Prevention: Water regularly and spray flowers in the morning. Tap plants to aid pollination.

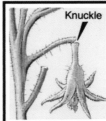

Knuckle

BLOSSOM END ROT

Leathery dark-coloured patch occurs at the bottom of the fruit. It is a frequent problem where growing bags are used.
Treatment: None.
Prevention: Never let the soil or compost dry out, especially when the fruit is swelling.

DRY SET

Growth of the fruitlet ceases when it reaches the size of a match-head. The trouble is due to the air being too hot and dry when pollination is taking place.
Treatment: None.
Prevention: Spray the plants daily with water in the morning or evening.

GHOST SPOT

Grey mould spores fall on or splash on to fruit. Small, transparent rings ('water spots') are formed.
Treatment: None. Affected fruit can be eaten.
Prevention: Provide good ventilation. Do not splash developing fruit when watering. Control grey mould.

GREENBACK

Area around the stalk remains hard, green and unripe. The cause is too much sunlight or too little potash.
Treatment: None.
Prevention: Apply shading material. Control heat of greenhouse. Feed regularly with tomato food. Resistant varieties are available.

HOLLOW FRUIT

There are several causes of hollow fruit — poor conditions for pollination (air too hot, too cold or too dry), too little potash in the soil or damage by a hormone weedkiller.
Treatment: None.
Prevention: Avoid factors listed above.

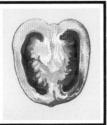

SPLIT FRUIT

A common complaint, both outdoors and under glass. It is caused by heavy watering or rain after the soil has become dry around the roots. The sudden increase in size causes the skin to split.
Treatment: None.
Prevention: Keep roots evenly moist.

STEM ROT (Didymella)

Lower leaves turn yellow and a sunken, brown canker appears at the base of the stem. Black dots develop in this cankered area. Disease may spread to other parts of the stem.
Treatment: None.
Prevention: Sterilise equipment between crops.

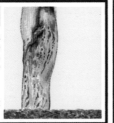

SUN SCALD

Pale brown, papery-skinned depression on the side of fruit facing the glass. Papery patches on leaves. Exposure to bright sun is the cause.
Treatment: None.
Prevention: Shade glass. Damp down adequately, but do not spray the plants at midday.

TOMATO LEAF MOULD

Purplish brown patches appear on the underside of the foliage — the top bears yellowish patches.
Treatment: Remove some of the lower leaves.
Prevention: Ventilate the greenhouse, especially at night. Avoid high temperatures when humidity is high.

TOMATO MOTH

Large green or brown caterpillars tunnel into fruit and stems. Young caterpillars eat holes in leaves.
Treatment: Too late for effective treatment at this stage. Destroy fruit.
Prevention: Spray with insecticidal soap when small caterpillars and holes appear on leaves.

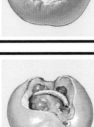

CUCUMBER TROUBLES

ANTHRACNOSE

Pale green sunken spots and patches appear near the blossom end of the fruits. The affected areas turn pink as mould develops over the surface, and eventually they become black and powdery. As the disease spreads the affected fruits turn yellow and die.
Treatment: None. Destroy infected fruit and dust weekly with sulphur.
Prevention: Grow Cucumbers in sterilised soil or compost. Make sure that the greenhouse is adequately ventilated.

CUCUMBER MOSAIC VIRUS

Misshapen small fruits bearing distinctive dark green warts. The surface is either white or yellow with patches or spots of green. The severity of the symptoms increases with the temperature of the greenhouse.
Treatment: None. Healthy plants should not be handled after infected fruit have been cut. However, there is no health risk if virus-affected Cucumbers or Marrows are eaten.
Prevention: Buy healthy seedlings.

GREY MOULD (Botrytis)

A grey furry mould appears on rotting fruit. Botrytis can cause serious losses outdoors in a wet season and under glass if the humidity is high. Stems are frequently infected, the point of entry being a damaged or dead area.
Treatment: Remove and burn infected fruit and leaves to prevent the infection of nearby plants.
Prevention: Avoid overwatering. Chemical sprays are no longer available.

GUMMOSIS

A serious disease of greenhouse Cucumbers grown under wet and cool conditions. Infected fruits develop sunken spots through which oozes an amber-like gum. A dark mould develops on the surface of this gum.
Treatment: Destroy all diseased fruit. Raise the temperature and reduce the humidity.
Prevention: Keep the greenhouse or frame warm and ensure adequate ventilation.

BITTERNESS

If the fruit is normal in appearance then one of the growing conditions is at fault. A sudden drop in temperature or soil moisture and a sudden increase in sunshine or pruning are all common causes. The second type of bitterness is associated with misshapen club-like fruits grown under glass. Here the cause is pollination; remember that male flowers must be removed. This tedious job can be avoided by growing an All-Female variety such as Pepinex. Bitter Cucumbers are generally unusable, but you can try the old practice of cutting the fruit a couple of inches from the blossom end and rubbing the cut surfaces together.

WITHERING OF YOUNG FRUIT

Cucumbers sometimes stop growing when they are only a few inches long and withering spreads back from the tip. Unfortunately there are many possible causes, such as draughts, heavy pruning and the use of fresh farmyard manure. The most likely reason is faulty root action due to poor drainage, overwatering or poor soil preparation. The secret is to maintain steady growth by careful watering. If withering of young fruit does take place, remove the damaged fruit and spray with a foliar feed. For the next week withhold water and ventilate the greenhouse, but keep the floor damp as usual.

PLANT COLLAPSE

There are scores of possible reasons which can account for the death of a plant in the greenhouse or conservatory. The commonest fatal factors are listed below.

● **DRYNESS** No life can survive without water. Many plants can cope with infrequent watering in winter but failure to provide sufficient water during the growing season can soon lead to wilting of the leaves and finally to the death of the plant.

● **OVERWATERING** The most usual cause of plant death in a heated house in winter is overwatering. The leaves of affected plants droop, and the owner thinks they are short of water. So the plants are thoroughly watered and collapse soon follows. It is vital to know how to separate the symptoms of drought and overwatering — see page 84.

● **SUB-MINIMUM TEMPERATURES** Many plants can withstand exposure for a short time to temperatures below the recommended minimum, but sub-zero temperatures will quickly kill a half hardy plant. It is not just a matter of the reading on the thermometer — the effect of a cold night is heightened if the plant is kept under warm or hot conditions during the day. It is often the sudden fluctuation in temperature rather than cold air which causes the damage.

● **DIRECT SUNSHINE** Some plants will quickly succumb if exposed to the direct rays of midsummer sun.

● **HOT AND DRY AIR** This can obviously be a problem in summer — the soil is baked and the roots are killed. It can also be a winter problem, as some plants need a cool resting period when light intensity is low.

● **PESTS AND DISEASES** Most pests and diseases are disfiguring rather than fatal, but some (e.g vine weevil, root rot, botrytis etc) are killers.

CHAPTER 6

CALENDAR

Many greenhouses are used to grow Tomato plants in summer, store a few house plants and produce seedlings in spring, and then little else for the rest of the year. Make your house earn its keep. Study this chapter and then plan for the year ahead — you can start at any time. Use charts like the ones below and mark on them the plants you propose to grow.

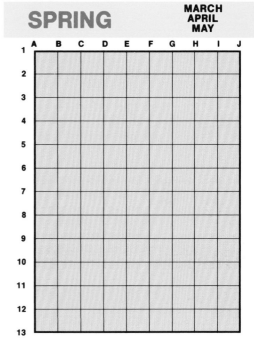

1 box = ½ x ½, 1 x 1 or 2 x 2 ft

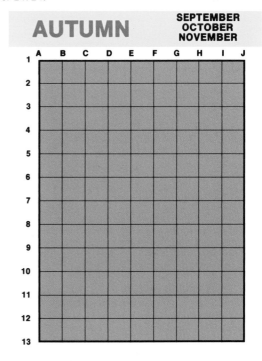

JANUARY

The start of a new year, but it's a slow start to the greenhouse year. The staging is usually at its emptiest — the Christmas pots went into the living room in December and the time for active seed sowing has not yet arrived. Only February is colder and only December has shorter days. Keep the greenhouse dry and reasonably cool and take the opportunity to get things ready for spring. This is a good time to take stock, checking on supplies and on the state of the structure. There are a number of jobs which can be done in January, but nearly all can be left until next month.

General Tasks

It is a good idea to draw up a plan for the coming year during this quiet period. Use the charts on page 99. Do grow more than just Tomatoes and bedding plants, but do not go to the other extreme of a jumble of plants with widely different requirements. Order seeds, composts etc. Check the greenhouse and its equipment. Block up all cracks which can lead to heat loss and draughts, and make sure that broken panes are quickly replaced. Inspect the heaters — paraffin stoves need regular filling and cleaning. Make sure that a max/min thermometer is installed at eye level.

•

Maintain a minimum temperature of 42°–45°F in the cool greenhouse if frost-sensitive plants are present. In a cold house it will be necessary to cover such specimens with matting, straw or newspaper if night frost is forecast. Do not aim for high temperatures — 55°–60°F during the day is high enough.

•

Maintain a dry atmosphere to prevent the onset of disease. Don't splash the floor, staging, leaves or the crowns of plants when watering. Pots should be watered sparingly — plants in flower should be watered more liberally. Water early in the day.

•

Inspect the plants. Keep pot plants which are in flower in a well-lit spot. Remove dead flowers and yellowing or diseased leaves. Spray if grey mould or whitefly has become a problem. Put down slug pellets if tell-tale shiny trails are seen.

•

Some ventilation is necessary, but do take care. The day should be dry and sunny — do not open ventilators on a damp or foggy day. Open ventilators on the side away from the wind — close the ventilators in mid-afternoon so as to conserve the heat of the sun before nightfall.

•

Complete insulation if not carried out last month — see General Tasks for December.

On Display

Arum Lily	Hyacinth
Azalea	Impatiens
Begonia	Iris
Browallia	Jasmine
Calceolaria	Lachenalia
Camellia	Narcissus
Carnation	Pelargonium
Cineraria	Poinsettia
Cyclamen	Primula
Eranthis	Saintpaulia
Euphorbia fulgens	Tulip
Freesia	Solanum capsicastrum

Azalea indica

Camellia japonica

Bulbs

Bring in the bowls of spring-flowering bulbs (Hyacinth, Narcissus, Crocus etc) from the plunge bed outdoors. Choose the ones showing the most growth — leave the other bowls outdoors. Feed with weak liquid fertilizer when you water — take care not to overwater.

Begin planting. Plant Hippeastrum, Gloxinia and Achimenes or wait until early spring.

Dust Gladiolus corms with sulphur if disease spots are present.

Other Ornamentals

Sow seeds of Begonia, Pelargonium and Streptocarpus in a propagator.

Take Fuchsia and Chrysanthemum cuttings.

Pot on seedlings and rooted cuttings of Pelargonium and Fuchsia. Look at the Pelargonium cuttings — remove diseased leaves and throw away plants if the base of the stem has turned black.

Bring in pots of Polyanthus and container-grown Roses from the garden.

Prune Fuchsia and Passion Flower — cut back Charm Chrysanthemum after flowering.

Bedding Plants

Inspect the pots of autumn-sown hardy annuals. Do not water unless the compost is distinctly dry on the surface.

Seed sowing of a number of bedding plants can begin in a heated propagator at the end of the month. Suitable types include Antirrhinum, Calceolaria, Canna, Carnation, Impatiens, Lobelia, Pelargonium and Verbena.

Garden Perennials and Shrubs

Look at the Dahlia tubers — dust with sulphur if disease spots are seen.

You can begin taking Chrysanthemum cuttings this month if growth is advanced. Use new shoots growing from the base (not the sides) of the stems on the stool. The cuttings should be about 3 in. long.

Tomatoes

The usual time for sowing Tomato seed is early March. However, in a heated greenhouse kept at a minimum night temperature of 50°–55°F, seed can be sown in a propagator in the first half of this month and then planted out in early March for a June crop.

Cucumbers No work to be done this month.

Vegetables

Sow French Bean (*Masterpiece* or *Flair*), Lettuce (*Emerald*), Carrot (*Amsterdam Forcing*), Onion (*Ailsa Craig*) and Leek (*Lyon-Prizetaker*). Sow Cauliflower (*Snowball*) and Cabbage (*Hispi*) in a heated propagator.

It is still not too late to pot up and force Chicory or box up and force Rhubarb — see page 78.

Plant up early Potatoes in pots for a May crop.

Harvest Lettuce, Radish, Mushroom, Mustard & Cress, Chicory and Rhubarb.

Fruit

Grape vines can be started into growth at the end of the month if a minimum night temperature of 45°F can be maintained.

Complete the planting of Peach, Nectarine and Apricot. If Peaches or Nectarines are to be grown in pots, make sure that they are grown on dwarf rootstocks. Keep established plants cool and well-ventilated.

Bring pots of Strawberry into the greenhouse — keep in a well-lit spot at 45°–55°F.

FEBRUARY

Both day length and jobs to be done increase this month, although the temperature outdoors is at its lowest ebb. Seed sowing begins in earnest — bedding plants which like a long time to establish are sown now and so are vegetables which are to be planted outdoors in cloche-warmed soil. There are Chrysanthemum and Dahlia cuttings to take, some potted shrubs to top dress and others to start into growth. It is still too early to sow Tomato seed for the cold house and it is not yet time for sowing Cucumber. The season has started, but the busy months are still to come.

General Tasks

Lengthening days mean that the frequency of watering should be increased slightly compared with December and January, but you will still have to take care. Throughout the whole of the November–February period the soil should be kept on the dry side and water should be kept off the leaves and crowns. Watering from below is recommended whenever possible. This calls for placing the pots in a bowl of water and leaving them there until the surface of the compost glistens. Remove the pots and allow to drain before returning them to their growing quarters. When watering from above put the spout of the watering can under the leaves and try to do this task before midday.

•

Cover tender plants on cold nights if you can't maintain a minimum temperature of 42°F. Try to avoid wide fluctuations — aim to keep the air within a fairly narrow (42°–60°F) temperature range.

•

Keep the atmosphere dry. Ventilate on bright days, following the instructions listed under General Tasks for January.

•

Inspect the plants. Keep plants which are in flower in a well-lit spot. Remove dead flowers and yellowing leaves. Spray if pests or diseases appear.

•

Make sure that pots and seed trays are sterilised before use — wash with a plant-safe garden disinfectant. Check that insulation is intact.

•

Label all seed trays clearly after sowing — don't trust to your memory. Remember to sow thinly in damp (not wet) compost and to cover the container until germination has taken place.

On Display

Azalea	Freesia
Begonia	Hyacinth
Calceolaria	Impatiens
Camellia	Iris reticulata
Carnation	Jasmine
Chionodoxa	Lapageria
Cineraria	Mimosa
Clivia	Narcissus
Columnea	Pelargonium
Crocus	Primula
Cyclamen	Saintpaulia
Dianthus	Tulip

Cineraria hybrid

Calceolaria herbeohybrida

Bulbs

Bring in the remainder of the bowls of spring-flowering bulbs from the plunge bed outdoors. Feed with weak liquid fertilizer when you water — take care not to overwater.

Place bowls under staging after flowers have faded.

Plant Begonia, Hippeastrum, Gloxinia, Gloriosa and Achimenes in a cool greenhouse.

Other Ornamentals

If you have a propagator a number of pot plants can be sown this month — Abutilon, Begonia, Celosia, Coleus, Streptocarpus, Saintpaulia, Pelargonium, Schizanthus and Solanum capsicastrum.

Take cuttings of Pelargonium, Carnation and Lorraine Begonias.

Pot on Ferns, Palms, Pelargonium, Fuchsia, Coleus and Schizanthus.

Prune Fuchsia, Bougainvillea and Pelargonium.

Dead-head Azaleas and Cyclamen after flowering.

Bedding Plants

Pot on the autumn-sown hardy annuals.

A wide range of half hardy annuals and other bedding plants can be sown this month rather than waiting until March. As a general rule small-seeded annuals are sown before the ones which have large seeds. Examples include Alyssum, Ageratum, Antirrhinum, Calceolaria, Celosia, Lobelia, Nicotiana, Pelargonium, Sweet Pea, Stocks and Verbena.

Garden Perennials and Shrubs

Continue taking cuttings of Chrysanthemums. It is now time to start Dahlia tubers into growth in order to produce new shoots for cuttings. Box up the tubers in a damp peat/sand mix. Place in a well-lit spot and cut the shoots when they are 2–3 in. high. Propagate in the way described on page 66.

Bring the pots of dormant Hydrangea, Heliotrope and Fuchsia on to the staging. Bring them into growth by watering and exposing to maximum light.

Take cuttings of Heliotrope and Fuchsia.

Top dress potted shrubs — remove the top inch of compost and replace with fresh material.

Tomatoes

Sow seed now if you failed to do so last month for planting in a cool greenhouse in late March or April.

Cucumbers   No work to be done this month.

Vegetables

Sow seeds for planting outdoors later in soil which has been covered with cloches. Included here are Broad Bean, early Pea, early Lettuce, Cauliflower, Carrot, Cabbage, Brussels Sprout, Onion, Parsnip and early Turnip.

Seeds can also be sown for growing to maturity in the greenhouse — examples are Lettuce and Aubergine.

Pot up and force Chicory.

Harvest Lettuce, Radish, Mushroom, Mustard & Cress, Chicory and Rhubarb.

Fruit

Sow Melon seed if heat can be provided — a minimum temperature of 60°F will be needed for the seedlings.

Bring potted Strawberry runners into the greenhouse. Grow in 5 in. pots, growing bags or Strawberry pots.

Train Grape vines which started to grow last month. Hand pollinate flowers — see page 106.

MARCH

March is the start of the busy season. Most bedding and greenhouse pot plants can now be sown. Some seeds like Tomato, Melon and Cucumber need a heated propagator — others such as Antirrhinum, Lobelia and Petunia do not. Softwood cuttings can now be taken and the seedlings produced by last month's sowings need to be pricked out. Established plants begin to grow actively, so cultural practices change. Watering now takes place on a more regular basis and damping down of the floor and staging should start in the middle of the month.

General Tasks

Wide temperature fluctuations can be a problem this month — a bright sunny day at the end of the month can result in serious overheating. Aim to keep the air at 45°–65°F — this calls for heating at night and ventilating plus damping down on cloudless days.

•

Feed growing plants with a liquid fertilizer — do not overfeed young plants. Use a balanced rather than a high-potash formula for leaf growth — use a high-potash feed for flowering plants.

•

Seedlings need good light, but young ones will need shade from the midday sun.

•

Insects start to become a problem this month — keep watch for greenfly, whitefly and red spider mite. Spray with a greenhouse insecticide such as derris or permethrin before the problem gets out of hand.

•

Damping off is a soil-borne disease of seedlings — see page 95. It is much less of a problem these days with the introduction of sterile composts, but it still occasionally appears. This may be due to incomplete sterilisation of a soil-based compost, but it is much more likely to be caused by overwatering, use of dirty seed trays or sowing too thickly. Act swiftly — remove all toppled seedlings and water the rest with Cheshunt Compound solution.

•

Keep pots of growing plants damp but not soaking wet. Capillary matting is a great help — see page 12.

•

Flowers of Peach, Nectarine and Strawberry must be pollinated by hand as pollinating insects are absent. See page 106 for instructions.

•

Now is the time to prepare hanging baskets for setting out in late May or June.

On Display

Begonia	Jasmine
Camellia	Mimosa
Carnation	Muscari
Cineraria	Narcissus
Clivia	Oxalis
Crossandra	Pelargonium
Cuphea	Primula
Cyclamen	Saintpaulia
Freesia	Schizanthus
Hippeastrum	Sparmannia
Hyacinth	Tulip
Impatiens	Veltheimia

Primula obconica

Schizanthus hybrida

Bulbs

Once the flowers have faded, plant spring-flowering bulbs outdoors — do not keep for planting in bowls next year.

Start the following bulbous types into growth — Achimenes, Tuberous Begonia, Caladium, Canna, Gloriosa, Gloxinia and Hippeastrum. Plant in trays and then pot on into small containers when shoots appear.

Sow Freesia seed.

Other Ornamentals

Pot on autumn-sown plants into 5 in. pots — stake if necessary. Prick out seedlings raised from seed sown last month.

Sow seed of the types listed last month. Additional ones for March include Asparagus Fern, Cacti, Campanula isophylla, Capsicum annuum and Grevillea robusta.

Bring overwintered established plants into growth by increasing watering and bringing into full light.

Pot on Regal Pelargonium. Cut back Poinsettia when flowers have faded — keep dry until June.

Take cuttings of Coleus, Fuchsia and Pelargonium.

Bedding Plants

Prick out seedlings raised from seed sown last month.

Most bedding plants can be sown this month. Use last month's list — additional ones include Begonia semperflorens, Callistephus, Campanula, Iberis, Kochia, Ornamental Maize, Petunia and Salvia.

Start overwintered plants into growth — see Other Ornamentals above.

Garden Perennials and Shrubs

Continue to strike Chrysanthemum and Dahlia cuttings — pot on rooted cuttings which were taken earlier in the year. Pinch out the growing tips of rooted cuttings of Chrysanthemum when they are about 6 in. high — this will induce bushiness.

Plant Dahlia tubers not used for producing cuttings. Put them in a damp peat/sand mixture until buds have formed. Then cut up the root into planting pieces, each with at least one stout tuber and one stout shoot at the top. Plant in multipurpose compost.

Tomatoes

Sow seed in a propagator for planting in a cold house in early May or for planting outdoors in late May or early June. The ideal germination temperature is 60°–65°F.

Prick out seedlings from a February sowing into 3 in. peat pots. Plant out seedlings from a December/January sowing when 6–8 in. high into growing bags or pots.

Cucumbers

Sow seed in a propagator for planting in a heated greenhouse in April.

Vegetables

A wide variety of seeds can be sown for planting out in the garden. See last month's list — extra ones include Courgette, Celery, Runner Bean, Sweet Corn, Leek and a number of herbs such as Parsley.

Seed can also be sown for growing to maturity in the greenhouse — examples include French Bean, Carrot, Lettuce, Capsicum, Aubergine and Beetroot.

Harvest Lettuce, Radish, Mushroom, Mustard & Cress and Chicory.

Fruit

Sow Melon and Cape Gooseberry.

Peach, Nectarine, Grape and perhaps Strawberry are in flower this month — hand pollinate as described in the General Tasks for April.

APRIL

Spring-flowering pot plants and bulbs in bowls should now provide an abundance of colour. Days are getting warmer, which means ventilation and damping down are necessary when the weather is sunny. There is lots of work to do. Seedlings must be pricked out before they become too large and cuttings must be potted on when new growth appears. This is the usual time to repot established plants and both Tomatoes and Cucumbers now need regular attention. Bedding plants must be prepared for their move outdoors at the end of next month or in early June.

General Tasks

High day temperatures can be a problem this month. Regular ventilation is essential. Open up the roof ventilators — don't use the bottom ones until the outside air gets warmer. Try to keep the greenhouse within the 45°–70°F range.

•

Some shading will be necessary in cloudless, sunny weather. This may mean coating part of the south-facing glass with shading paint or covering small seedlings, newly-potted plants and rooted cuttings with newspaper during the heat of the day.

•

Check plants regularly to see if watering is needed. You may have to water actively-growing plants several times a week.

•

Keep watch for pests. Greenfly, whitefly, vine weevil and red spider mite are all active now. So are slugs, which can quickly destroy a trayful of seedlings.

•

Regular feeding of growing plants is essential. Follow the instructions on the package or bottle carefully. Little and often is the general rule — overfeeding can cause distortion, leaf damage or root scorch.

•

The need for night heating is reduced this month, but do take care. Young growth is especially susceptible to low temperatures — always ensure that the heaters are working whenever a frost is forecast. However, severe and prolonged frosts are not likely in the South, which means that insulation can now be removed as maximum illumination is essential.

•

Hand pollinate fruit. This calls for transferring pollen with a soft brush or a ball of cotton wool — do this work at midday. Repeat the procedure for several days to ensure success.

On Display

Saintpaulia ionantha

Stephanotis floribunda

Early Annuals
Azalea
Calceolaria
Carnation
Cineraria
Clivia
Coleus
Freesia
Fuchsia
Hippeastrum
Impatiens
Jasmine
Lantana
Pelargonium
Primula
Rose
Saintpaulia
Schizanthus
Schlumbergera
Stephanotis
Streptocarpus
Streptosolen
Tibouchina
Tulip

Bulbs

Plant Tuberous Begonia and Gloxinia (hollow side up) in trays of compost. Plant Canna and Gloriosa in pots.

Reduce watering when Cyclamen flowers fade. Remove and dry the corms — store for planting in autumn.

Other Ornamentals

Sow seeds of the types listed for February and March if this was not done at the recommended time. Prick out seedlings raised from seed sown last month.

Bring Hydrangea into growth by providing extra watering and warmth. Take stem cuttings.

Take cuttings of Pelargonium and Fuchsia if not done last month. Pinch out growing tips to induce bushiness.

April is the popular time for repotting house plants and greenhouse pot plants. Follow the rules on page 87. With some types clumps can be divided when repotting.

Bedding Plants

Sow seeds of the types listed for February and March if this was not done at the recommended time. Sow Zinnia, Nemesia and Marigold.

Prick out seedlings raised from seed sown last month. Begin hardening off for planting outdoors at the end of next month.

Garden Perennials and Shrubs

Plant up Dahlia tubers if this was not done last month.

Pot on rooted cuttings. Take softwood cuttings.

Tomatoes

Plant out seedlings in a cold house — the Tomato plants should be about 6–8 in. high at this stage and the flowers of the first truss should be beginning to open. Seedlings which have not yet reached this stage should be potted on into 3 in. peat pots for planting out in May. Plants destined for planting outdoors in late May should be hardened off this month.

Tomatoes in growing bags need regular and frequent watering — follow the instructions carefully. Feed with liquid tomato food — use the amount and timing stated on the package.

Pinch out side shoots. Mist plants at midday and tap the supports occasionally to aid pollination and fruit set.

Cucumbers

Plant out seedlings in a heated greenhouse before the end of the month. Sow seed to produce Cucumber seedlings for planting out in a cold house at the end of May.

Vegetables

Sow Marrow, Courgette, Runner Bean, Celery, Celeriac and French Bean for planting out in the garden at the end of next month or early June.

Plant Capsicum and Aubergine seedlings in growing bags.

Harvest Carrot, Lettuce, Radish, Mushroom, Mustard & Cress, Potato and Chicory.

Fruit

Plant March-sown Melon — sow seed now if this job was not done last month.

Start Grape vine into growth in a cold greenhouse — do this by increasing water and closing down ventilators.

Hand pollinate flowers as they appear. Thinning of young fruit of Grape, Peach, Nectarine and Strawberry may be necessary — do this in stages. Water liberally and regularly once fruit has started to swell.

Harvest Strawberry.

MAY

Shortage of space is often a problem this month. There are trays and pots of bedding plants, vegetables, shrubs and pot plants everywhere, and on the floor there are growing bags filled with Tomatoes and Cucumbers. The answer is to transfer bedding plants and vegetables into a cold frame to harden off for their move into the open garden at the end of the month. Much less heat will be required to keep the cool house above the minimum temperature, but do not put the heater away. Remember to space out pots so that fresh air will circulate round them.

General Tasks

Between November and April the major temperature problem was to keep the atmosphere above freezing point on cold nights. Now the main task is to keep the temperature of the air below 75°–80°F during warm and sunny spells.

•

Shading becomes important. Use blinds if you have them — otherwise cover the glass with shading paint. Only the south-facing panes need to be treated at this stage — rub off if weather turns dull and cool.

•

In most parts of the country a heater will no longer be required during the day. But night frosts are still a possibility, so don't switch off at this stage.

•

Ventilation is vital this month. Open bottom or side ventilators as well as roof ones if the temperature is over 75°F — open the door if necessary.

•

Damp down the floors and staging in the morning when the weather is sunny. This water has two roles — the air temperature is lowered when it evaporates and the relative humidity is raised. See page 82 for more details.

•

Plants are now actively growing but roots in pots or growing bags cannot extend to seek out extra food as in the open garden. Regular feeding is therefore required — little and often is the golden rule. For general purposes use a balanced formula with nitrogen, phosphates and potash in roughly equal proportions. To stimulate leaf growth use a high-nitrogen feed — for plants in flower or fruit use a high-potash fertilizer.

•

Regular and thorough watering is essential — some plants will need daily attention. You must check the dryness of the compost every day if automatic watering is not installed.

On Display

Achimenes	Hoya
Annuals	Impatiens
Begonia	Lily
Bougainvillea	Medinilla
Calceolaria	Pelargonium
Carnation	Primula
Celosia	Saintpaulia
Cineraria	Schizanthus
Clianthus	Spathiphyllum
Coleus	Stephanotis
Dianthus	Streptocarpus
Fuchsia	Zantedeschia

Achimenes hybrida

Impatiens wallerana

Bulbs

Plant Begonia, Canna and Gloxinia.

Reduce watering of Arum Lily, Freesia, Lachenalia and Nerine once the flowers have faded.

Other Ornamentals

It is now time to sow the seeds of plants for winter display in the home. Included here are Asparagus Fern, Calceolaria, Cineraria, Primula and Schizanthus.

Prick out seedlings raised from seed last month.

Take cuttings of house plants. Cuttings of Azalea, Coleus and many succulents are taken this month, but July and August are the usual months for striking Pelargonium cuttings.

Pot on rooted cuttings.

Bedding Plants

The main activity this month is hardening off. This calls for moving the seedlings into a cooler and fresher environment to get them used to the conditions they will have to face outdoors. This is done in several stages — the ideal steps are to place the trays in the coolest part of the greenhouse, then into a cold frame and finally a sheltered part of the garden for a few days before planting out.

Make up hanging baskets and tubs for moving out of doors next month.

Sow Viola and Pansy for bedding out in autumn.

Garden Perennials and Shrubs

Plant out rooted Chrysanthemum cuttings at the beginning of the month. Rooted Dahlia cuttings are planted out at the end of the month or in June. Harden them off during May to prepare the plants for outdoor conditions.

Tomatoes

In the cold greenhouse finish planting into growing bags seedlings which have just started to flower.

Established plants are now growing actively. Feed regularly once the first fruits have started to swell and make sure that the compost is never allowed to dry out.

Train the stems up the vertical string. Remember to turn the twine around the stem, not the other way around.

Tap the supports or flowers daily to aid pollination. Pinch out the side shoots which appear where the leaves join the stem.

Cucumbers

Plant seedlings into growing bags in a cold greenhouse at the end of this month. Water carefully at first, keeping the compost damp but not wet. Increase watering when the plants start to grow actively — 2 pints a day per growing bag may be needed when the plants are in full growth.

Train the stems up vertical supports and pinch out unwanted growth — see Cucumber notes for June.

Vegetables

This is a time for cropping rather than sowing. Harvest Beetroot, Carrot, French Bean, Lettuce, Mushroom, Mustard & Cress and Potato.

Fruit

Plant Melon sown last month. Established plants need warm and humid conditions — damp down regularly.

Hand pollinate Melon and Grape vine when flowers appear. Thinning of Peach, Nectarine and Grape may be necessary — do this in stages using The Fruit Expert as your guide.

Pruning and training of Peach, Nectarine, Grape and Melon must be carried out this month. Don't guess what to do — follow carefully the rules set out in The Fruit Expert.

Continue to harvest Strawberry.

JUNE

There is a marked change this month. Most of the pots and trays disappear in June as the vegetable seedlings, bedding plants, summer-hardy pot plants, tender shrubs, rooted perennials and hanging baskets are moved to their outdoor quarters. Tomatoes and Cucumbers now come into their own and there is much work to do — picking of the first fruits starts in the heated greenhouse. Heaters are switched off this month except in the colder part of the country — clean and overhaul heating equipment now instead of waiting until the onset of winter.

General Tasks

Sun scorch can be a problem this month — growth slows down, flowers lose their colour and leaves are scorched. Shading is the answer — use a proprietary paint.

•

Regular ventilation now becomes essential — open all ventilators and the door as required to keep the temperature down. Ventilation during the morning and evening should be carried out on warm days and it may be necessary to open a ventilator on warm nights. Automatic ventilation is a great aid, especially if you take long holidays and there is nobody to look after the greenhouse when you are away. Install it this month if you intend to buy one — do not wait any longer.

•

Check watering requirements daily. Some plants may need water twice a day. Feed at regular intervals.

•

You must damp down the greenhouse regularly by spraying the floor and staging in the morning or early afternoon. Apart from moistening the air and cooling the greenhouse there is the added benefit of discouraging red spider mite which can be a menace at this time of the year.

•

Plants destined for the garden are moved out this month — make sure that the danger of frost has gone before putting out half hardy plants and also make sure that greenhouse-grown specimens have had a period of hardening off before the move into the garden. Some greenhouse plants can be stood out in the open garden during the June–early October period — this improves their health and gives you more space under glass.

•

Clean up after the big move outdoors. Do not leave dirty pots, discarded plants or dead leaves laying about.

On Display

Achimenes	Gloxinia
Annuals	Hippeastrum
Begonia	Hydrangea
Bougainvillea	Hymenocallis
Caladium	Impatiens
Callistemon	Lily
Carnation	Pachystachys
Celosia	Pelargonium
Clivia	Saintpaulia
Cobaea	Stephanotis
Eucomis	Strelitzia
Fuchsia	Streptocarpus

Streptocarpus hybrida

Hydrangea macrophylla

Bulbs

Sow Cyclamen — pot on seedlings raised earlier.

Reduce watering of Arum Lily when flowering has finished — dry and store bulbs.

Other Ornamentals

Continue sowing seeds of plants which will provide a winter and early spring display. Add Impatiens, Grevillea and Zinnia to last month's list. You can also sow seed of many exotic house plants such as Strelitzia at this time, but only if you are willing to wait several years for the flowering stage.

Take semi-ripe or leaf cuttings of popular pot plants such as Bougainvillea, Oleander, Passiflora, Streptocarpus, Begonia rex, Saintpaulia, Ivy and Philodendron.

Rooted cuttings of Pelargonium, Fuchsia, Carnation etc should now be in their final pots for autumn display.

Cut back Regal Pelargonium — stop Chrysanthemum stems.

Move summer-hardy types such as Carnation, Chrysanthemum, Zygocactus etc outdoors.

Support lax growth with canes — dead-head faded flowers.

Bedding Plants

Move summer-flowering plants into the garden. Place hanging baskets outdoors. Prick out Viola and Pansy which were sown last month.

Garden Perennials and Shrubs

This is a good time to take cuttings of a number of garden perennials such as Gypsophila, Delphinium, Pinks, Lupin, Penstemon, Linum etc.

Sow hardy perennials now if you intend to raise them from seed.

Move out tender shrubs such as Citrus which have overwintered in the greenhouse. Also move out summer-hardy greenhouse shrubs such as Camellia and Hydrangea once flowering has finished.

Tomatoes

Continue to follow the rules laid down for May. Regular watering and feeding become even more important and so does the regular watch for pests and diseases.

Train the stems up the vertical supports — do this job in the morning. At midday tap the supports or mist the flowers gently to aid pollination. Continue to remove side shoots and cut off yellow leaves which are immediately below a fruit truss.

In a heated greenhouse the first fruits will be due for picking. See page 72 for instructions on how to tell when the fruit is ready for harvesting.

Cucumbers

In the cold house finish planting seedlings into growing bags.

Continue to follow the rules laid down for May. Regular watering and feeding are essential. Daily damping down is necessary. The tip of each side shoot should be pinched out at 2 leaves beyond a female flower. Pinch out tips of flowerless side shoots when 2 ft long. Remove all male flowers.

Picking starts this month in a heated greenhouse.

Vegetables

Sow French Bean and Mustard & Cress.

Harvest Beetroot, Carrot, French Bean, Lettuce, Mustard & Cress, Parsley, Radish and Mushroom.

Fruit

Water, feed and train Peach, Nectarine, Grape and Melon. Hand pollinate Melon.

Thin Grape bunches — see The Fruit Expert for details.

JULY

Often the hottest month of the year, and one of the busiest in the greenhouse. Watering is a tiresome job which has to be done every day — so is the constant opening and closing of the ventilators. Still, this must be done if you do not have automatic systems installed — Tomatoes and Cucumbers can seriously suffer if subjected to one or two days' dryness, and a fully closed-down greenhouse in the middle of a heat wave can lead to damage or death of many plants. Holidays are a problem — you will need a friend or neighbour to take care of the plants in the greenhouse.

General Tasks

The major problem is keeping the temperature low enough during a hot spell. Ventilation now becomes vitally important and will be necessary at night as well as during the day. Opening all the ventilators and propping the door open may not be enough. Damping down and shading will help, but the answer may be to install an extractor fan or to bring in an electric fan to provide forced ventilation.

•

As in June sun scorch can be damaging. Some form of shading is essential for many plants — flowering pot plants, rooted cuttings, Cucumbers in flower etc. Inside blinds are difficult to use when tall-growing plants such as Tomatoes and Cucumbers are present. A shading paint is an easier and less expensive answer.

•

Compost must be felt every day and watering carried out without fail. Daily damping down is needed.

•

Keep watch for pests and diseases. Red spider mite, greenfly, whitefly, thrips, grey mould and mildews are the major headaches — spray promptly if you see them, but read the rules for safe spraying (page 93) before you begin. Hang up yellow greenhouse fly catchers. Birds and egg-laying butterflies entering through open ventilators and door can pose a problem.

•

Routine feeding is necessary as most plants are now growing vigorously. A liquid feed at fortnightly intervals is suitable as a basic treatment, but fruit-bearing plants such as Cucumbers and Tomatoes need feeding every 7–10 days.

•

July is a good time for taking cuttings — roots usually form quickly in the warm conditions.

On Display

Achimenes	Heliotrope
Begonia	Hibiscus
Cacti	Hoya
Calceolaria	Impatiens
Callistemon	Ipomoea
Campanula	Ixora
Canna	Nerium
Carnation	Passion Flower
Celosia	Pelargonium
Fuchsia	Saintpaulia
Gloriosa	Schizanthus
Haemanthus	Streptocarpus

Celosia plumosa

Heliotrope hybrida

Bulbs

Summer-flowering bulbs make a fine show at this time of the year — Lilies, Gloxinia, Achimenes, Begonia, Canna, Gloriosa etc. When flowering has finished remove the seed pods before they develop so that all the energy is diverted away from the pods and into building up the underground storage organs.

Plant up Cyclamen and Freesia.

Other Ornamentals

Sow Stocks and Mignonette for winter scent and colour. Sow Coleus, Cineraria, Calceolaria, Schizanthus and Primula for a bright display next spring.

Prick out and pot up seedlings of winter-flowering annuals sown in May and June.

Pot on Fuchsia and Pelargonium.

Take cuttings of Regal Pelargonium, Saintpaulia, Impatiens, Coleus, Fuchsia and foliage house plants.

Stake and train climbing plants as necessary. Disbud large-flowering Begonia and Carnation for maximum display.

Move Solanum capsicastrum outdoors to stimulate berry formation.

Shade pot plants in flower.

Move out summer-hardy shrubs which were not transferred to the garden last month. It is important to move pot-grown Roses outdoors — others which should be strengthened by a stay outdoors include Camellia, Azalea, Jasmine and Solanum.

Bedding Plants   No work to be done this month.

Garden Perennials and Shrubs

Cuttings of many garden shrubs can be taken this month — use semi-ripe wood and dip the ends in rooting hormone before inserting in the compost. Examples include Cotoneaster, Forsythia, Hydrangea, Philadelphus, Pyracantha and Weigela.

Tomatoes

Continue feeding, watering, damping down and ventilating as noted last month.

The plants will now be in full fruit and picking will be necessary nearly every day. Remove side shoots as they appear, but only remove the lower leaves if the greenhouse is well shaded.

Remove the tip at 2 leaves above the top truss when the plant reaches the top of the greenhouse or when 7 trusses have set. Top dress plants growing in pots with fresh compost.

Cucumbers

The plants are now in full fruit — see page 73 for instructions on how to tell when the fruit is ready for harvesting.

Pinch out the growing point when the main stem reaches the roof.

Continue watering, damping down and ventilating as noted for May and June. Feed regularly with a tomato fertilizer.

Vegetables

Sow Parsley and Mustard & Cress. Potatoes should be set out for sprouting, ready for planting next month for a Christmas crop.

Harvest Lettuce, Radish, Capsicum, Mustard & Cress and Parsley.

Fruit

Train, feed and water as for June.

Thin Grape bunches — vines prefer a dry atmosphere.

Support Melon fruits with netting. Peg down Strawberry runners to produce new plants for next season.

Harvest Melon, Peach and Nectarine.

AUGUST

A well-planned greenhouse is an attractive sight in August — staging filled with colourful pot plants and a background of climbers, fruit, Tomatoes and Cucumbers. The problem of keeping the temperature down still remains, but this warmth means that the pots can be stood outdoors without coming to any harm. Because of this, August is often recommended as a painting and repair month, the plants being returned once the work is over. Use a water-based and not a solvent-type wood preservative for treating a wooden greenhouse.

General Tasks

Watch for grey mould — if leaves, fruit and flowers are attacked you should destroy affected parts, spray with a systemic fungicide and improve ventilation. Make sure that the plants are not splashed in the evening and never leave old leaves and fruit laying about. Dead-head flowering plants regularly to extend the flowering season.

•

Ventilation remains a vital task. Open all the ventilators and the door on warm days — during the night open only the roof ventilator.

•

Continue with the chore of regular watering. Daily soakings will still be needed for vigorous plants in small containers.

•

Routine feeding of actively-growing plants remains a necessity. Use a potash-rich feed to prolong and improve fruiting and flowering — leave 10–14 days between feeds. Holidays can be a problem — without a helpful neighbour you will need automatic ventilating and watering equipment.

•

This is a good month for taking cuttings for plants in the garden. There are three groups — alpines such as Armeria, shrubs such as Weigela and half hardy types such as Pelargonium. Don't take many more cuttings than you will be able to handle, but always strike a few extra as failures do occur.

•

The annual round of planting bulbs begins this month — make sure you have an adequate supply of pots, bowls and bulb fibre.

On Display

Abutilon	Impatiens
Achimenes	Ipomoea
Allamanda	Lantana
Anthurium	Lily
Begonia	Passion Flower
Campanula	Pelargonium
Campsis	Plumbago
Canna	Saintpaulia
Carnation	Schizanthus
Celosia	Streptocarpus
Fuchsia	Thunbergia
Heliotrope	Vallota

Begonia multiflora

Campanula isophylla

Bulbs

Sow Cyclamen seed for flowering at Christmastime next year.

Plant up Freesia, Lachenalia, Nerium, Vallota, Cyclamen, Arum Lily and Iris reticulata.

At the end of the month plant up specially prepared bulbs of Hyacinth and Narcissus for blooming at Christmas.

After flowering dry off and store Hippeastrum, Achimenes, Gloxinia and Begonia.

Other Ornamentals

A key job this month is to sow a variety of hardy and half hardy annuals to provide a spring display in the greenhouse. Choose from Schizanthus, Nemesia, Phlox, Clarkia, Primula, Salpiglossis, Cineraria, Larkspur and Sweet Scabious.

Prick out seedlings from July sowing — pot up rooted cuttings.

Take cuttings of greenhouse plants and climbers if these were not taken last month.

Pot up Cineraria and Primula for Christmas flowering.

Prune back climbing plants if the shade effect on other plants is becoming a problem.

Take cuttings of alpines.

Bedding Plants

Take cuttings from the tender bedding plants growing in the garden — Pelargonium, Fuchsia etc. The rooted cuttings are overwintered in the greenhouse for bedding out in late May-early June next year.

Garden Perennials and Shrubs

Continue to take cuttings this month of outdoor shrubs. Add Hebe, Escallonia, Laurus, Kerria, Hypericum, Euonymus, Erica, Cytisus and Lavender to last month's list.

Tomatoes

Follow the cultural practices noted under May, June and July. Regular watering is vital — irregular watering reduces yield, produces cracked fruit and induces blossom end rot. Ventilation is needed to keep the temperature below 80°F.

Check that the wires and other supports are strong enough to support the weight of the plants and crop.

Never leave fruit on the ground — moulds will develop and the growing crop can be affected.

Continue with a regular feeding programme. Follow the manufacturer's instructions — choose a liquid fertilizer with which you feed every time you water.

Cucumbers

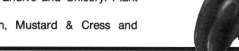

Continue to water, damp down, ventilate and feed as described for May, June and July. You must feed regularly — use a tomato fertilizer every 2 weeks.

Vegetables

Sow Winter Lettuce (*Kwiek* or *Marmer*), Carrot, Endive and Chicory. Plant sprouted Potatoes in tubs.

Harvest Lettuce, Capsicum, Aubergine, Radish, Mustard & Cress and Mushroom.

Fruit

Water and feed Grape vine — use a tomato fertilizer.

Reduce watering of Melon once the fruits have started to ripen.

Pot on rooted Strawberry runners — stand the pots outdoors for bringing into the greenhouse in January.

Harvest Melon, Grape, Nectarine, Peach and Apricot.

SEPTEMBER

Days are shorter and nights are colder — the first days of autumn arrive this month. Many plants will still be actively growing, but the colourful summer display declines as the month progresses. Now is the time to start bringing in frost-sensitive plants from the garden and to prepare for the coming winter. Check the heating system — you may need to use it if there are early frosts. The Cucumber season finishes in September and most Tomato plants are removed — September is a good month for cleaning and disinfecting the greenhouse.

General Tasks

Temperature has to be carefully controlled this month. In an Indian summer you will have to open up all the ventilators and perhaps the door to avoid overheating, but during a cold snap all the ventilators should be closed. Aim to keep the temperature in the 50°–70°F range — close down the ventilators in early evening to retain some of the sun's warmth overnight.

•

Damping down as well as ventilation are reduced this month. Only spray the floor and staging on warm days, and even then make sure that the job is completed by midday.

•

Compost stays moist longer as temperatures fall — growth becomes less active. Reduce the frequency of watering accordingly. Keep watch for fungal diseases which tend to appear this month.

•

Remove shading in late September — maximum illumination is now more important than heat control, but maintain some form of shading in areas where shade-lovers such as ferns are present.

•

There may be a gap between clearing out the Tomatoes and Cucumbers and bringing in the frost-sensitive plants from outside. This may be at the end of this month or the beginning of October, and it is an excellent opportunity to fumigate the structure with a fungicidal smoke.

•

Don't wait too long before bringing in tender specimens —one sharp frost may kill them. Make sure that the pots of Chrysanthemum, Fuchsia etc are free from pests before the move indoors.

On Display

Abutilon	Habranthus
Aphelandra	Impatiens
Begonia	Ipomoea
Beloperone	Lapageria
Bougainvillea	Passion Flower
Capsicum	Pelargonium
Carnation	Petunia
Cobaea	Plumbago
Exacum	Saintpaulia
Fuchsia	Stephanotis
Gloriosa	Streptocarpus
Gloxinia	Thunbergia

Bougainvillea glabra

Pelargonium hortorum

Bulbs

Finish potting up prepared Hyacinth and Narcissus bulbs for Christmas flowering. Keep the bowls in a dark, frost-free shed or plunge them under a layer of peat or ashes outdoors.

Plant up Freesia, Lily, Cyclamen, Lachenalia, Hippeastrum and Arum Lily.

Finish sowing Cyclamen seed for flowering at Christmastime next year.

Other Ornamentals

Pot up the annuals sown last month for spring display — it is still not too late to sow seeds if you failed to do so in August.

Bring in pot plants which have stood outdoors over the summer months. There is no great hurry if the weather is mild, but you should complete the task before the first frosts arrive. Plants involved include Chrysanthemum, Carnation, Azalea, Primula, Cineraria, Camellia, Zygocactus and Solanum capsicastrum.

Disbud Chrysanthemum.

Prune back climbers which have finished flowering.

Bedding Plants

Take cuttings of frost-sensitive bedding plants growing in the garden to provide material for planting out next year. Take cuttings of Fuchsia varieties which are recommended for training as standards.

Plants such as Pelargonium, Heliotrope, Canna and Fuchsia which have not been used for cuttings should be dug and potted up. These plants are kept cool and on the dry side over the winter months, prior to bedding out again next year.

Sow hardy annuals such as Sweet Pea and Pansy for spring bedding in the garden.

Garden Perennials and Shrubs

Begin to bring in the tubs of tender shrubs and trees (e.g Orange and Lemon) which have stood outdoors throughout the summer months. Timing depends on beating the arrival of the first frosts.

September is a good month for taking cuttings of evergreens. Some types are difficult to propagate.

Tomatoes

Despite the cooler days it is as vital as ever to make sure that the compost never dries out. Ventilate to keep the temperature below 80°F on warm days and damp down as necessary.

Continue to pick fruit regularly. Remove leaves which are covering ripening fruits and never leave discarded Tomatoes laying about.

Cropping can continue until October but picking often stops at the end of this month. Place any remaining fruit on the windowsill to ripen. Remove old plants, growing bags, pots etc promptly — dead leaves encourage diseases which can affect other greenhouse plants.

Cucumbers

The season is drawing to a close — the plants are cleared at the end of the month. Until then water regularly, damp down on warm days and pick regularly.

Vegetables

Sow Carrot, Lettuce, Radish, Endive and Mustard & Cress.

Prick out Lettuce.

Harvest Capsicum, Aubergine, Radish, Mustard & Cress and Mushroom.

Fruit

Harvest Melon and Grape. Judging the right time to pick Grapes is not straightforward —the bunches must be left on the vine for a week or two or even a couple of months after the fruit appears ripe. See The Fruit Expert for details.

OCTOBER

There is much less work to do in the greenhouse now that the summer crops and summer heat have gone. No more daily waterings, no more constant syringing of floor and walls and no more Tomatoes and Cucumbers to look after. Chrysanthemums and Perpetual-flowering Carnations provide most of the colour and it is now time to start worrying about heating and insulation. The annual clean-up must take place in the September–November period — early October is an excellent time for this task. Complete the clean-up before bringing in the frost-sensitive plants for winter protection.

General Tasks

Heating now starts in the cool house — maintain a minimum night temperature of 42°–45°F. If frost is forecast you may have to protect tender specimens with matting, straw or newspaper.

•

Stop damping down — the extra humidity which was so necessary in the summer months is now no longer required. In fact moist air can pose a problem by encouraging grey mould. Some ventilation is therefore necessary, its purpose being to create fresh and moving air rather than to cut down the temperature.

•

Ventilate a little each day between mid-morning and early afternoon. Use the roof ventilators only. Close down at night, although you will have to leave a small gap if a paraffin stove is used. Do not ventilate on damp or foggy days.

•

Water with care — make sure that the pot requires watering before applying it. Do not splash the water about — keep it off the floor, staging, leaves and crown of the plants. Do this watering before midday which will allow time for splashes to dry before sunset.

•

Inspect the plants. Remove dead flowers and yellowing or diseased leaves. Put down slug pellets if slime trails or damaged foliage is seen. Spray if grey mould or whitefly has become a problem — do this spraying in the morning.

•

Make sure that all the half hardy plants have been brought inside.

•

Insulation can be carried out this month in cold districts — see page 13. Leave this task until November or December in mild areas.

On Display

Abutilon	Heliotrope
Campanula	Impatiens
Canna	Jacobinia
Capsicum annuum	Nerine
Carnation	Pelargonium
Celosia	Plumbago
Chrysanthemum	Primula
Cyclamen	Saintpaulia
Datura	Salpiglossis
Erica	Smithiantha
Exacum	Solanum capsicastrum
Fuchsia	Tibouchina

Plumbago capensis

Salpiglossis sinuata

Bulbs

Plant the traditional spring-flowering bulbs — Tulip, Hyacinth, Narcissus, Snowdrop, Muscari, Crocus, Chionodoxa and so on for display in the greenhouse or living room.

Dry off Begonia, Hippeastrum, Gloxinia, Lily, Achimenes, Canna etc once flowering has finished.

Water and feed Lachenalia, Cyclamen and Freesia.

Prick out Cyclamen seedlings.

Other Ornamentals

Prick out last month's sowing of annuals for spring display. Pinch out the growing tips of older seedlings to induce bushiness.

Pot on Cineraria, Calceolaria and Schizanthus.

Reduce watering of established plants — avoid waterlogging at all costs.

Cut Chrysanthemums and Perpetual-flowering Carnations for arranging indoors. Keep watch for grey mould and earwigs on Chrysanthemums.

Make sure that the last of the tender pot plants have been brought inside. Keep the compost almost dry.

Bring in pots of Azaleas in bud to provide winter blooms.

Bedding Plants

Garden Pelargonium and Fuchsia which were potted up and brought inside last month for overwintering should be stored under the staging and kept quite dry. They will be brought back into growth next spring and bedded out again in May or June.

Pot on rooted cuttings.

Sow Sweet Peas for planting out in the spring.

Garden Perennials and Shrubs

Continue to take cuttings of evergreens. Always use a rooting hormone. Use a propagator or cover pot with a polythene bag — see page 88.

Pot up Lily bulbs in 8 in. pots for planting out next spring.

Dahlias should be lifted from the border when the first frosts have blackened the foliage. Complete this lifting by the end of the month. Cut down to 6 in. and label with the colour and name of variety. Box up the tubers as described on page 66 and store under the staging until the spring when the young shoots will be used as cuttings.

Tomatoes

Continue picking if plants were not lifted last month. Pick all fruit before the middle of the month. Ripen in a drawer or bag — see page 72. Remove plants and containers when cropping stops.

Cucumbers
No work to be done this month.

Vegetables

Remove Aubergine and Capsicum plants when cropping stops. Plant up seedlings sown last month.

Sow a spring-cropping Lettuce such as *May Queen*.

Harvest Capsicum, Aubergine, Radish, Mustard & Cress and Mushroom.

Fruit

Reduce watering. Ventilation is required for established Peach and Nectarine — these trees require cool and dry air in order for the wood to ripen.

Prepare ground for planting Peach, Nectarine, Apricot or Grape vine next month.

Harvest Grapes.

NOVEMBER

The Tomatoes have gone and November heralds the end of the autumn growing season. A quiet time in the greenhouse, but there is a reasonable amount of work to do if you are using the space properly. Pots will need careful watering and proper ventilation is a tricky job — there must be enough air movement to reduce the risk of disease but not enough to chill the plants. November is a suitable month for the annual clean-up — don't leave this essential task until the depths of winter.

General Tasks

Maintain a minimum temperature of 42°–45°F in the cool greenhouse if frost-sensitive plants are present. In a cold house it will be necessary to cover such specimens with matting or newspaper if night frost is forecast.

•

If the day is dry and sunny, open a ventilator away from the wind. Close down the ventilator in mid-afternoon so the sun's heat will be conserved before nightfall. Keep the ventilators closed on damp or foggy days.

•

Try to keep the air on the dry side — don't splash the floor, staging or leaves when watering. Pots should be watered sparingly except for plants which are in flower.

•

Inspect the plants. Space out pots to ensure maximum illumination. Remove dead flowers and yellowing or diseased leaves. Spray if grey mould or whitefly has become a problem.

•

This is a good time for the annual clean-up. Choose a bright and dry day — begin work about mid-morning as there may be a lot to do. The basic jobs are listed here, but for full details see page 90. Place pots in a safe place in the garden — move tender types indoors. Remove rubbish from inside the house and scrub the staging and shelves with a garden disinfectant. Use a stiff brush to clean aluminium frames. Remove all traces of shading from the glass and clean thoroughly, both inside and out. If wood is unsightly paint with a plant-safe wood preservative. Dig if you plan to grow in the border soil. When the clean-up is over bring back the plants from their temporary outing in the garden.

•

Clean-up time is an ideal opportunity for carrying out minor repairs and for insulating the house.

On Display

Abutilon
Begonia
Browallia
Capsicum annuum
Carnation
Cassia
Chrysanthemum
Cyclamen
Erica
Exacum
Hedychium
Impatiens

Jacobinia
Kalanchoe
Lantana
Nerine
Pelargonium
Pentas
Primula
Saintpaulia
Salvia
Solanum capsicastrum
Tetranema
Zygocactus

Zygocactus truncatus

Capsicum annuum

Bulbs

Finish planting up the spring-flowering bulbs — include Tulip, Iris reticulata and Lily of the Valley.

Look at the bowls you have plunged outdoors. If shoots are about 1 in. high bring some inside to induce earlier flowering.

Other Ornamentals

Pot up cuttings of Pelargonium, Fuchsia, Heliotrope, Helichrysum, Campanula, Plumbago etc which were struck in autumn.

Bring in pots of Fuchsia, Hydrangea, Begonia and Pelargonium from outdoors — store under staging and keep the compost almost dry.

Pot up a few hardy plants from the garden for Christmas display — examples are Polyanthus and Helleborus niger.

Cut Chrysanthemums and Perpetual-flowering Carnations for arranging indoors. Keep watch for grey mould and earwigs on Chrysanthemums.

Bedding Plants

Pot on the hardy annuals which were sown in autumn for spring bedding — examples include Pansy and Sweet Pea. Use small 3 in. pots — small plants in large pots can result in root rot. Pot on Pelargonium and Fuchsia cuttings for bedding out next year — see Other Ornamentals above.

Pack plants taken from hanging baskets into boxes containing slightly damp peat.

Garden Perennials and Shrubs

Perennials such as Chrysanthemum and Dahlia should be lifted from the border before the end of the month and packed into peat-filled boxes. Label and cut down before boxing, then place under the staging until the spring when the young shoots will be used as cuttings. For details see pages 66 and 67 — check occasionally during winter to ensure that they are not rotting.

Bring tubs of tender shrubs and perennials (Agapanthus, Osteospermum etc) into the greenhouse — prune as necessary.

Tomatoes   No work to be done this month.

Cucumbers   No work to be done this month.

Vegetables

Plant out into the border or into growing bags Lettuce seedlings raised from a September or early October sowing. A minimum of 45°F will be necessary. Plant out Mushroom spawn.

Harvest Lettuce and Mushroom.

Pot up and force Chicory. For instructions on how to do this see page 78.

Box up and force Rhubarb at the end of the month. Lift crowns of well-established plants from the open garden and leave exposed to frost. Then place crowns in a peat-filled box and cover with black polythene sheeting. Small and succulent shoots will be ready for pulling in about 4 weeks.

Lift from the garden and pot up Chives, Parsley and Mint for a supply during the winter months.

Fruit

Plant Peach, Nectarine and Apricot. Established bushes or fans should be ventilated during dry days — heat is not necessary.

Plant Grape vines. Prune established vines once all the leaves have fallen — see The Fruit Expert (page 91) for full instructions.

DECEMBER

The greenhouse owner reaps the benefit of earlier work this month. Pots of Cyclamen, Primula, Cineraria etc are brought into the living room for Christmas decoration — so are bowls of forced Narcissi and Hyacinths. In addition Christmas lunch can include home-grown Carrots, Mushrooms and Potatoes plus a Lettuce and Chicory salad. A satisfying month, then, but also a difficult one. December is not the coldest month, but it is the darkest one. This means that growth is sluggish and light is the controlling factor. Without supplementary lighting keep the soil on the dry side and the air at less than 60°F.

General Tasks

Watch the temperature carefully. In a cool house aim for a minimum night temperature of 42°–45°F and a maximum day temperature of 55°–60°F. High temperatures lead to soft and lanky growth.

•

Some ventilation will be necessary to remove condensation and to keep the air moving. Do this job carefully or you will create plant-killing draughts and a dangerous drop in temperature. Avoid problems by following the instructions set out in the General Tasks section for November.

•

You must keep the soil rather dry at this time of the year if the plants are not in flower — this is especially true for Cacti, Succulents and Pelargonium. Only damp down the floor and staging if it is really necessary, and do this job in mid-morning.

•

Inspect the plants. Remove dead flowers and yellowing or diseased leaves. Spray if grey mould or whitefly has become a problem. Put down slug pellets if tell-tale shiny trails are seen.

•

Although the coldest weather has not yet arrived, it is essential to insulate your greenhouse before the end of the month. This task is doubly important if the structure is an all-glass one rather than the traditional type with brick or wood covering the space below the staging. The general principles of insulation are outlined on page 13. Attaching plastic sheeting to an aluminium structure is not an easy task. With some models there are slots in the glazing bars in which you can push insulating plugs. If these are not available use double-sided sticky pads. Whichever method you use it is necessary to avoid blocking the ventilators.

•

Trim the wicks of paraffin heaters to prevent the production of plant-toxic fumes.

On Display

Cyclamen persicum

Acacia
Azalea
Begonia
Bromeliads
Camellia
Capsicum annuum
Carnation
Chrysanthemum
Cineraria
Columnea
Cyclamen
Freesia

Hippeastrum
Hyacinth
Impatiens
Jacobinia
Narcissus
Pelargonium
Poinsettia
Primula
Saintpaulia
Scilla
Solanum capsicastrum
Zygocactus

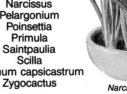

Narcissus 'Paperwhite'

Bulbs

Bring in more bowls of bulbs from outside to hasten growth. The buds of forced bulbs will start to show colour this month — move the bowls into the living room for Christmas or New Year decoration.

Plant Lilies. Support stems of Freesia and Lachenalia.

Other Ornamentals

Move the Christmas pot plants to the warmest part of the greenhouse at the beginning of the month. Water carefully, adding a liquid feed. Take into the living room for the festive season — examples include Azalea, Cineraria and Primula.

Sow Campanula isophylla. Propagate Perpetual-flowering Carnations and stake Lorraine Begonias.

Bring in pot-grown Roses. Cut the stems to about 3–4 buds above the compost, or leave until next month.

This is a good time to get seed trays and pots ready for use in the New Year. Throw away broken ones — wash the remainder thoroughly with a garden disinfectant and stack neatly. Buy a multipurpose compost.

Pot up shrubs for greenhouse decoration in spring. Examples include Forsythia, Hebe, Lilac and Weigela. A number of herbaceous perennials can be planted in pots. Suitable types are Lupin, Aquilegia, Delphinium and Gaillardia.

Bedding Plants

A quiet time here — sowing of half hardy types begins in January. Inspect the pots of autumn-sown hardy annuals. Make sure that they get maximum light and do not water unless the compost is distinctly dry on the surface.

Garden Perennials and Shrubs

Complete the cutting back of Chrysanthemums and Dahlias which were lifted and brought into the greenhouse last month. Keep these roots cool and fairly dry until they are brought into growth in January or February.

Tomatoes

The usual time for sowing Tomato seed is early March. However, in a heated greenhouse kept at a minimum night temperature of 50°–55°F, seed can be sown in a propagator in late December and planted out in early March for a June crop.

Cucumbers

No work to be done this month.

Vegetables

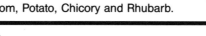

Sow Lettuce, Carrot, Mustard & Cress and French Bean — choose varieties recommended for growing under glass. Plant out October-sown Lettuce seedlings into the border or into growing bags.

Pot up and force Chicory — box up and force Rhubarb. See Vegetables section for November.

Harvest Lettuce, Carrot, Radish, Mushroom, Potato, Chicory and Rhubarb.

Fruit

Plant Peach, Nectarine, Apricot and Grape vine. Prune established Grape vines if not carried out last month — see The Fruit Expert (page 91) for full instructions.

These fruit trees do not make ideal companions for tender plants. Peach, Nectarine etc need unheated conditions and they also need to be ventilated freely on dry days.

CHAPTER 7

PLANT INDEX

Acknowledgements

The author wishes to acknowledge the painstaking work of John Woodbridge, Gill Jackson, Paul Norris, Linda Fensom, Angelina Gibbs and Constance Barry. Grateful acknowledgement is also made for the help or photographs received from Pat Brindley, Harry Smith Horticultural Photographic Collection, Joan Hessayon, Norman Barber, Tania Midgley, Carleton Photographic, Brian Carter/The Garden Picture Library, John Glover/The Garden Picture Library, Steven Wooster/The Garden Picture Library, Brock/Robert Harding Syndication and Hugh Palmer/Robert Harding Syndication.

John Dye provided both artistry and design work. The artist who contributed was Roger Shipp.